Whitewater Rafting
in Western North America

Whitewater Rafting
in Western North America
A Guide to Rivers and Professional Outfitters

■

by Lloyd D. Armstead

An East Woods Book

The
Globe
Pequot
Press

Chester, Connecticut

Maps by Joann Krupa
Photographs with no credit line were taken by the author.

Library of Congress Cataloging-in-Publication Data

Armstead, Lloyd Dean, 1943–
    Whitewater rafting in western North America : a guide to rivers and professional outfitters / by Lloyd D. Armstead.
        p.   cm.
    "An East Woods book."
    Includes index.
    INDEX 0-87106-490-1
    1. Rafting (Sports)—West (U.S.)—Guide-books. 2. Rafting (Sports)—Canada, Western—Guide-books. 3. West (U.S.)—Description and travel—1981–   —Guide-books. 4. Canada, Western—Description and travel—Guide-books. I. Title.
    GV776.W3A76   1990
    797.1'22'097—dc20   90-35933
                                                                          CIP

$13.95

Manufactured in the United States of America
First Edition/First Printing

CONTENTS

American (South Fork) • American (Middle Fork) • American (North Fork) • Yuba (North Fork) • Truckee • Carson (East Fork) • Mokelumne • Stanislaus • Tuolumne • Merced • Kings • Kern • Kaweah • Klamath (Upper) • Klamath (Lower) • Scott • Salmon • Wooley • Trinity • Eel (Middle) • Sacramento (Upper) • Cache Creek

WORDS OF CAUTION

To Whitewater Rafters

Whitewater rafting is one of the safest and most enjoyable sporting activities in western America. In any sport, however, there are certain elements of risk. Unforeseen accidents and injuries occasionally occur while whitewater rafting, but by using professional outfitters and heeding the advice of their guides, you can reduce to a minimum the chances of injury. While the author assumes no liability for accidents to any reader engaged in whitewater rafting, readers are cautioned to respect the dangers of swift-flowing rivers and whitewater rafting and thereby increase their enjoyment of this sport many times over.

ABOUT THE AUTHOR

Lloyd Armstead started rafting the rivers of North America nearly a dozen years ago. Realizing that little information was available on the whitewater sport, he began organizing pertinent river data for rafters. Today he is respected by river outfitters and rafting enthusiasts for his accurate and detailed research.

Mr. Armstead works for the federal government in Washington, D.C., and lives in nearby Fairfax County, Virginia. An avid rafter and kayaker, he is a member of both American Rivers and the Canoe Cruisers of Washington.

FOREWORD

Little known just two decades ago, whitewater rafting has become one of North America's most popular and fastest growing outdoor sports. The continent's rich diversity of rivers and large number of professional outfitters afford everyone from child to senior adult the choice of a comfortable level of whitewater exposure and the opportunity to enjoy, safely, otherwise inaccessible canyons and wild areas.

Whitewater rafting in the western United States and Canada includes challenge, excitement, and even a pioneerlike sense of adventure and exploration. Whitewater rafting also encompasses somewhat more subdued river journeys that allow both the time and opportunity for wildlife and scenery to be enjoyed in a more relaxed atmosphere. Multiday or vacation rafting itineraries, of course, extend the greatest latitude for one to capture a total river experience comprised of off-river adventure time, quiet time, interaction and reflection time, as well as time to eat and play.

Confluence '89, a national gathering of the professionals and leaders in outfitting and resource management in New Orleans in December 1989, was organized as a "window to the future of river recreation." Presented jointly by the Western River Guides Association, Eastern Professional River Outfitters Association, the Bureau of Land Management, the National Park Service, and the U.S. Forest Service, the historic conference focused on the emerging trends in marketing, customer service, liability and safety, and the federal policies that will influence river preservation and recreation into the twenty-first century.

I, like hundreds of other professional rafting outfitters, welcome *Whitewater Rafting in Western North America* as a well-researched and valuable link between the rivers of western America and those of us who are fortunate enough to provide you incredibly enjoyable and long-remembered whitewater and wilderness experiences. It is the business of professional rafting outfitters to do our utmost to make each 'and every river trip safe and enjoyable.

SHERI GRIFFITH
President
Western River Guides Association

PREFACE

Whitewater Rafting in Western North America is intended as a non-technical guide for first-time as well as frequent rafters.

This book details the enjoyable, exciting, and sometimes daring sport of whitewater rafting. It is a literary bridge connecting nearly 500 professional outfitters with 200 rafting trips on 140 rivers in thirteen western states and three Canadian provinces. As such it is the most complete and authoritative source of whitewater rafting information for the rivers and professional rafting outfitters of western North America.

As with my earlier, companion, guide, *Whitewater Rafting in Eastern North America*, I wrote this book with the desire to introduce people to not only the sport of rafting and the excitement of whitewater but also to the total river experience—the grandeur and solitude of isolated mountain and desert canyons, the imprints of past civilizations, and an incredible oneness with nature. W. Kent Olson, president of American Rivers, succinctly penned the mood of the river experience, which often leaves me without words: "Rivers are refuges for the soul, places of spiritual refreshment where the natural flow and play of running water mirror the movement of life itself. They provide for elemental, relatively unadorned experiences in which man and nature can come together. . . ."

Because of the assistance of the following people, *Whitewater Rafting in Western North America* became a reality. Consequently, I extend my heartfelt appreciation and thanks to: my wife, Connie, for her encouragement and help with so many aspects of the book; my son, Rodney, for his valuable and often needed computer assistance and support; my daughter, Jolene, for preparing countless questionnaires for mailing; my friend Genie Bata for hours of volunteer effort to help meet the publisher's deadlines; and the many agencies and bureaus of the U.S. and Canadian governments for providing the names and addresses of outfitters having permits to run rivers on federal lands.

Thanks, too, to the professional rafting outfitters of western America whose information, photos, and suggestions are responsible for a major portion of this book. Those deserving special credit are: Sheri Griffith, Sheri Griffith River Expeditions; George Wendt, O.A.R.S.; Bill McGinnis, Whitewater Voyagers; Marty McDonnell, Sierra Mac River Trips; Chip Sharp, Trinity River Rafting Center; David Mills, Rocky Mountain River Tours; Betsy Barrymore Stoll, The River Company; Jerry Hughes, Hughes River Expeditions; Bill Dvorak, Bill

Dvorak's Raft and Kayak Expeditions; Dawn Benner, Rocky Mountain Outdoor Center; Mike Buck, Keystone Raft and Kayak Adventures; Aaron Underwood, Osprey Expeditions; Bernie Fandrich, Kumsheen Raft Adventures; and Mike Mitrovic, Mirage Adventure Tours.

I am also indebted to the regional river authors who willingly reviewed the manuscript and added much-needed suggestions: Doug North, *Washington Whitewater I* and *Washington Whitewater II*; and Jim Cassady, *California Whitewater* and *Western Whitewater*.

Lastly, I thank the publisher for making it possible for me to share the whitewater rivers of western America with you.

RIVER PRESERVATION

While rivers all across the continent face threats to their free-flowing and ecological existence, the greatest whitewater river losses have been in the water-thirsty West. Giant hydro and irrigation projects have dramatically altered or eliminated the natural flow of several of the West's greatest rivers—the Colorado, Snake, and Columbia. Stretches of countless other important, but perhaps lesser-known whitewater rivers, such as California's Stanislaus, have likewise been silenced. Presently, many popular whitewater playgrounds such as Oregon's Klamath, California's North and Middle Forks of the American, Idaho's North Fork Payette, and Colorado's Animas and South Platte face similar destruction.

Two decades after the 1968 enactment of the National Wild and Scenic Rivers Act by the U.S. Congress, the list of federally protected rivers has increased from 8 to its present 121. Leading river preservationists note two important phases in the types of rivers thus far protected by the historic conservation act. Initially, the new legislation protected those large and obvious segments already well known for their scenic qualities and high level of recreational use. Among these were Oregon's Rogue, Idaho's Middle Fork of the Salmon, and New Mexico's Rio Grande. A second list of protected rivers of equal wild, scenic, and recreational qualities is now emerging as a result of land use planning by the U.S. Forest Service and Bureau of Land Management. Recently protected were some forty rivers in Oregon and twenty-five in Alaska. As many as twenty-three rivers in Michigan are slated for federal protection.

Wild and scenic status for rivers during the decade of the 1990s will frequently depend upon the ability of river preservation organizations to achieve recognition for waterways surrounded by economic enterprises such as manufacturing, farming, grazing, mining, logging, and residential development. Thus, the political success of river conservationists will increasingly require the confidence and cooperation of private landowners as well as other resource users.

The most effective forces in river preservation are those nearest the source. No river—no matter how beautiful, appreciated, used, or enjoyed—will be protected without action by the people who raft or canoe it, fish in it, and live along it. Although many rafters admire and enjoy the resource they use, few are aware of the constant threats to rivers and the work required by national, state, and local organizations to preserve them.

American Rivers, the only national organization dedicated exclusively to preserving outstanding natural rivers, has been amazingly

Preservation of the free-flowing rivers of America should be a priority for everyone.
Photo by John Blaustein

successful in its fight to preserve what remains of America's heritage of free-flowing streams. Founded in 1973 to help expand the five-year-old, but sluggishly growing Wild and Scenic Rivers System, this organization helps shape national and state rivers' policy from its office in Washington, D.C. American Rivers also works to combat unneeded hydropower development and acts as a resource, catalyst, and counselor for river protection efforts across the country. It has a growing national membership and relies largely on the support of members to make certain that free-flowing rivers continue to have a voice in Washington, D.C.

A regional river preservation organization with similar goals to those of American Rivers, California-based Friends of the River was created in 1973 in an attempt to save the Stanislaus River from needless burial behind the New Melones Dam. One of the most beautiful and popular rivers in the West, the Stanislaus was eventually lost, but its spirit kept flowing, inspiring Friends of the River to continue its work to prevent similar tragedies from happening again.

In the years that followed, Friends of the River grew into the largest grass-roots river conservation organization in the nation and successfully fought for the preservation of the Tuolumne, Kings, Kern, Merced, and other rivers now protected by the federal Wild and Scenic program. Friends of the River's "100 Rivers Campaign" is an unprecedented cooperative effort with eighteen local conservation groups to save what's left of California's wild river heritage. It is a long-term campaign to win permanent protection for more than 100 stretches of rivers and streams flowing through national forests and other public lands.

Membership in these organizations is one of the more basic ways to become involved in river conservation. For more information, call or write: American Rivers, 801 Pennsylvania Avenue, S.E., Suite 303, Washington, D.C. 20003, (202) 547–6900; and Friends of the River, Fort Mason Center, Building C, San Francisco, CA 94123, (415) 771–0400.

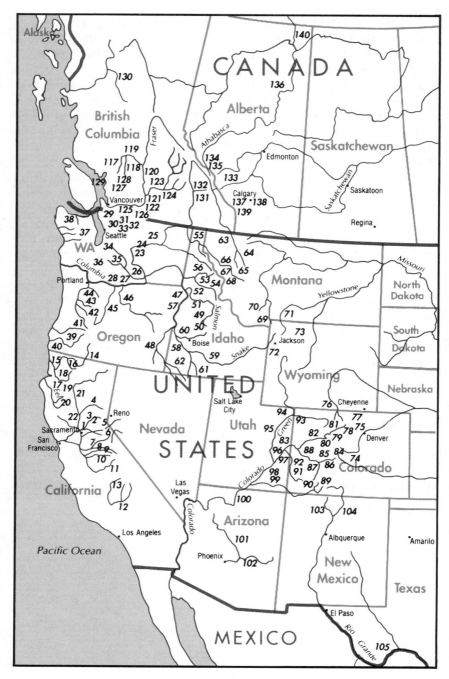

For river locations in Alaska, see page 172.

California

1.	American (South Fork)	California
2.	American (Middle Fork)	California
3.	American (North Fork)	California
4.	Yuba (North Fork)	California
5.	Truckee	California
6.	Carson (East Fork)	California–Nevada
7.	Mokelumne	California
8.	Stanislaus	California
9.	Tuolumne	California
10.	Merced	California
11.	Kings	California
12.	Kern	California
13.	Kaweah	California
14.	Klamath (Upper)	Oregon–California
15.	Klamath (Lower)	California
16.	Scott	California
17.	Salmon	California
18.	Wooley	California
19.	Trinity	California
20.	Eel (Middle)	California
21.	Sacramento (Upper)	California
22.	Cache Creek	California

The Pacific Northwest States

23.	Wenatchee	Washington
24.	Methow	Washington
25.	Stehekin	Washington
26.	Tieton	Washington
27.	Klickitat	Washington
28.	White Salmon	Washington
29.	Nooksack (North Fork)	Washington
30.	Sauk	Washington
31.	Suiattle	Washington
32.	Skagit	Washington
33.	Skykomish	Washington

34. Green	Washington
35. Cispus	Washington
36. Toutle	Washington
37. Olympic Rain Forest	Washington
38. Elwha	Washington
39. Rogue	Oregon
40. Illinois	Oregon
41. North Umpqua	Oregon
42. McKenzie	Oregon
43. North Santiam	Oregon
44. Clackamas	Oregon
45. Deschutes	Oregon
46. John Day	Oregon
47. Grand Ronde	Oregon–Washington
48. Owyhee	Oregon

The Northern Rocky Mountain States

49. Salmon (Middle Fork)	Idaho
50. Salmon (Upper Main)	Idaho
51. Salmon (Main)	Idaho
52. Salmon (Lower)	Idaho
53. Lochsa	Idaho
54. Selway	Idaho
55. Moyie	Idaho
56. St. Joe	Idaho
57. Snake (Hells Canyon)	Idaho–Oregon
58. Snake (Birds of Prey)	Idaho
59. Snake (Middle)	Idaho
60. Payette	Idaho
61. Jarbidge–Bruneau	Idaho
62. Owyhee	Idaho–Oregon
63. Flathead (North Fork)	Montana
64. Flathead (Middle Fork)	Montana
65. Flathead (South Fork)	Montana
66. Flathead (Lower)	Montana
67. Clark Fork	Montana
68. Blackfoot	Montana

69. Gallatin	Montana
70. Madison	Montana
71. Yellowstone	Montana
72. Snake (Upper)	Wyoming
73. Shoshone	Wyoming

The Southwest States

74. Arkansas	Colorado
75. Clear Creek	Colorado
76. North Platte	Colorado–Wyoming
77. Cache la Poudre	Colorado
78. Blue	Colorado
79. Eagle	Colorado
80. Roaring Fork	Colorado
81. Colorado (Upper)	Colorado
82. Colorado (Glenwood)	Colorado
83. Colorado (Horsethief–Ruby)	Colorado
84. Taylor	Colorado
85. Slate	Colorado
86. Gunnison	Colorado
87. Gunnison (Lake Fork)	Colorado
88. Gunnison (Gorge)	Colorado
89. Piedra	Colorado
90. Animas	Colorado
91. Dolores	Colorado–Utah
92. San Miguel	Colorado
93. Yampa	Colorado
94. Green (Dinosaur Nat'l Monument)	Colorado–Utah
95. Green (Desolation)	Utah
96. Colorado (Professor Valley)	Utah
97. Colorado (Westwater)	Utah
98. Colorado (Cataract)	Utah
99. San Juan	Utah
100. Colorado (Grand Canyon)	Arizona
101. Verde	Arizona
102. Salt	Arizona

103. Rio Chama	New Mexico
104. Rio Grande	New Mexico
105. Rio Grande	Texas

Alaska

106. Alsek–Tatshenshini	Yukon–British Columbia–Alaska
107. Chitina–Copper	Alaska
108. Lowe	Alaska
109. Tonsina	Alaska
110. Tazlina	Alaska
111. Talkeetna	Alaska
112. Nenana	Alaska
113. Fortymile	Alaska
114. Brooks Range (East)	Alaska
115. Brooks Range (Central)	Alaska
116. Brooks Range (West)	Alaska

Western Canada

117. Chilko	British Columbia
118. Taseko	British Columbia
119. Chilcotin	British Columbia
120. Fraser	British Columbia
121. Thompson	British Columbia
122. Nahatlatch	British Columbia
123. Clearwater	British Columbia
124. Adams	British Columbia
125. Chehalis	British Columbia
126. Chilliwack	British Columbia
127. Cheakamus	British Columbia
128. Birkenhead	British Columbia
129. Squamish	British Columbia
130. Babine	British Columbia
131. Illecillewaet	British Columbia
132. Kicking Horse	British Columbia
133. Red Deer	Alberta
134. Maligne	Alberta
135. Athabasca (Upper)	Alberta

Paddle rafts allow guests to participate actively in their whitewater river adventure.
Photo courtesy of Four Corners Expeditions

CHAPTER 1

Preparations

HISTORY APTLY RECORDS the canyon explorations of John Wesley Powell and his brave companions as being among the first legitimate river running expeditions of western North America. Written accounts of their whitewater journeys through the spectacular canyons of the Southwest's Green and Colorado rivers in 1869 have fascinated the armchair traveler for more than a century. Only in the past twenty-five years, however, has it been possible for tens of thousands of rafters a year to experience these same whitewater canyons.

After Powell, nearly a half-century passed before other adventure-seeking boaters regularly navigated these forbidding canyon waters. While many entrepreneurial boatmen, including Bus Hatch and Norman Nevills, successfully operated commercial whitewater trips in wooden boats in Utah, Idaho, and Oregon during the 1930s and 1940s, their unusual river exploits received little attention outside their local area.

The birth of modern commercial rafting in the mid-1950s is largely attributable to the determination and innovativeness of a Chicago-born woman, Georgie de Ross-Clark. Georgie, unwilling to believe that river running was for men only, successfully lashed surplus World War II Army bridge pontoons together, creating the first oar-guided rubber raft. News of her successful Grand Canyon of the Colorado whitewater boat adventures rapidly spread, attracting guests as well as competing river outfitters. In just a decade, at least two dozen professional outfitters were offering whitewater trips in rubber rafts on numerous western rivers. Yet another two decades later, in 1990, there are hundreds of professional outfitters offering 200 whitewater raft and float trips in western North America.

The multifold growth of the whitewater rafting industry in the western United States and Canada has led to numerous equipment innovations. The variety of rafts and other river equipment available to western river outfitters make it possible for almost anyone to safely participate in some level of whitewater rafting. Outfitters, using state-of-the-art self-bailing rafts, offer energetic rafters an opportunity to run rivers that just a few years ago were considered unrunnable. Oar-guided rafts with lightweight aluminum rowing frames make it possible for senior citizens and families with young children to safely enjoy both single- and multiday Class II–III whitewater trips. Motorized rafts enable those with less time to experience the otherwise inaccessible canyons of the Colorado, Green, Snake, lower Salmon rivers in the western United States and the Thompson and Fraser in British Columbia. In addition, there are dories or drift boats for the explorer-minded rafter and inflatable kayaks for the thrill-seeking solo rafter.

Many outfitters have made a remarkable effort to make whitewater rafting both possible and affordable for the disabled and disadvantaged populations. On several of the popular river trips of moderate difficulty, such as California's South Fork American, Utah's Green and Colorado, and Colorado's Arkansas, it is not at all uncommon to see paraplegics, quadriplegics, the deaf, and even the blind experiencing the unique thrill of the whitewater.

The lure of western whitewaters and the unique access to the spectacular canyons provided by rafting have also created an international market. In addition to the high percentage of rafters from Midwest and East Coast population centers, outfitters attract increasingly large numbers of customers from England, France, Germany, Japan, Australia, and elsewhere. Bilingual guides are employed by many of the outfitters to better serve their foreign clientele. While the multiday Grand Canyon of the Colorado rafting adventure has been the traditional favorite of foreign visitors, each year more and more of them are discovering the equally fascinating wilderness canyon river adventures of Idaho, Colorado, and Utah as well as the wild rivers of Alaska and British Columbia.

Competition among outfitters has also spurred creative approaches to maintain or increase their market share and to enhance the river experience for customers. This is particularly shown by the growing number of specialty rafting trips including gourmet dinners and wine tastings, storytellers, concerts in the canyon, and personal and professional development seminars and workshops. Multiday trips are offered on many rivers and continually grow more popular as rafters realize that such trips offer the best and often the only way to see, enjoy, and experience many isolated western river canyons. They also allow one the opportunity to enjoy the wilderness without carrying food and heavy equipment. Many rafters find the quiet solitude of the wilderness canyons as much a part of the river experience as the whitewater.

WHO SHOULD GO?

Every year more people of all ages and occupations are finding white-water rafting to be one of the most challenging and exciting forms of recreation they have ever enjoyed. Other persons have found that rafting offers a perfect escape from the pressures and tensions of their daily routines. No matter who you are or what your career, if you feel comfortable around water, chances are you will enjoy whitewater rafting and will want to go again and again. Almost anyone can enjoy some level of whitewater rafting in the western United States and western Canada.

Rafting is fun to do alone, but it is even more enjoyable when you go with friends or family. It is an ideal sporting activity for persons

Oar-guided rafts enable guests of all ages to enjoy rafting through the Green River's Split Mountain Gorge in Dinosaur National Monument.

Specially equipped oar-guided rafts make it possible for the disabled to appreciate many of the West's whitewater river canyons.
Photo courtesy of S'Plore

from your plant or office, church or school group, or civic or social organization. Likewise, each year more families are finding that whitewater raft and float trips add a new and long-remembered dimension to their summer vacation.

For safety and insurance reasons, rafting outfitters often have minimum-age requirements on each river where they operate. These age limits, usually between the ages of ten and eighteen, have been set after careful consideration of river conditions by experienced outfitters. In recent years an increasing number of relatively easy whitewater trips allow children ten years old and sometimes younger to enjoy rafting. Often a child's size—whether or not the smallest life jacket will fit—determines whether an outfitter will allow a child to participate.

The maximum age for rafting can only be determined by a person's physical health and enthusiasm for adventure. Persons with a heart condition, shortness of breath, or serious physical disabilities should consult their physician as well as the river outfitter before attempting a raft trip. Many people more than ninety years old enjoy moderate-level whitewater each year.

Should a nonswimmer go whitewater rafting? Many nonswimmers go rafting each year. On less demanding rivers, outfitters often leave the decision to the individual, after pointing out that life jackets provide adequate flotation and standard swimming techniques are not used in the rapids. Whatever is decided, it is important not to coax or dare someone to go whitewater rafting against his wishes. Fear of water may lead to moments of panic should a nonswimmer fall overboard in fast-moving rapids. The ability to swim is recommended for all Class IV and above whitewater rivers.

BEST TIMES TO GO

Rain or shine, you can go whitewater rafting; you probably will get wet regardless of the weather.

The rafting season for most western rivers is from April to October. Outfitters who wear wet suits, however, begin rafting the snow runoff in March and, if fall water levels permit, run raft trips well into November. Understandably, it is difficult to say what time of year is best for whitewater rafting. If you are interested in big whitewater action, the early spring runoff should provide it. Days following periods of extended rain during the summer and fall offer the same thrills, but the water is hard to catch at sustained levels.

During a lunch break Sacramento-area friends relive an unexpected swim through Tuolumne's Class IV–V Clavey Falls.

If scenery is a prime consideration, two of the most beautiful times of year are when the rhododendron and mountain laurel bloom, which is usually from mid-May through early June, and during the fall colors. Rafting during the summer usually provides a welcome relief from unpleasant heat as well as an enjoyable opportunity to swim and relax.

There are three advantages to weekday rather than weekend rafting trips: most outfitters offer reduced rates on weekdays; more popular rivers usually have fewer rafters on weekdays; and many outfitters fill up their weekend reservations far in advance. Weekday trips are usually available on much shorter notice.

Rafters frequently find it enjoyable to raft the same river during different seasons and water levels. The complexity and characteristics of the rapids vary dramatically with water levels, thereby offering very different challenges.

High water after periods of heavy rain, or low water after extended dry periods in the late summer and fall, can temporarily halt river rafting. This is particularly true of the uncontrolled or free-flowing rivers. When making reservations, ask the outfitter about cancellation and rescheduling policies in the event of high or low

During the summer's lower waters, many of the West's raft trips afford time for a refreshing swim.
Photo courtesy of Turtle River Rafting Company

water. Often this information is stated in the outfitter's brochure. If you have any questions about water levels or conditions, it is also advisable to check with your outfitter a day or two before your scheduled trip.

EQUIPMENT

One of the primary reasons commercial whitewater rafting is so popular is its simplicity. On guided trips, you do not have to buy any special equipment, carry a heavy pack, bring lunch, or worry about extra supplies. In fact, there are few easier ways to enjoy the wilderness. The outfitter provides the basic items of equipment: the raft, the life jacket, and the paddle on paddle-raft trips. Helmets are furnished on many river trips. Buckets or containers for bailing excess water are provided with each raft unless it is self-bailing.

On multiday trips requiring overnight camping, outfitters will provide dry bags for personal belongings, meals, beverages, cooking ware, and coolers. Camping gear such as sleeping bags and tents, if not included in the price of the trip, can normally be rented from the outfitter.

The Raft

Professional outfitters use a variety of rafts and other craft on the whitewater rivers of western North America. Most rafts are paddle rafts (those paddled by guests), oar rafts with aluminum rowing frames (those controlled by guides), or paddle/oar rafts (those paddled and controlled by both guests and guides). Highly maneuverable and stable inflatable kayaks (paddled by one or two guests) are also becoming increasingly available for river rafting customers, particularly during lower water levels.

While the type of raft or boat used on many rivers is frequently determined by the difficulty of the whitewater and the age and physical condition of rafters, the individual preference of potential customers often determines whether the raft is paddled by guests or is guided by an oarsman.

Rafts may hold four to six persons or eight to twelve persons. Large motorized rafts are more commonly used on some of the high-volume rivers in Arizona, Utah, and British Columbia.

Most rafts are made of neoprene, or nylon, polyester or Hypalon (a DuPont product). Although the rafts are flexible and can bend and bounce off rocks, rafters are expected to exercise care so rafts will not be permanently damaged.

In addition to rafts and inflatable kayaks, a few outfitters use wooden dories, similar to those popularized by John Wesley Powell, or the McKenzie whitewater drift boats, popularized by Oregon steelhead fishing outfitters. Dories are most commonly seen on Idaho's Salmon and Snake rivers, Idaho's and Oregon's Owyhee River, and on the Grand Canyon of the Colorado, whereas the McKenzie drift boat is used on several Oregon and Idaho rivers.

The Life Jacket

Without question, the most important item of personal equipment on any river is the life jacket. The guide will provide you with one at the beginning of your trip. Make sure it fits properly and fastens securely. Ask either a friend or guide to help you with necessary adjustments.

Life jackets should be worn and securely fastened while on the river.

Should you fall into swift-moving water, a loose fitting life jacket can slip up around your face and disorient and confuse you.

Wear the life jacket at all times. Do not risk being without it while swimming or wading in calm waters as undiscernible currents or channel dropoffs may be present. It is also advisable to wear your life jacket when climbing on rocks near the water's edge so it can cushion your body if you fall. Remind your rafting companions to wear their jackets; do not be offended if someone politely reminds you to do the same.

The Paddle

The single-bladed paddle (not an oar) is an important item in making your whitewater outing in a paddle raft a success. During the orientation and safety talk, the guide will demonstrate how to use the paddle. Pay careful attention to the guide's instructions for propelling and maneuvering the raft with the paddle. Your quick mastery of the

Raft guide demonstrates proper paddle-raft techniques during pretrip orientation.

correct paddle techniques will add greatly to your enjoyment and enhance your value as a team member. On paddle-raft trips, the use of the paddle is not optional. You are expected to do your share of the paddling.

Helmets

Plastic or fiberglass helmets are worn on most Class IV–V western rivers to prevent potential head injuries from rocks or flailing paddles. The use of helmets on any river is the decision of the outfitter. If helmets are provided, however, rafters will be required to wear them and keep them fastened during whitewater stretches.

Surprisingly, even on some of the most difficult western rivers, some outfitters feel helmets are unnecessary. If you desire the added safety that a helmet provides, you can make this a priority when selecting an outfitter, or you can bring one of your own.

The Bailer

Although an ever-increasing number of rafts used on western rivers are self-bailing, most are not. These rafts are usually supplied with one or more bucketlike containers for removing water from the floor of the raft. Rafters normally share the job of bailing.

Water weighs one kilogram per liter (or more than eight pounds a gallon). Unless water is removed from a raft, the added weight will slow the raft and reduce its maneuverability.

If you enjoy water fights with other rafters, use the bailer and not the paddle to throw water! Paddle blades can be sharp and can inadvertently injure someone.

CLOTHING AND PERSONAL EQUIPMENT

Wearing the proper clothing is essential to the enjoyment of a river outing. Season, location, water temperature, and both forecasted and unforecasted weather should be considered when selecting clothing for rafting trips. Afternoon thunderstorms, common in mountain areas, can suddenly drop the temperatures as well as deliver heavy downpours.

Other than tennis shoes or sneakers, which are required for all rafting trips, you should plan your dress according to three general types of water and weather conditions: warm, cool, and cold.

The following clothing suggestions are for half- and one-day trips in western America. Additional clothing and equipment may be required for multiday trips.

Helmets are often worn to prevent head injuries by rocks or flailing paddles.

Warm-weather Clothing
■ Swimming suit and/or shorts or cutoffs
■ T-shirt and windbreaker
■ Tennis shoes or sneakers

In addition to anticipated daytime temperatures, you should consider three other factors when choosing clothing. In the late-spring, early summer, or early fall water temperatures can be considerably colder than air temperatures. If water is released from a dam or reservoir, it probably will be many degrees colder than expected. Many rivers pass through narrow, steep-walled gorges, which remain shaded and cool during much of the day. Even on warm days, especially on northern rivers, and during the cool morning hours or along the shaded portions of the river, you may feel more comfortable wearing a light jacket, pants, or windbreaker. Most outfitters have dry bags to carry extra clothing.

Cool- and Rainy-weather Clothing

- Long wool underwear and pants
- Wool, polyester, or acrylic sweater
- Heavy windbreaker, poncho, or rain jacket
- Wet suit
- Tennis shoes or sneakers
- Wool socks
- Wool hat
- Gloves

Short of a wet suit, wool provides the best protection against the cold because it absorbs less water and retains body heat better than cotton.

Wet suits enable rafters to enjoy their sport during the spring snow runoff or on cold days.

Cold-weather Clothing
- Wet suit
- Wet suit booties or tennis shoes
- One or two pairs of wool socks
- Wool hat
- Gloves

Rafting in a wet suit is becoming increasingly common on western rivers. Wet suits enable rafters to take advantage of exciting whitewater during the spring snow runoff. Rafters also use them during chillier fall temperatures. If you feel a need for a wet suit and your outfitter does not rent them, they can be rented from many dive shops. It is best to wear a pair of shorts or cutoffs over the wet suit to minimize the contact of the rubber suit with the raft, which causes unnecessary wear to both the wet suit and the raft.

The importance of being properly dressed for both cool- and cold-weather rafting cannot be overemphasized. Unfortunately many rafters have had otherwise enjoyable trips ruined because they were miserably cold and wet.

If there is any question about weather and water temperatures, be sure to take along extra clothing. Check with your outfitter prior to the trip about the best river attire. Being improperly prepared for cold water and air temperature can also lead to hypothermia—a dangerous lowering of body temperature. A little extra thought about your river wear should guarantee an enjoyable time during almost any rafting season or weather.

Nonclothing Items

For half- and one-day rafting trips, the less you take, the better. Other than what you are wearing, try to get by with as few extra items as possible. If you wear glasses or sunglasses, be sure to include a safety strap or string to keep them securely fastened. Unless you absolutely need them, you may find the streaked and fogged lenses that result from splashing water make glasses an annoyance. Waterproof sunscreens should be in a pocket-size plastic or metal container.

Try to leave your car keys with the outfitter. If you must take keys, put them in a zippered pocket or bag. It is a good idea to hide an extra key with the car.

Almost all outfitters furnish lunch on one-day trips, high energy snacks on half-day trips, and all meals for two-day or longer trips. Information pertaining to river meals is either described in an outfitter's brochure or can be obtained from the outfitter.

Almost anytime you take a camera, you are taking a risk. Remember, most cameras are not waterproof. All too often, expensive cameras have been damaged or lost because of careless or improper handling or packing. No rafting outfitter can be held responsible for a lost or damaged camera. If you take a camera that is not waterproof, follow these guidelines:

■ Carefully cushion your camera in a waterproof bag. Although many outfitters provide these bags, none will guarantee the bag is waterproof. Make sure the container is watertight before you begin the trip. Most outfitters do not allow ammunition boxes for cameras because they might puncture a raft or injure a rafter.

■ Carefully secure your camera container to the raft with a rope or strap.

■ Use extreme caution when taking a photograph from a raft. Survey your downriver situation very carefully before taking out your camera. Sit in a stable position on the raft. Make sure nearby rafters know you are using your camera. Sudden water fights or horseplay may catch you by surprise. It is best to photograph from the riverbank.

■ If your camera becomes thoroughly wet or submerged, get it to an authorized repair shop as soon as possible.

■ Many outfitters employ river photographers who offer color prints of your raft trip. These photos are usually of fairly high quality and fully guaranteed.

EXPENSES

Few generalizations can be made about the cost of whitewater rafting in the western United States and Canada. Rafting trips normally cost from $15 to $40 for a half-day trip, $40 to $125 for a full-day trip, and $75 to $150 per day for multiday trips. The cost of expedition-type raft trips in Alaska and Canada may be somewhat higher. A trip's price depends on the day of week, the time of the year, the difficulty of the river, the number of guides needed, the length of shuttle transportation required, and the competing outfitters.

Wet suit rentals from the outfitters normally cost an additional $5 to $15 a day. A security deposit may be required at the time of the wet suit rental.

The cost of all rafting trips and the terms of payment—including group, weekday, and special season discounts—are detailed in each company's brochure. Although it is a good idea to compare the prices of trips offered by companies competing on the same rivers, cost should not be the only criterion used to select an outfitter. Chapter 8 lists several criteria for selecting an outfitter.

In addition to payment by cash, traveler's checks, or personal checks, most outfitters accept major credit cards.

TRIP RESERVATIONS

Reservations are recommended for all rafting trips. They enable outfitters to carefully plan food and equipment for each river trip and ensure an adequate number of guides. Even on the popular one-day river trips, there may be weekdays and some weekends when "walkons" can join a rafting trip, but it is advisable to check in advance.

While many of the more popular multiday trips are booked weeks, and even months, in advance, late cancellations do occasionally make it possible for a person to join a trip, such as one on the Grand Canyon or Salmon River, on fairly short notice. Outfitters often keep standby lists of those wishing to join already booked multiday trips. Although whitewater outfitters have differing reservation policies and requirements, some general observations can be made.

The sooner you make reservations, the greater your chance of obtaining the rafting dates of your choice. Most outfitters will accept an initial reservation by telephone, but will send a final confirmation only after receiving your deposit or, in many cases, full payment. Outfitters normally require a deposit soon after your reservation, and full payment from fourteen to thirty days prior to the scheduled trip. To avoid any possible confusion, always ask the outfitter to confirm your reservation in writing. An outfitter's brochure details the specific terms for reservations.

In the event that a trip is cancelled by the outfitter, due to high water or a lack of water, a refund or rescheduling almost always can be arranged to the mutual satisfaction of the rafter and the outfitter. Many outfitters reserve the right to run alternate rivers or sections of rivers when unfavorable water conditions prevail.

Notable exceptions where advance reservations are frequently not required are the family- and tourist-oriented rafting trips near national parks and other popular tourist centers. Outfitters are normally able to accommodate visitors on numerous daily rafting excursions lasting from one to four hours. Such river trips include:

- Flathead (Middle Fork); Glacier National Park
- Snake (upper); Grand Teton National Park
- Yellowstone; Yellowstone National Park
- Colorado (Glenwood Canyon); Glenwood Springs, Colorado
- Colorado (Professor Valley); Moab, Utah
- Animas (lower); Durango, Colorado
- Arkansas; Buena Vista and other locations in south-central Colorado
- Rogue (recreation section); Galice, Oregon
- Nenana; Denali National Park, Alaska

- Lowe (Keystone Canyon); Alaska
- Bow; western Alberta

ORGANIZING GROUP TRIPS

Whitewater rafting is more enjoyable in the company of friends. Numerous office and professional groups, church and school groups, social and civic clubs, and other organizations have found rafting provides an ideal activity for recreational outings.

Outfitters prefer one person to serve as trip leader or organizer. The trip leader should make the group's reservation, deposit, and payment as required. He should also handle all arrangements with the outfitter. The selection of the right person as trip leader greatly influences the success of the planned rafting trip. A well-organized individual who pays careful attention to detail should find trip planning a relatively easy task. For another person, organizing a group rafting trip may be a frustrating and unpleasant experience.

To those organizing a group rafting trip for the first time, the following suggestions should be beneficial:

- Begin your planning months in advance. Start with an initial interest survey to determine approximately how many reservations you will need. The size of your group may well influence which outfitter and river you select.

- Learn as much about your group as you can before selecting a river trip. Carefully consider the likely participants, their age, experience, and physical limitations; don't plan a trip beyond their abilities. Unless the group has been rafting before, it may be best to plan a late spring or summer trip.

- Select an outfitter, river, date, and time and begin promoting the trip. Several large outfitting services have films, photographs, posters, and other informative materials to assist in the organization and promotion of group trips. Request an adequate supply of outfitter brochures or reproduce the pertinent information for everyone. Early planning may enable you to take advantage of your organization's newsletter and bulletin boards.

- Obtain either a check or cash from interested participants when they sign up. Only those who have paid should be considered definite participants. If you have a specific number of guaranteed reservations, persons should be informed in advance that after a certain date their money can be refunded only if someone is found to replace them.

- As the date of the actual trip nears, make sure all drivers and participants have necessary trip information, including a detailed

Whitewater rafting is an ideal activity for group recreational outings.

map with the location, name, and telephone numbers of the outfitter. Advise anyone who has unexpected car trouble or illness on the day of the trip to call the outfitter to avoid unnecessary delay for the rest of the group.

Outfitters offer varying price reductions or incentives for group rafting; trip leaders should decide how these savings can be passed on to participants. Some outfitters offer percentage discounts above a specified number of rafters. Others offer a free space for every rafter over a certain number. No one should object when a trip leader accepts a free trip in exchange for his time and organizational efforts. Finally, it may become necessary for a trip leader to include a per-rafter charge to cover out-of-pocket expenses such as long-distance telephone calls, promotional materials, or postage.

RIVER GUIDES

Competent, experienced, and friendly guides are essential for the safety and enjoyment of whitewater rafting trips. Outfitters provide a trip leader and one or more guides on each river trip depending on the size, age, and physical condition of the group. On more difficult rivers, at least one guide will be in each raft. On more moderate paddle-raft trips, guides may only ride in selected rafts.

Professional guides like Sobek's Mike Boyle are responsible for the safety and enjoyment of all rafting guests.

The guides' responsibilities include much more than safely maneuvering the rafts down the river. Prior to each trip, rafts and equipment must be packed and transported and food and supplies must be readied. During multiday trips, they must select and prepare campsites and meals, and be able to repair boats and equipment. They are also responsible for the comfort and enjoyment of guests on and off the river.

At the beginning of paddle-raft and paddle-assisted oar-raft trips, guides will explain and demonstrate a basic system of commands for controlling the raft and give you an opportunity to practice your responses. If your raft is unguided, your group should select a leader with previous rafting or canoeing experience and practice responding to the commands for maneuvering the raft.

In addition to being experienced in trip organization and management, paddling techniques, raft control, and river reading, most guides have had extensive training in first aid, cardiopulmonary resuscitation (CPR), and rescue methods. Before running difficult rapids, guides will often scout the best routes for existing water conditions and may even set up rescue procedures and safety throw lines. Once these decisions have been made, the guides will assemble the rafts and explain the selected route through the rapids.

Guides are selected not only for their whitewater skill, but also for their leadership, judgment, maturity, amiability, and organizational skills. Most are quite knowledgeable about the unique features of the particular river, such as its ecology, wildlife, geology, geography, history, and folklore. Guests are entertained by their musical talents and river stories and tales. You will find few professions in which persons enjoy their work more than do river guides.

RIVER ORIENTATION AND SAFETY

Prior to all river trips, the outfitter's trip leader will give an orientation and safety talk. It is important to pay close attention as guides discuss the river, the proper use of the equipment, mistakes to avoid, and safety procedures. Guides generally provide additional information during the river trip.

The orientation and safety talk may vary depending on the use of oar-guided or paddle rafts, but it should cover the following key points:

■ A general description of the river and the rapids you will run.

■ An explanation of the basic equipment: raft, life jacket, and paddle.

■ A demonstration of the basic techniques for paddling and controlling the raft.

Prior to each rafting trip, guides give a detailed orientation-and-safety briefing.

- A discussion of the potential hazards you may encounter.
- A demonstration of what to do if you fall in.
- An introduction to the ecology of the river including the flora and fauna.
- Information about the care and conservation of the river (including sanitation procedures).
- An opportunity for any questions.

Do not be alarmed if during the orientation and safety talk the guides exaggerate tales and joke about the upcoming trip. It is often an effective psychological method to "break the ice" with a group, and it sometimes helps tense rafters relax.

The outfitters and guides conducting your trip will take the necessary precautions to ensure a safe and enjoyable trip for all rafters. Your chances of sustaining an injury requiring medical attention are slight if you follow a few basic rules. Listen for additional guidelines given by your guides.

- Always wear your life jacket on and near the river. Make sure it fits correctly and is securely fastened.
- Do not take drugs or drink alcoholic beverages either before or during the river trip.
- Always wear tennis shoes or sneakers.
- Avoid wearing or carrying sharp objects.
- Be careful with your paddle when going through rapids.

Hold onto it with both hands; if you must release it with one hand, keep it outside the raft. Many rafters' injuries result from flailing paddles.

Should you fall from your raft, or if it should capsize, get out from under it. Once in the water, lean back, point your feet downstream, and let the water carry you. Don't try to stand up in swift water or your feet may become lodged between rocks. Try to propel yourself toward a raft, calm water, or shore. Keep your feet up.

LIABILITY WAIVER

Although whitewater outfitters and guides make every effort to provide safe trips, river rafting does include some danger. Due to the potential hazards of whitewater rafting, the terms are that you participate at your own risk. You can, however, minimize the risks by using good personal judgment and by following your guides' instructions.

You will be given an "Assumption of Personal Liability" form prior to your trip. You must read and sign it, and responsible adults must sign for children. Among other things, it simply states that you are expected to follow the outlined rules on the river. Also you agree that you will not hold the rafting outfitter liable for any personal injuries, loss of property, or damages resulting from your river trip. If you have any handicaps or medical problems that might hinder your ability to watch out for your own safety, you should inform the guides before the trip.

The personal-liability form may ask your permission to use photographs taken of you on the river for publicity or other purposes. Last, and perhaps one of the most important reasons for the form, it provides outfitters with names and addresses for mailing lists of rafters arriving with groups or with other individuals.

River rapids in North America are rated on a scale from one to six. Class I is the smallest of rapids and waves, and Class VI are extremely difficult rapids.
Photo courtesy of Four Corners Expeditions

RAPIDS CLASSIFICATIONS

Whitewater rapids in western America are rated on a scale of one to six, based on relative difficulty (usually written in Roman numerals). Class I is the smallest of rapids and waves, and Class VI is extremely difficult rapids. An earlier Class I to X rating scale, still referred to by some outfitters on the Colorado River, is a different scale rather than a continuation of difficulty for the International Class I–VI classification system.

A river's rating varies considerably with fluctuating water levels. Although higher water levels normally increase the difficulties of rapids, high water occasionally covers rocks sufficiently to wash out rapids. Conversely, some rapids become more difficult at lower water levels because more rocks are exposed.

Outfitters and guides are familiar with rapids classification and are always glad to explain the rating system in more detail.

Class I: Very small rapids with low waves, slow current, no obstructions.

Class II: Fairly frequent rapids of medium difficulty, few or no obstructions.

Class III: Difficult, large, irregular waves up to four feet, numerous rapids. The course requires some maneuvering of the raft.

Class IV: Very difficult, long extended rapids that require careful maneuvering of the raft; powerful irregular waves and dangerous rocks are common. The course is hard to determine and scouting is necessary.

Class V: Long and violent rapids. Large waves that are unavoidable and irregular. Extremely difficult and complex course. Scouting is essential.

Class VI: Maximum difficulty. Nearly impossible and extremely dangerous. Class V carried to the limit of navigability. Involves risk of life.

RIVER MEMORIES

Long after the final splash of the last rapid, you will likely remember the excitement and fun of your raft trip. With your rafting buddies you will relive the river, your passage through the whitewater, what you did right, what you did wrong, and how you will run it the next time. During each retelling of the story the rapids become more savage, your raft maneuvering more exacting, and the lure of the river stronger.

The challenge of whitewater rafting seems to draw you back. You want to run the river again, improve your technique or have a second shot at the big one. The wilderness solitude and beauty strengthen the magnetic force. You remember stretches of quiet water dotted with

Cliff swallows nest along the Texas Rio Grande River.
Photo by Nancy Jane Reid

sunlight, wildflowers adorning the shoreline, or the woods vibrant with fall colors. You savor the thrill of fast water—the incredible feeling of the natural river high. You want to remember it all.

Perhaps it is the intensity of these feelings that makes a river runner try to capture a bit of the river, to hold onto those memories.

Color photography is the most lasting visual reminder. Because of the difficulty of getting good pictures while on the water, many outfitters offer the services of a photographer positioned at key points along the river. In such cases, color prints of your raft can be ordered

Memories of the river experience linger long after the splash of the last rapid.

from the outfitter following the river trip. On some rivers, photographers also capture the excitement of your whitewater trip on video. Copies of the video may be purchased through the outfitter.

Probably the most popular river souvenirs are the colorful and artistic T-shirts sporting river slogans or river maps. Several outfitters use the proceeds from T-shirt sales for river conservation and preservation projects.

Other prevalent memorabilia available at outfitters and nearby shops are posters, postcards, frisbees, insignia patches, key chains, and photographs.

The excitement and pleasure of rafting are addicting. Once you've run a river, you will likely be hooked. At the conclusion of your river trip chances are, as you shed your life jacket and say goodbye to your friends, you also add, "until next time."

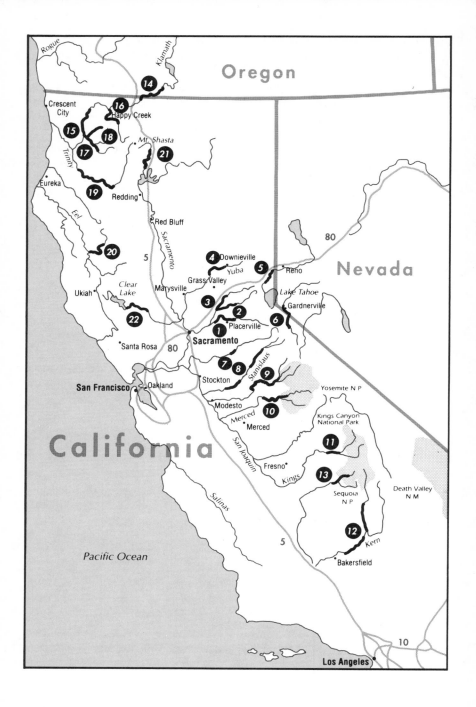

CHAPTER 2

California

CALIFORNIA, THE NATION'S MOST POPULOUS STATE also has some of the country's best whitewater rivers. Outfitters offer at least thirty-five rafting trips on more than twenty rivers in the mountain canyons and foothills of the central and southern Sierra Nevada and in the coastal mountain ranges of northern California.

California's most popular rafting rivers are in the western Sierra, near the agricultural-rich central valley. Here, free-flowing snowmelt from the high Sierra and controlled water releases from irrigation reservoirs and power dams are the sources of many of California's most well-known Class III–IV+ whitewater rivers, such as the Stanislaus, Tuolumne, Merced, Kern, and Kings. The most popular trip for first-time rafters is the dam-controlled South Fork of the American, which is in the historic gold country between Auburn and Placerville.

The rain-fed rivers of northern California's Pacific Coast mountains provide reliable all-season rafting and action-packed spring-season whitewater excitement for the adventurous rafter. Five of California's most challenging Class IV–V+ whitewater trips—the upper Klamath, Scott, Salmon, Wooley, and Trinity's Burnt Ranch Gorge—are within 75 miles (120 km) of the California–Oregon border. On a more relaxed scale, outfitters offer exciting, yet more moderate, Class II–III whitewater trips to rafters on the lower Klamath and Cache Creek.

Two reasons explain the rapid growth and popularity of California's whitewater market during the past decade. The obvious is the close proximity of many of the state's fine rivers to major population centers. Perhaps equally as important has been the aggressiveness with which outfitters have promoted their sport in the urban markets. This keen competitiveness among outfitters to obtain a larger share of the urban recreational market has generated a variety of whitewater trips. Such offerings include half-, single-, and multiday trips and trips geared to children, families, senior citizens, and the disabled.

Many outfitters also promote charter-bus trips for customers from San Francisco, Los Angeles, and other population centers. Interested rafters will find information about these trips described in outfitters' brochures.

1. AMERICAN RIVER (South Fork), CALIFORNIA

Section:	Chili Bar and Gorge runs
Location:	El Dorado County, central California between Auburn and Placerville
Distance:	9 miles (14 km) (Chili Bar)
	12 miles (19 km) (Gorge) distances for each section may vary between outfitters
Class:	II–III
Trip Options:	Mostly paddle raft, oar-guided raft upon request; one day on either section or two-day overnight including both sections
Season:	April–October
Outfitters:	A.B.L.E. Rafting Company
	Access to Adventure
	Action Adventures Wet 'n Wild
	Action Whitewater Adventures
	Adventure Connection
	All-Outdoors Adventure Trips
	American River Recreation
	American River Touring Association
	Beyond Limits Adventures
	California Adventures
	California River Trips
	Chili Bar Outdoor Center
	Earthtrek Expeditions
	ECHO: The Wilderness Company
	Environmental Travelling Companions (E.T.C.)
	Gold Country River Runners
	Gold Rush River Runners
	Libra Whitewater Expeditions
	Mariah Wilderness Expeditions
	Mother Lode River Trips
	O.A.R.S.
	Operation Challenge
	Outdoor Adventures–M.U. Recreation
	River Mountain Action

The South Fork of the American River, which flows through nineteenth-century gold rush country, is the site of California's most popular rafting trip.

River Rat and Company
River Riders Whitewater Tours
River Runners–California
Rollinson River Rafting
Rubicon Whitewater Adventures
Sierra Western Adventure Trips
South Bay River Rafters
Tributary Whitewater Tours
Turtle River Rafting Company
W.E.T. (Whitewater Expeditions and Tours)
Whitewater Connection
Whitewater Excitement
Whitewater Voyages
Wild River Tours
Zephyr River Expeditions

The South Fork of the American River, between Chili Bar and Folsom Lake, is California's most frequently rafted whitewater stretch. South Fork American maintains its popularity because of its exciting whitewater, beautiful scenery, historical setting, and proximity to population centers. The river's put-ins are an hour's drive from Sacramento and less than three hours from the San Francisco area. Many outfitters arrange charter-bus transportation from as far away as Los Angeles and San Diego.

Each year more than 80,000 rafters enjoy the South Fork's exciting, yet not too difficult, rapids in the heart of California's gold country. More than fifty Class II–III rapids, such as Meat Grinder, Racehorse Bend, African Queen, Triple Threat, Ambush Island, Swimmers, Troublemaker, Satan's Cesspool, Lower Haystack, Bouncing Rock, and Hospital Bar, test the skills of beginning and intermediate rafters. In addition to raft trips for groups, children, families, and first-timers, many outfitters are very accommodating to the disabled and disadvantaged populations.

South Fork American rafters may choose between one-day trips on the upper Chili Bar Run and the lower Gorge Run, and two-day camping trips that cover the 21-mile stretch from Chili Bar to Folsom Lake. On two-day trips outfitters offer many of the comforts of home: gourmet meals, saunas, and volleyball games.

The South Fork American flows past the historic town of Coloma, where John Marshall discovered gold and started the famed California Gold Rush of 1849.

2. AMERICAN RIVER (Middle Fork), CALIFORNIA

Section: Oxbow to Mammoth Bar
Location: Placer County, central California between Auburn and Foresthill
Distance: 26 miles (42 km) or less
Class: II–IV +
Trip Options: Paddle raft, oar raft; one to three days
Season: April–October
Outfitters: A.B.L.E. Rafting Company
                 Access to Adventure
                 Action Adventures Wet 'n Wild
                 Action Whitewater Adventures
                 Adventure Connection
                 All-Outdoors Adventure Trips
                 American River Recreation
                 American River Touring Association
                 Beyond Limits Adventures
                 California River Trips
                 Chili Bar Outdoor Center
                 Earthtrek Expeditions
                 Libra Whitewater Expeditions
                 Mariah Wilderness Expeditions
                 Mother Lode River Trips
                 Outdoors Unlimited River Trips
                 RAM River Expeditions
                 River Rat and Company
                 Rollison River Rafting
                 Tributary Whitewater Tours
                 W.E.T. (Whitewater Expeditions and Tours)
                 Whitewater Connection
                 Whitewater Excitement
                 Whitewater Voyages
                 Wild River Tours

The Middle Fork of the American River, in the western Sierra foothills, provides rafters with the unique opportunity to experience a wilderness river in California's gold rush country. Numerous beaches, side creeks, and waterfalls alternating with exciting whitewater provide a variety of adventure for river lovers. Along the calmer areas of the river, the chances of seeing deer, black bears, otters, and bald and golden eagles are excellent. On overnight trips, rafters generally have ample time to fish for the river's trout.

One of the first rapids encountered on the Middle Fork is Tunnel Chute, a fast, steep, narrow piece of water leading into a 30-yard granite tunnel, which was blasted through the mountainside by early miners. Because of a potential for injury at some water levels, outfitters may not always run Tunnel Chute. Downstream, most Class II–III rapids, such as Karma, Gumby, and Bus Wreck, are more civilized. The exceptions are Ruck-A-Chucky and Murderer's Bar rapids that are usually portaged.

An energetic group of paddle rafters navigate the Class IV + Tunnel Chute on the Middle Fork American.
Photo by Curt Smith

3. AMERICAN RIVER (North Fork), CALIFORNIA

Section:	Chamberlain Falls and Giant Gap
Location:	Placer County, central California near Iowa Hill
Distance:	9 miles (14 km) (Chamberlain Falls)
	14 miles (22 km) (Giant Gap)
Class:	IV + (Chamberlain Falls)
	V (Giant Gap)
Trip Options:	Mostly paddle raft; paddle only on the Giant Gap run; one and two days
Season:	April–June
Outfitters:	A.B.L.E. Rafting Company

Access to Adventure
Action Adventures Wet 'n Wild
Action Whitewater Adventures
Adventure Connection
All-Outdoors Adventure Trips
American River Recreation
American River Touring Association
Beyond Limits Adventures
California River Trips
Chili Bar Outdoor Center
Earthtrek Expeditions
ECHO: The Wilderness Company
Libra Whitewater Expeditions
Mariah Wilderness Expeditions
Mother Lode River Trips
O.A.R.S.
Outdoor Adventures-M.U. Recreation
RAM River Expeditions
River Rat and Company
River Riders Whitewater Tours
River Runners–California
Rollison River Rafting
Rubicon Whitewater Adventures
Tributary Whitewater Tours
W.E.T. (Whitewater Expeditions and Tours)
Whitewater Connection
Whitewater Excitement
Whitewater Voyages
Wild River Tours

The North Fork of the American River, Chamberlain Falls run, offers a spectacular whitewater run through a wilderness canyon that is protected under the California Wild and Scenic Rivers Act. During the first half of the 9-mile (14 km) trip, the river drops through narrow boulder-filled Class III–IV + rapids such as Chamberlain and Bogus Thunder falls, Staircase, Nose Stand, and Entrance Exam. On the more mellow lower half of the trip, the river has numerous relaxing and enjoyable Class II–III rapids.

Rafting on the free-flowing North Fork American depends upon snowmelt from the Desolation Wilderness region of the Sierras, west of Lake Tahoe. Considered a step up from the Class II–III South Fork American, outfitters prefer rafters to have had previous Class III whitewater experience.

The North Fork American, Giant Gap run, is yet another step up in difficulty. It is one of California's finest and most technical whitewater stretches. For nearly 14 miles from Eucre Bar to the Iowa Hill Bridge take-out, rafters challenge one Class V rapid after another in a 2,000-foot canyon. Now included in the National Wild and Scenic River System, the Giant Gap run has just recently been opened to a limited number of raft trips. To reach the Eucre Bar put-in, rafters must hike 2 miles into a steep ravine.

4. YUBA RIVER (North Fork), CALIFORNIA

Section:	Union Flat Run (upper)
	Goodyear's Bar Run (lower)
Location:	Sierra County near Downieville, north-central California
Distance:	10 miles (16 km) (upper)
	18 miles (29 km) (lower)
Class:	V (upper); III–IV (lower)
Trip Options:	Paddle raft, oar raft; one day (upper). Paddle raft, oar raft; one and two days (lower).
Season:	April–June
Outfitters:	Beyond Limits Adventures
	Tributary Whitewater Tours
	Whitewater Voyages

The North Fork of the Yuba River features almost 30 miles (48 km) of exciting free-flowing whitewater near the historic Gold Rush town of Downieville. Its steep Class V upper or Union Flat section, which cascades for 10 miles (16 km) through numerous boulder gardens containing narrow chutes, concludes with the Class V Rosasso Ravine just above Goodyear's Bar, where the gradient exceeds 100 feet a mile.

North Yuba's 18-mile (29 km) lower, or Goodyear's Bar, run offers rafters the choice between a one-day, 9-mile (14 km) run to Fiddle Creek or a two-day trip that ends in the placid waters of New Bullards Bar Reservoir. The highlight of the Goodyear's Bar run is the spectacular Class V, Maytag Rapid, just upstream from Fiddle Creek.

Tahoe National Forest's issuance of commercial rafting permits to only three outfitters on the Yuba River assures an uncrowded experience for those who raft on this beautiful Sierra river. California Route 49, which parallels much of the river, provides several vantage points from which to take photographs of the north Yuba's exciting rapids.

Rafters on the Yuba should allow extra time to visit Downieville, one of the state's most charming and picturesque gold rush mining towns.

5. TRUCKEE RIVER, CALIFORNIA

Section:	Floriston to Crystal Peak Park
Location:	Nevada and Placer counties near Lake Tahoe, east-central California
Distance:	12 miles (19 km)
Class:	III–IV
Trip Options:	Paddle raft, oar raft; one and two days
Season:	April–October
Outfitter:	RAM River Expeditions

The Truckee River, only a 20-minute drive from Reno, Nevada, provides rafters with beautiful eastern Sierra scenery and lively whitewater, just below nearly 11 miles (18 km) of the historic Donner Trail. While the Truckee's most challenging whitewater trips result from the spring snowmelt from Lake Tahoe during May and June, rafting is usually possible until early October.

Interested rafters should ask travel agents at Reno and Lake Tahoe-area hotels to assist them with information about whitewater rafting on the Truckee River.

6. CARSON RIVER (East Fork), CALIFORNIA/NEVADA

Sections:	Cave Rock to Hangman's Bridge (upper)
	Hangman's Bridge to Ruhenstroth Dam (Wilderness Run)
Location:	Alpine County, southeast of Lake Tahoe, east-central California near Markleeville
Distance:	7 miles (11 km) (upper)
	20 miles (32 km) (Wilderness Run)

Class:	III (upper); II (Wilderness Run)
Trip Options:	Paddle raft, oar raft; one and two days
Season:	April–June
Outfitters:	Access to Adventure
	Action Adventures Wet 'n Wild
	American River Recreation
	Beyond Limits Adventures
	California Adventures
	California River Trips
	Environmental Travelling Companions (E.T.C.)
	O.A.R.S.
	RAM River Expeditions
	River Journey
	Tributary Whitewater Tours
	W.E.T. (Whitewater Expeditions & Tours)
	Whitewater Voyages
	Wild River Tours
	Zephyr River Expeditions

The East Fork Carson River, named for the explorer Kit Carson, affords rafters two relatively easy, yet very scenic, whitewater trips down the semiarid eastern slopes of the California Sierra in Toiyabe National Forest. Outfitters offer the Class III swift-moving upper East Fork Carson above Markleeville as a one-day trip and the Class II Wilderness Run from Markleeville to the desert near Gardnerville, Nevada, as a two-day trip with overnight camping.

Except for during early spring, the mildness of the East Fork Carson below Markleeville makes it an idea river trip for families and first-time rafters. Unfortunately, without an unusually heavy winter snowfall in the Sierras, the rafting season lasts only from April until late June.

7. MOKELUMNE RIVER, CALIFORNIA

Section:	Electra Run
Location:	Calaveras County near Jackson and Mokelumne Hill, central California
Distance:	5 miles (8 km)
Class:	II +
Trip Options:	Paddle raft, inflatable kayak; half-day
Season:	March–September
Outfitters:	Great Valley Canoe and Raft Trips
	O.A.R.S.
	Sunshine Outdoor Center
	Tributary Whitewater Tours

Just an hour's drive east of Sacramento, the Mokelumne River's Electra run is a short and easy, yet very popular, whitewater run for beginners. Its mostly Class II rapids enable families with children as young as eight years old an opportunity to experience the excitement of whitewater. Outfitters also offer inflatable kayak trips when water levels are low during the summer. Many rafters take advantage of the trip's short length and run the river twice in one day.

8. STANISLAUS RIVER, CALIFORNIA

Section: North Fork, Sourgrass to Calaveras Big Trees State Park
Location: Calaveras County near Dorrington; central California
Distance: 5 miles (8 km)
Class: III–IV; experience highly recommended
Trip Options: Paddle raft; one day
Season: April–June
Outfitters: A.B.L.E. Rafting Company
                All-Outdoors Adventure Trips
                Beyond Limits Adventures
                Whitewater Voyages

The North Fork Stanislaus River is nestled within the breathtaking granite gorges of Stanislaus National Forest and Calaveras Big Trees State Park in the heart of the mother lode. Along the banks of the whitewater run, giant sequoias tower above the beautiful azaleas, dogwoods, and side canyon waterfalls.

The North Fork Stanislaus, however, is not a river for first-time rafters. The many technical Class III–IV + pool-drop rapids leave little time to enjoy some of the river's most spectacular scenery. While the North Fork's lack of water has limited summertime rafting in the past, outfitters expect that more dependable water releases from upstream reservoirs will greatly expand the season of this run.

Rafters on the North Fork Stanislaus should allow enough time to wander through the North Grove of Calaveras Big Trees State Park and visit the nearby Mercer Caverns and the historic gold rush towns of Columbia and Murphys.

Section: Middle Fork
Location: Calaveras County near Dorrington, central California
Distance: 10 miles (16 km)
Class: IV–V + ; Class IV experience required
Trip Options: Paddle raft, oar raft; one and two days
Season: April-June
Outfitters: A.B.L.E. Rafting Company
              All-Outdoors Adventure Trips
              Beyond Limits Adventures
              River Journey
              Tributary Whitewater Tours

The Middle Fork Stanislaus River, like the Upper Tuolumne and the Giant Gap run on the North Fork American, offers sensational Class V + whitewater action that should be attempted only by the experienced rafter. Its numerous Class IV–V + rapids are normally rafted, sometimes walked, from late April until June.

Hidden at the bottom of a seemingly inaccessible gorge, the put-in for the Middle Fork Stanislaus is nearly as difficult as the river itself. A 2-mile hike down a switchback trail is the only access to the river, which is some 3,000 feet below the roadway.

The upper canyon of the Middle Fork Stanislaus is a relatively new whitewater run. Under experimental permits from the Stanislaus National Forest, three professional outfitters have offered rafting trips since 1986. The take-out is at Camp Nine, a forest camp just upstream from the New Melones Reservoir. The impoundment covers what was widely acclaimed to be one of America's most beautiful stretches of whitewater.

Section: Lower: Goodwin Canyon to Knight's Ferry
              Knight's Ferry to Orange Blossom
Location: Stanislaus and Calaveras counties near Knight's Ferry, central California
Distance: Goodwin Dam to Knight's Ferry: 4.5 miles (7 km)
              Knight's Ferry to Orange Blossom: 8 miles (13 km)
Class: Goodwin Dam to Knight's Ferry: III–IV +
              Knight's Ferry to Orange Blossom: I–II
Trip Options: Paddle raft, oar raft; one day
Season: June–October
Outfitters: Adventure Connection
              Beyond Limits Adventures
              Great Valley Canoe and Raft Trips
              River Journey

Sunshine Outdoor Center
Tributary Whitewater Tours

The lower Stanislaus River offers a challenging 4.5-mile (7 km) Class III–IV+ whitewater stretch, which runs through the beautiful Goodwin Canyon Gorge from Goodwin Dam to Knight's Ferry. Below Knight's Ferry, the lower Stanislaus mellows into a relatively calm but swift flowing 8-mile (13 km) Class I–II stretch that is an ideal introduction to whitewater for families with children.

9. TUOLUMNE RIVER, CALIFORNIA

Section:	Main: Lumsden Launch to Ward's Ferry Bridge
Location:	Tuolumne County, northwest of Yosemite National Park near Groveland, central California
Distance:	18 miles (29 km)
Class:	III–IV+ ; IV–V in high water
Trip Options:	Paddle raft, oar raft, oar/paddle raft; one, two, and three days
Season:	April–October
Outfitters:	Action Adventures Wet n' Wild
	All-Outdoors Adventure Trips
	American River Touring Association
	ECHO: The Wilderness Company
	O.A.R.S.
	Outdoor Adventures
	Sierra Mac River Trips
	Whitewater Voyages
	Zephyr River Expeditions

The Tuolumne, a National Wild and Scenic River since 1984, has all of the features that any river adventurer could want: remoteness, beauty, wildlife, and swift-flowing and demanding whitewater. In addition, its banks and side canyons are awash with the folklore of the Miwok Indians and early California gold seekers.

For more than two decades, the classic 18-mile (29 km) main Tuolumne has been one of California's premier whitewater trips. Following a breathtaking shuttle ride down the steep canyon to Meral's Pool near Lumsden put-in, the river trip drops to 760 feet at Ward's Ferry Bridge. This steep gradient, varying between 30 and 70 feet per mile, creates fifteen major Class IV–IV+ rapids. Tuolumne's noted rapids include Sunderland's Chute, Hackamack's Hole, Ram's Head, The Squeeze, Clavey Falls, Grey's Grindstone, and Hell's Kitchen. The most exciting rapid is Clavey Falls, a breathtaking Class IV+ plunge, one of the major drops on western rivers.

Paddle-assisted oarsman successfully avoids large hydraulic below the Tuolumne's Class IV–V Clavey Falls.

Section:	Upper: Cherry Creek
Location:	Tuolumne County, northwest of Yosemite National Park near Groveland, central California
Distance:	9 miles (14 km)
Class:	IV–V + ; Class IV rafting experience is highly recommended
Trip Options:	Paddle raft, paddle/oar raft; one day
Season:	April–August
Outfitters:	See list for main Tuolumne section

Rafters wanting an even greater challenge than the main Tuolumne should ask outfitters about the river's upper run from Cherry Creek to Meral's Pool. Known as the Cherry Creek trip, unbelievable Class V + rapids cascade and drop almost continuously (at times up to 150 feet per mile), for nearly 9 miles (14 km) to the start of the main Tuolumne trip. Class IV–V + rapids, such as Mushroom, Miracle Mile, Lewis's Leap, Flat Rock, and Horseshoe Falls, will excite even the most experienced rafter.

Self-bailing rafts and more experienced outfitters make it possible to descend the upper Tuolumne, previously thought unrunnable. Persons interested in the one-day Cherry Creek or upper Tuolumne raft trip should contact any of the outfitters who offer trips on the main Tuolumne.

10. MERCED RIVER, CALIFORNIA

Section: Cranberry Gulch to Lake McClure near Bagby
Location: Mariposa County near El Portal, central California
Distance: 27 miles (43 km)
Class: III–IV + ; experience recommended during spring high water
Trip Options: Paddle raft, oar raft; one and two days
Season: April–July
                A.B.L.E. Rafting Company
Outfitters: All-Outdoors Adventure Trips
                American River Touring Association
                Earthtrek Expeditions
                Mariah Wilderness Expeditions
                Merced River Trips
                O.A.R.S.
                Whitewater Excitement
                Whitewater Voyages
                Wild River Tours
                Zephyr River Expeditions

Just west of Yosemite National Park's Arch Rock entrance, the Merced River begins a spectacular Class III–IV whitewater journey through a non-glaciated V-shaped canyon alongside California's Route 140. This is in sharp contrast to the tranquil section of the Merced River seen by the millions of persons who visit the park's glaciated valley floor each year. Merced Canyon was added to the National Wild and Scenic River System in 1987.

The Merced is one of the Sierra's more popular whitewater rivers. Dropping at rates of up to 70 feet per mile, the high waters of April and May often push many of its terrific rapids into the Class IV + range.

11. KINGS RIVER, CALIFORNIA

Section: Garnet Dyke to Kirch Flat
Location: Fresno County, east of Fresno, central California
Distance: 10 miles (16 km)
Class: III–IV
Raft Options: Paddle raft, oar raft; one and two days
Season: April–August
Outfitters: Kings River Expeditions
                Spirit Whitewater
                Zephyr River Expeditions

The Kings River is the largest of the Sierra's many fine whitewater rivers. It is free flowing during its westward descent through Kings Canyon National Park and Sequoia National Forest until it enters Pine Flat Lake, nearly due east of Fresno.

Generally rafters find the King's best whitewater from early May through June. During this peak springtime runoff, more than 25 rapids, many in the Class III–IV range, provide a thrilling intermediate-advanced run with numerous large waves and fast currents. Although considerably less intense during July and August, the Kings still offers fine whitewater and beautiful mountain canyon scenery.

12. KERN RIVER, CALIFORNIA

The remarkable Kern River, unlike most Sierra waters, flows north-to-south instead of east-to-west for 100 of its 165 miles (264 km). Outfitters offer nearly 60 miles (96 km) of exciting whitewater and beautiful Sierran scenery on the Kern River between Sequoia National Park and Bakersfield.

Skilled oarsman guides raft through Vortex Rapid on California's Class IV–V + Forks of the Kern.
Photo by Curt Smith

Section: Forks of the Kern
Location: Tulare County, south of Sequoia National Park, south-
                 central California
Distance: 18 miles (29 km)
Class: IV–V + ; Class IV experience required
Trip Options: Paddle raft, oar raft; two and three days
Season: April–July
Outfitters: Chuck Richard's Whitewater
                 Kern River Tours
                 Outdoor Adventures
                 Whitewater Voyages

The Forks of the Kern run, which is formed by the confluence of the
Little Kern and the main Kern, is rated by whitewater experts as one
of the most technically demanding runs in California. Its almost
equally difficult access—a 2-mile (3 km) downhill trail—requires
pack horses and mules. The Forks, as the river is called by outfitters,
has a gradient of nearly 64 feet per mile creating numerous Class IV–
V + rapids, many of which must be scouted and, during high water,
sometimes must be portaged.

Section: Upper: Johnsondale to Kernville
Location: Kern and Tulare counties, north of Kernville, south-
                 central California
Distance: 20 miles (32 km) or less
Class: III–IV + ; Class IV paddling experience required
Trip Options: Paddle raft, oar raft; one and two days
Season: May–July
Outfitters: Chuck Richard's Whitewater
                 Kern River Tours
                 Outdoor Adventures
                 Sierra South (family trip near Kernville only)
                 Whitewater Voyages

The upper Kern River, between Johnsondale Bridge and River Kern
Beach at the top of Lake Isabella Reservoir, is less demanding than the
Forks run, but has plenty of exciting whitewater of varying difficulty.
The Class III–IV Limestone run above Fairview Dam is just a warm-
up for the whitewater in the dam's tailwaters. The 17 miles (27 km)
from the dam to Kernville includes the Fairview and Goldledge, or
Thunder Run stretches, which offer numerous Class III–V rapids.
Some outfitters now offer family and first-timer float trips through
Class II–III Powerhouse, Big Daddy, and Ewings rapids beginning
just above Kernville.

Section:	Lower: Lake Isabella to Democrat Beach
Location:	Kern County, east of Bakersfield, south-central California
Distance:	21 miles (34 km) or less
Class:	III–IV
Trip Options:	Paddle raft, oar raft; one and two days
Season:	May–October
Outfitters:	Chuck Richard's Whitewater
	Kern River Tours
	Outdoor Adventures
	Whitewater Voyages

The Lower Kern River runs from Lake Isabella through the Greenhorn Mountain canyons to the central valley's floor. Outfitters offer rafters several one- and two-day trip options. While most rapids in this section are class III–IV, Royal Flush is rated a Class V + and is normally portaged.

13. KAWEAH RIVER, CALIFORNIA

Section:	Gateway Bridge to Terminus Reservoir
Location:	Tulare County, east of Visalia, south-central California
Distance:	12–20 miles (19–32 km)
Class:	III–V + ; experience and wet suits required
Trip Options:	Paddle raft; one and two days
Season:	April–June
Outfitters:	Adventure Connection
	Libra Whitewater Expeditions
	Tributary Whitewater Tours

The Kaweah River, which drains the 12,000-foot high peaks of Sequoia National Park, is one of California's steepest and most challenging whitewater runs. The incredibly beautiful river, which parallels California Route 198, is also very close to southern California's metropolitan centers. It is just a three-and-one-half-hour drive from Los Angeles. The Kaweah offers an excellent opportunity to combine a whitewater adventure with a trip to Sequoia or Kings Canyon national parks.

Outfitters reserve the stretch of the Kaweah River, between the East and North forks, as an expert run for physically fit and adventurous rafters. During spring's high waters, many of the Class IV–V + rapids are scouted; some must be portaged.

While the excitement of Kaweah's whitewater will long be remembered, its season is usually short. Prospective rafters should make reservations early and maintain close contact with their outfitter just prior to the scheduled trip.

14. KLAMATH RIVER (Upper), OREGON/CALIFORNIA

Section: Hell's Corner Gorge
Location: Klamath County, southern Oregon, and Siskiyou County, northern California
Distance: 18 miles (29 km)
Class: IV–V; Class IV experience recommended
Trip Options: Paddle raft, oar raft, paddle/oar raft; one and two days
Season: May–September
Outfitters: A.B.L.E. Rafting Company
Adventure Connection
All-Outdoors Adventure Trips
American River Recreation
American River Touring Association
Beyond Limits Adventures
Eagle Sun
Headwaters River Adventures
Ken Warren Outdoors
Munroe's Wilderness Adventures
Noah's World of Water
Ouzel Outfitters
Rogue/Klamath River Adventures
Sierra Whitewater Expeditions
Tributary Whitewater Tours
Trinity River Rafting Center
Turtle River Rafting Company
W.E.T. (Whitewater Expeditions and Tours)
Whitewater Connection
Whitewater Voyages

The upper Klamath, between the John Boyle Powerhouse near Klamath Falls, in southern Oregon, and Copco Lake in northern California, features the 200-mile-long (320 km) river's most exciting and challenging whitewater. It is little wonder that so many of central California's outfitters include the upper Klamath on their list of river selections.

The moderate Class I–II waters at the beginning of the upper Klamath are used to practice maneuvering rafts and hone paddling skills. Once the river enters the volcanic Hell's Corner Gorge, the river is transformed into a very challenging and demanding Class IV–V whitewater stretch with more than forty major rapids and waterfalls. During one 6-mile (9 km) stretch, the river's gradient averages 85 feet per mile. Many of these rapids are known by colorful western names: Old Hooch, Gunsmoke, Stageline, Branding Iron, Wild Card, Jackass, Ambush, and Ol' Bushwacker.

Hell's Corner Gorge is well known for its consistent year-round water flows. Many outfitters accordingly promote the gorge trip as California and Oregon's best all-season Class IV + trip. While river guides do their best to help rafters enjoy the beautiful scenery of Klamath National Forest, its abundant wildlife, and quaint nineteenth century cabins and ranches in the gorge, this is not always an easy task, due to the demanding nature of the river trip.

Most outfitters require rafters in paddle boats to have had Class IV whitewater experience. Except for the colder spring months, wet suits are normally not required.

15. KLAMATH RIVER (Lower), CALIFORNIA

Section:	Happy Camp to Ti Bar
Location:	Del Norte County, northern California
Distance:	35 miles (56 km) or less
Class:	II–III
Trip Options:	Paddle raft, oar raft, paddle/oar raft, inflatable kayak; one to three days
Season:	May–September
Outfitters:	A.B.L.E. Rafting Company
	All-Outdoors Adventure Trips
	American River Touring Association
	Beyond Limits Adventures
	California Adventures
	Cooley River Expeditions
	Electric Rafting Company
	Environmental Travelling Companions (E.T.C.)
	Klamath River Outdoor Experiences
	Klamath River Outfitters
	MG Whitewater Adventures
	Mother Lode River Trips
	Munroe's Wilderness Adventures
	Noah's World of Water
	O.A.R.S.
	Orange Torpedo Trips

Oregon River Experiences
Oregon Whitewater Adventures
Outdoor Unlimited River Trips
Ouzel Outfitters
River Country Rafting
Rivers West Whitewater Specialists
Rogue–Klamath River Adventures
Rubicon Whitewater Adventures
The Somes Bar Lodge
Sunrise Expeditions
Sunshine Outdoor Center
Ti Bar Guide Service
Tributary Whitewater Tours
Trinity River Rafting Center
Turtle River Rafting Center
W.E.T. (Whitewater Expeditions & Tours)
Whitewater Voyages
Wild River Tours

The lower Klamath gives families and first-time rafters a unique opportunity to enjoy either a single-day or multiday whitewater trip. The scenic river, with deep-wooded canyons and abundant wildlife, is protected by both California and National Wild and Scenic River legislation.

Children learn the techniques of paddle rafting on northern California's lower Klamath River.
Photo courtesy of Turtle River Rafting Company

Challenging Class II–III rapids alternating with quiet stretches offer a near-perfect blend of rafting, swimming, hiking, fishing, and relaxing on the trip beginning at Happy Camp. Its flow, along with that of the upper Klamath, is dam-controlled; it has consistently reliable water levels throughout the summer.

Rafting enthusiasts seeking a Klamath adventure that combines both the upper and lower sections should ask outfitters about the five- or six-day river extravaganza.

16. SCOTT RIVER, CALIFORNIA

Section:	Kelsey Creek and Klamath River confluence
Location:	Siskiyou County, near Etna, northern California
Distance:	18 miles (29 km) or less
Class:	IV–V
Trip Options:	Paddle raft, paddle/oar raft; one and two days
Season:	April–June
Outfitters:	A.B.L.E. Rafting Company
	Adventures Whitewater
	All-Outdoors Adventure Trips
	Beyond Limits Adventures
	Eagle Sun
	Mother Lode River Trips
	Munroe's Wilderness Adventures
	Noah's World of Water
	Tributary Whitewater Tours
	Turtle River Rafting Company
	W.E.T. (Whitewater Expeditions and Tours)
	Whitewater Voyages

The beautiful Scott River, nestled in northern California's Marble Mountains, is aptly described as a whitewater jewel. After a serene passage through the pastoral Scott valley, the river plunges into a gorge with numerous long, difficult, and powerful Class IV–V boulder drops rapids. During the Scott's downward tumble to the Klamath, the gradient sometimes exceeds 100 feet per mile. Its technical Class IV–IV+ rapids—Boulder Creek Falls, Schuler Gulch, White House, and Tompkins and Canyon creeks—are several of California's finest.

The free-flowing Scott has a relatively small drainage area; therefore, outfitters normally run whitewater trips on the river for a few weeks each spring. Early reservations are essential because of the limited number of trips.

Rafters should be experienced, physically fit, and ready for cold water, cold weather, and superb whitewater excitement.

17. SALMON RIVER, CALIFORNIA

Section: Forks of Salmon to Somes Bar
Location: Siskiyou County, east of Orleans, northern California
Distance: 18–21 miles (29–34 km)
Class: IV–V; experience required by most outfitters
Trip Options: Paddle raft, oar raft, paddle/oar raft; one and two days
Season: April–July
Outfitters: A.B.L.E. Rafting Company
               Adventures Whitewater
               All-Outdoors Adventure Trips
               American River Recreation
               American River Touring Association
               Beyond Limits Adventures
               Eagle Sun
               ECHO: The Wilderness Company
               Electric Rafting Company
               Great Out of Doors
               Klamath River Outfitters
               Mother Lode River Trips
               Munroe's Wilderness Adventures
               Noah's World of Water
               O.A.R.S.
               Outdoor Adventures-MU Recreation
               Ouzel Outfitters
               Rubicon Whitewater Adventures
               Sierra Whitewater Expeditions
               The Somes Bar Lodge
               Sunrise Expeditions
               Ti Bar Guide Service
               Tributary Whitewater Tours
               Turtle River Rafting Company
               W.E.T. (Whitewater Expeditions & Tours)
               Whitewater Excitement
               Whitewater Voyages

The Wild and Scenic "California Salmon," so referred to by river outfitters to avoid confusion with the famed Idaho Salmon, is near the Trinity River's Burnt Ranch Gorge. After a deceptively easy start near the community of Forks of the Salmon in the Klamath National Forest, northeast of Eureka, the Salmon drops into an incredibly beautiful and rugged gorge with vertical granite walls decorated by hanging ferns, wildflowers, and sparkling waterfalls. Snowmelt waters from the Trinity Alps passing over and through large boulder gardens generate more than fifty exciting rapids that include numerous Class IV rapids. Also in this stretch are three dynamic Class V rapids: Cascade, Last Chance, and Freight Train.

Outfitters normally run one-day trips on both the upper and lower sections of the Salmon. On two-day trips, the 10-mile Class III–IV lower, or Butler Creek section, is frequently used as a preparatory run to the Class IV–V Nordheimer section.

Rafters must not take the California Salmon lightly. Its steep gradient exceeds that of the main Tuolumne. Most outfitters require rafters to be at least sixteen years old and have Class IV rafting experience.

The "California Salmon" is one of the state's many excellent Class IV–V whitewater rivers.
Photo by Curt Smith

18. WOOLEY CREEK, CALIFORNIA

Section: Fowler Cabin to the California Salmon River confluence
Location: Siskiyou County near Somes Bar, northern California
Distance: 9 miles (14 km)
Class: V; experience required
Trip Options: Paddle raft; one to three days
Season: April–June
Outfitters: A.B.L.E. Rafting Company
               Munroe's Wilderness Adventures

Wooley Creek, located in northern California's Marble Mountain Wilderness Area, is a recent addition to the state's growing list of fine whitewater runs. First commercially rafted in 1985, it is now revered as one of California's finest wilderness creek opportunities.

The Class V Wooley Creek cascades downward through an extremely narrow gorge to the California Salmon. In some stretches the creek reaches an electrifying gradient of more than 100 feet per mile. The trip concludes with a 5-mile (8 km) journey on the Class I–II waters of the Salmon just above its confluence with the Klamath.

Wooley Creek is for experienced whitewater paddlers who are at least eighteen years old and in good physical condition. Self-bailing rafts and scouting major rapids are essential for a safe trip.

The natural beauty of Wooley Creek is superb. Giant trees, moss-covered logs, and breathtaking canyon walls—sometimes rising abruptly for 200-feet—complement the fantastic whitewater for a truly memorable wilderness experience.

19. TRINITY RIVER, CALIFORNIA

Section:	Upper
Location:	Trinity County, west of Weaverville, northern California
Distance:	25–36 miles (40–58 km) or less
Class:	II–III +
Trip Options:	Paddle raft, oar raft; one to five days
Season:	April–October
Outfitters:	Beyond Limits Adventures
	Electric Rafting Company
	Great Out of Doors
	Headwaters River Adventures
	Munroe's Wilderness Adventures
	Rubicon Whitewater Adventures
	Tributary Whitewater Tours
	Trinity River Company
	Trinity River Rafting Center
	Turtle River Rafting Company
	Whitewater Voyages

The upper Trinity River offers an excellent introduction to whitewater rafting in Salmon–Trinity Alps Wilderness and the Trinity National Forest. Trips of varying lengths enable families, senior citizens, and the disabled to enjoy the beautiful mountain scenery and exciting, but not too difficult, rapids. California Route 299, which parallels much of the Trinity, provides several excellent photographic views of the scenic river.

Regular water releases from Lewiston Dam, in the Whiskeytown Shasta–Trinity National Recreation Area, usually ensure ample water levels for rafting throughout the summer season.

Section:	Burnt Ranch Gorge
Location:	Trinity County near Burnt Ranch, northern California
Distance:	9 miles (14 km)
Class:	IV–V; Class IV experience required
Trip Options:	Paddle rafts; one and two days
Season:	June–September
Outfitters:	Beyond Limits Adventure
	Headwaters River Adventures
	Tributary Whitewater Tours
	Whitewater Voyages

The most spectacular stretch of the Trinity River is known as the Burnt Ranch Gorge, near the small town of Burnt Ranch. First run by Whitewater Voyages in 1983, many professional outfitters had previously considered this Class V section unrunnable. Today with the use of self-bailing paddle rafts and more experienced guides, outfitters regularly schedule trips through the Class IV–V technical waters of the nearly 2,000-foot deep gorge.

Many whitewater experts rate the 9-mile (14 km) Burnt Ranch Gorge as California's most challenging raft trip. Five Class IV–IV +

rapids within the first 2.5 miles (4 km) are a necessary prerequisite to the seven Class V–V + rapids—Upper, Middle, and Lower Burnt Ranch Falls, Hennessey and Gray falls, Origami, and Table Rock—that follow.

Water releases from Lewiston Dam provide the best summer-season Class V rafting in the state. As on the California Salmon and the Scott rivers, only experienced and physically fit rafters are permitted on the Trinity's Burnt Ranch Gorge whitewater trip.

20. EEL RIVER (Middle), CALIFORNIA

Section: Black Butte River to Dos Rios
Location: Mendocino County, north of Ukiah, northern California
Distance: 30 miles (48 km)
Class: I–III
Trip Options: Paddle raft, oar raft, inflatable kayak; one to three days
Season: April–June
Outfitters: River Country Rafting
                Rubicon Whitewater Adventures
                Tributary Whitewater Tours
                Turtle River Rafting Company

The Middle Fork of the Eel River provides one of the best wilderness raft trips in California. Trips begin at the Middle Eel's confluence with the Black Butte River in Mendocino National Forest and end 30 miles (48 km) later at the small town of Dos Rios.

On oar-guided trips, families and inexperienced paddlers can enjoy this beautiful mountain stream. An uncontrolled river, its beauty normally can only be enjoyed during the spring rains and runoff. The trip starts out as an easy Class II and gradually increases to Class III by the last one-third of the river. Coal Mine Falls, a Class IV–V + drop near the end of the trip is usually portaged.

About a three-hour drive north of the Bay Area, the Middle Eel is an excellent multiday springtime raft trip. In addition to its several waterfalls, occasional wildlife may be seen.

21. SACRAMENTO RIVER (Upper), CALIFORNIA

Sections: Sims Flat to Dog Creek
Location: Siskiyou and Shasta counties near Dunsmuir, northern California
Distance: 35 miles (56 km) or less
Class: III–IV
Trip Options: Paddle raft, oar raft; one to three days
Season: April–June
Outfitters: Great Out of Doors
                 Mother Lode River Trips
                 Munroe's Wilderness Adventures
                 Tributary Whitewater Tours
                 Turtle River Rafting Company
                 W.E.T. (Whitewater Expeditions and Tours)

Just below northern California's snowcapped Mount Shasta, and parallel to Interstate 5, the upper Sacramento River features nearly fifty rapids during its 35-mile (56 km) descent from the Box Canyon Dam north of Dunsmuir to Shasta Reservoir. The two most popular whitewater runs on the upper Sacramento are the 6-mile (10 km) Class IV upper canyon trip from the dam to Dunsmuir and the 14-mile (22 km) Class III–IV trip from Sims Flat to Dog Creek near Shasta Lake. Both of these stretches contain numerous rapids that drop between pools.

In most years, the upper Sacramento can only be rafted in the spring. Early reservations are recommended because the season is short and the number of raft trips are limited.

22. CACHE CREEK, CALIFORNIA

Sections: Bald Eagle Run (upper)
                 Rumsey Run (lower)
Location: Yolo County, between Route 20 Bridge and Rumsey, north-central California
Distance: 23 miles (37 km) (upper)
                 8.5 miles (14 km) (lower)
Class: II–III
Trip Options: Paddle raft; one and two days (upper)
                 Paddle raft; one day (lower)
Season: May–September
Outfitters: Cache Canyon River Trips
                 MG Whitewater Adventures
                 Whitewater Voyages

A two-hour drive north of San Francisco, Cache Creek offers an ideal introduction to whitewater rafting. With guide-escorted trips, families and inexperienced paddlers can enjoy this relatively easy trip through a picturesque canyon in Lake and Yolo counties. Rafters may choose between one- and two-day paddle trips on the upper, or Bald Eagle, section and the lower, or Rumsey Run, section.

Cache Creek, fed by irrigation releases from Clear Lake and the Indian Valley Reservoir, normally has sufficient water to provide rafting throughout the summer.

Cache Creek trips are run in small 8- to 12-foot rafts and inflatable kayaks. These small boats provide an exciting trip on this small stream.

CHAPTER 3

The Pacific Northwest States

MOST RIVERS THAT ARE RAFTED in Washington and Oregon originate in the high elevations of the Cascade Mountains, which divide the states from north to south. As rivers drop through glacially formed valleys to Puget Sound, the Columbia River, or the Pacific Ocean, countless miles of exciting whitewaters await rafting enthusiasts.

Most of Washington's whitewater trips are fairly challenging one-day adventures. Melting snows and spring rains tumbling through steep valleys generally result in sustained water flows until midsummer. Six rivers on the eastern slopes of the Cascades offer the advantage of the warmer and drier climate of central Washington:

■ The Wenatchee, the state's most popular commercial raft river, and its sister river the Methow, with large and powerful waves, will excite both beginning and experienced rafters.

■ The Stehekin, an extremely remote and scenic river, can only be rafted after a 40-mile (64 km) boat ride across Lake Chelan.

■ Each September, after most rivers are too low for rafting, controlled water releases from the dam at Rimrock Lake generate almost continuous Class II–III + rapids on the Tieton River.

■ The Klickitat and White Salmon, tributaries of the Columbia, are popular Class III–IV rivers with whitewater fans from Washington and Oregon.

Western Washington's exciting rivers include:

■ Four rivers in the north Cascade's—the Nooksack, Sauk, Suiattle, and Skagit—provide an excellent choice of Class II–IV whitewater thrills within three hours of Seattle. A popular eagle-watching trip on the Skagit River is also available during the winter.

■ The Skykomish and the Green, two of Washington's most technically demanding whitewater trips, are near Everett, Seattle, and Tacoma.

■ The lovely Cispus of southwest Washington, although not frequently rafted, is a scenic gem near Mt. Adams.

■ Transformed by the devastating volcanic eruption of Mount St. Helens in 1980, the Toutle passes through one of America's most unusual river landscapes.

■ Rafters of all ages can safely enjoy scenic raft trips on the Elwha and the unforgettable rain-forest rivers of the Olympic Peninsula.

Favorite Oregon whitewater rivers include:

■ Southern Oregon's Rogue River encompasses both the multiday Wild and Scenic section and the popular recreation section with half- and one-day trips on the middle Rogue. While rafters must choose from almost forty outfitters licensed to run the river, only three run the Illinois River, the Rogue's pristine tributary.

■ The North Umpqua, which passes through southern Oregon's scenic forests, is becoming an increasingly popular river for both rafts and inflatable kayaks.

■ Three tributaries of western Oregon's Willamette River—the McKenzie, North Santiam, and Clackamas—provide excellent one-day rafting opportunities within two hours of Portland, Salem, and Eugene.

■ In central Oregon rafters head for the Deschutes and John Day rivers. The Deschutes, Oregon's most popular river, offers single and multiday trips through semi-arid surroundings. The John Day, another tributary of the Columbia, offers multiday moderate whitewater journeys through arid, basalt canyons.

■ The Grand Ronde, which flows through the Blue Mountains of northeast Oregon to the Snake River along the Washington–Idaho border, is a perfect multiday trip for families with young children.

■ The Owyhee, a remote and steep-walled tributary of the Snake, affords both technical and easy whitewater. The middle section should be attempted only by true whitewater enthusiasts, but the lower section may be enjoyed by anyone.

23. WENATCHEE RIVER, WASHINGTON

Section:	Leavenworth to Cashmere or Monitor
Location:	Chelan County near Cashmere, eastern Washington
Distance:	15–21 miles (24–34 km)
Class:	II–III +
Trip Options:	Paddle raft, oar raft; one day
Season:	April–July
Outfitters:	Blue Sky Outfitters
	Downstream River Runners
	Leavenworth Outfitters
	Leierer's Outdoors Limited
	North Cascades River Expeditions
	Northern Wilderness River Riders
	Orion Expeditions
	Reachout Expeditions
	River Drifters
	River Recreation
	Rivers Incorporated
	Watershed
	Wenatchee Whitewater and Scenic River Trips
	Wildwater River Tours

The Wenatchee River, which provides the water for much of Washington's famous apple growing region, accounts for nearly one-half of the state's annual raft trips. Roller coaster whitewater action, big waves, and usually sunny spring weather can be enjoyed by novice and experienced rafters. Exciting Class II–III + rapids, such as Boulder Bend, Rock 'n Roll, Gorilla Falls, Drunkard's Drop, and Snowblind, provide plenty of thrills as the Wenatchee winds its way adjacent to U.S. Highway 2.

Visitors to the Wenatchee River should plan enough time to see the apple orchards and scenic bluffs they probably missed during their raft trip. A visit to any of the neo-Bavarian shops and restaurants of Leavenworth is recommended.

24. METHOW RIVER, WASHINGTON

Section:	McFarland Creek to Pateros near Columbia River confluence
Location:	Okanogan County, northwest of Brewster, eastern Washington
Distance:	16 miles (26 km)
Class:	III–IV
Trip Options:	Paddle raft, oar raft; one and two days
Season:	April–July
Outfitters:	Blue Sky Outfitters
	Downstream River Runners
	North Cascades River Expeditions
	Northern Wilderness River Riders
	Orion Expeditions
	River Recreation
	Rivers Incorporated
	Wenatchee Whitewater and Scenic River Trips
	Wildwater River Tours

The Methow, a tributary of the Columbia River in eastern Washington, features some of the Northwest's largest whitewaters.
Photo by Lorrie North

Whitewater enthusiasts seeking big-wave action, rather than technical rock and boulder rapids, will find the Methow River, in eastern Washington's Okanogan National Forest, to be a utopia.

The Methow, adjacent to Washington Route 153 and just a few miles upriver from its confluence with the Columbia River near Brewster, is best known for a superb stretch of whitewater called the Black Canyon, which has become a favorite of guides and adventurous rafters. Fortunately, there are nearly 8 miles (13 km) of Class I–II rapids to hone your paddling skills before the steep-walled Class IV Black Canyon. During the next 6 miles (9 km), huge waves, big holes, and powerful hydraulics provide everyone with a thrilling and memorable Class III–IV whitewater ride.

Although outfitters promote the 16-mile (26 km) Methow's normally sunny weather, its cold north Cascade's origins necessitate wearing wet suits.

25. STEHEKIN RIVER, WASHINGTON

Section:	Stehekin Valley Ranch to Lake Chelan
Location:	Chelan County in the Lake Chelan National Recreation Area, north-central Washington
Distance:	10 miles (16 km)
Class:	I–II
Trip Options:	Paddle raft, oar raft; one day
Season:	May–August
Outfitters:	Stehekin Adventure Company

North-central Washington's Stehekin River offers the state's most remote whitewater stretches. Nestled between the Lake Chelan National Recreation and Glacier Peak Wilderness areas above Lake Chelan, the Stehekin valley, although homesteaded in the late nineteenth century, has no road access. Both residents and rafters must arrive via boat across Lake Chelan.

Despite its remote locale, the river's whitewater is not difficult. Raft trips begin just below Class IV Cascade Rapids, the 10-mile (16 km) run usually has easy Class I–II whitewater. The outfitter allows children as young as six years old on all but early season trips. A superb photographic opportunity on the trip is the spectacular 312-foot Rainbow Creek Falls.

Because of the time required to reach the river, many rafters overnight at the Stehekin Valley Ranch, which is about 1 mile (1.5 km) below the put-in. Ranch guests often combine their rafting adventure with horseback riding, hiking, and fishing.

26. TIETON RIVER, WASHINGTON

Section: Tieton Dam to Windy Point
Location: Yakima County, west of Yakima, south-central Washington
Distance: 13 miles (21 km)
Class: II–III + ; paddle-raft experience recommended
Trip Options: Paddle raft, oar raft; one-day
Season: September
Outfitters: Blue Sky Outfitters
                  Downstream River Runners
                  Leavenworth Outfitters
                  North Cascades River Expeditions
                  Northern Wilderness River Riders
                  Orion Expeditions
                  River Recreation
                  Wenatchee Whitewater and Scenic River Trips
                  Wildwater River Tours

The Tieton River, a mere trickle in the summer, roars with excitement each September when the dam gates of Rimrock Lake are opened to provide water for the Yakima Valley and the salmon run up the Yakima River. The swift-flowing Tieton drops at rates exceeding 50 feet a mile in a stretch flowing over countless stairstep ledges. While most of the river's numerous technical drops are Class II–III, the continuous nature of the rapids and its steep gradient makes it closer to a Class IV run.

Located southeast of Mt. Rainier, the Tieton whitewater run parallels U.S. Highway 12 for 13 miles (21 km) from the Tieton Dam to the Windy Point Campground.

27. KLICKITAT RIVER, WASHINGTON

Section: Glenwood to Lendl Bridge
Location: Yakima and Klickitat counties near Glenwood, southern Washington
Distance: 15 miles (24 km)
Class: III–IV; experience recommended
Trip Options: Paddle raft, oar raft; one and two days
Season: April–June
Outfitters: Blue Sky Outfitters
                  Downstream River Runners
                  Exodus Whitewater Adventures
                  North Cascades River Expeditions

Northern Wilderness River Riders
Phil's Guide Service
River Recreation
Rivers Incorporated
Sierra Whitewater Expeditions
Wildwater River Tours

The Klickitat River, like the White Salmon River 30 miles (48 km) to its west, flows south from the slopes of Mt. Adams into the Columbia River gorge. Because of the difficult access to the Klickitat, however, its excellent whitewater and breathtaking beauty can be viewed only from the river. Scrub oak and pine trees cling precariously to the 200-foot columnar basalt cliffs of the lower gorge.

Most of the Klickitat's more technical rapids—Rattler, Diamondback, Hatchery Drop, and Borde—are in the first half of the trip, but interesting Class II–II + whitewater continuously fills the remainder of the ride. Some outfitters offer the Klickitat as a two-day overnight trip or as a Klickitat–White Salmon combination two-day trip.

28. WHITE SALMON RIVER, WASHINGTON

Section: BZ Corners to Northwestern Lake
Location: Klickitat County near Trout Lake, southern Washington
Distance: 8 miles (13 km)
Class: III–IV +
Trip Options: Paddle raft, oar raft; one day
Season: May–August
Outfitters: Blue Sky Outfitters
                Downstream River Runners
                Exodus Whitewater Adventures
                Leierer's Outdoors Limited
                McCann's Northwest River Guides
                North Cascades River Expeditions
                Northern Wilderness River Riders
                Orion Expeditions
                Phil's Guide Service
                River Drifters Whitewater Tours
                River Recreation
                Rivers Incorporated
                Shaull's Whitewater Experience
                Wenatchee Whitewater and Scenic River Trips
                Wildwater River Tours

Whatever a raft trip on the White Salmon River may lack in distance, it makes up for in beauty and whitewater thrills. Its several technical Class III rapids—Grasshoppper, Shark's Fin, Waterspout, and Corkscrew and Stairstep falls—are at the bottom of a narrow gorge with steep lava cliffs. Rafts must be lowered by a cable system 150 feet to the river. Beyond the canyon's intense rapids, you have little time to enjoy the calmer waters and scenic pastoral surroundings before reaching the last major rapid, the Class IV + Husum Falls.

The White Salmon, on the dry eastern side of Washington's southern Cascades, is fed by glacier melt and numerous springs as it flows from the slopes of 12,278-foot Mt. Adams to the Columbia River near the town of White Salmon. The White Salmon has long been a popular river stretch for canoe and kayak races. The Slalom Races are held as part of the Husum Days celebration each July.

29. NOOKSACK RIVER (North Fork), WASHINGTON

Section: Douglas Fir Camp to Maple Falls
Location: Whatcom County, east of Bellingham, northwest Washington
Distance: 8 miles (13 km)
Class: II–III
Trip Options: Paddle raft, oar raft; one day
Season: July–September
Outfitters: Blue Sky Outfitters
Downstream River Runners
North Cascades River Expeditions
River Recreation

Western Washington's North Fork of the Nooksack is the state's most northern rafting river. The source of the Nooksack's challenging whitewater is the glacier slopes of the north Cascades, so its best whitewater occurs in late summer, after most other Cascade rivers are too low for rafting.

Outfitters normally begin the 8-mile (13 km) North Fork Nooksack trip at the Douglas Fir Camp about 2 miles (5 km) east of Glacier, a popular lodging village for skiers at Mt. Baker. The Nooksack's seven or eight Class III rapids are within the first 3 miles (5 km) of the run. Downstream, less intense Class II rapids and flat stretches provide rafters the opportunity to enjoy numerous views of the impressive snowcapped Mt. Baker and the scenic farm country of central Whatcom County.

30. SAUK RIVER, WASHINGTON

Section: White Chuck Campground to Darrington
Location: Snohomish County, southeast of Darrington, western
                  Washington
Distance: 10 miles (16 km)
Class: II–IV
Trip Options: Paddle raft, oar raft, inflatable kayak; one day
Season: May–July
Outfitters: Downstream River Runners
                  Orion Expeditions

The middle section of the Sauk River, between its confluence with the White Chuck and Suiattle rivers near Darrington, is becoming one of western Washington's more popular waters for rafting trips. Beautiful Mt. Baker National Forest and mountain scenery provide a gorgeous backdrop to the exciting, but not overly difficult whitewater.

The Sauk's numerous boulder-filled Class II rapids; Class III Alligator Drop, Whirlpool, Popeye, and Sue; and Class III–IV Jaws, provide ample opportunity for paddlers to improve their navigational skills. Many early-season rafters often return when summer water levels are too low for rafting and test their paddling skills during inflatable kayak trips.

While Glacier Peak, the origin of the Sauk's glacial waters, cannot be seen from the river, its cold waters most certainly can be felt. Wet suits are a must for rafters.

31. SUIATTLE RIVER, WASHINGTON

Section: Rat Trap Bridge to Sauk River
Location: Snohomish and Skagit counties near Darrington,
                  western Washington
Distance: 13 miles (21 km)
Class: I–III
Trip Options: Paddle raft, oar raft; one day
Season: May–August
Outfitters: Blue Sky Outfitters
                  Downstream River Runners
                  North Cascades River Expeditions
                  Northern Wilderness River Riders
                  Reachout Expeditions
                  River Drifters
                  River Recreation
                  Rivers Incorporated
                  Wildwater River Tours

The Suiattle River, a scenic tributary of the North Cascade's Sauk River, is an excellent trip for persons who want a relatively simple introduction to whitewater rafting. The lower 13 miles (21 km) of the Suiattle are neither intimidating nor strenuous. Its whitewater, with the exception of the Class III Coyote Crossing and Hurricane rapids, is all Class I–II. Its wilderness scenery, which on a clear day includes the 10,541-foot snowcapped Glacier Peak, is incredibly beautiful.

The Suiattle starts in the melting ice of Glacier Peak and flows through the Mt. Baker National Forest to the Sauk River. Braided channels, gravel bars, and fallen alder trees often change channel courses during high water. Extensive log jams often line the channels and occasionally must be cut out. Suiattle's cold waters, which still carry a large volume of glacial silt, necessitate wearing wet suits.

The Class II–III waters of the Suiattle River in the North Cascades afford a perfect introduction to whitewater rafting.
Photo by Verne Huser

*Midwinter float trips on the Wild and Scenic Skagit River in Washington's
North Cascades enable guests to photograph bald eagles.*
Photo by Verne Huser

32. SKAGIT RIVER, WASHINGTON

Sections: Newhalem to Copper Creek (upper)
                Marblemount to Rockport (lower)
Location: Whatcom and Skagit counties near North Cascades
                National Park, western Washington
Distance: 9 miles (14 km) (upper)
                8 miles (13 km) (lower)
Class: II–III (upper)
                I–II (lower)
Trip Options: Paddle raft, oar raft, one day (one-half day, lower)
Season: July–September (upper)
                December–February (lower)
Outfitters: Blue Sky Outfitters
                Downstream River Runners
                North Cascades River Expeditions
                Orion Expeditions
                Pacific Northwest Float Trips
                Reachout Expeditions
                River Drifters
                River Recreation
                Rivers Incorporated
                Wildwater River Tours

Near North Cascades National Park in western Washington, the upper Skagit River offers a very scenic intermediate-level whitewater opportunity for venturesome first-time rafters. Except for a one-half-mile section of whitewater that includes the Class III rapids Jack-the-Ripper and Wavy Gravy, the upper Skagit has a low gradient and easy Class I–II rapids.

The flow of upper Skagit, controlled by water releases from Seattle City Light's Ross, Diablo, and Gorge dams, generally has adequate water for rafting from midsummer until early fall.

On the lower Skagit, outfitters now promote winter float trips from December to February for wildlife enthusiasts who wish to see bald eagles. Migrating south from Alaska and Canada, as many as 300 eagles now congregate in the Skagit Preserve, adjacent to Washington Route 20, to feed on the river's spawning salmon. Sightings of the magnificent and endangered birds are very frequent because the eagles have become accustomed to seeing river rafts.

33. SKYKOMISH RIVER, WASHINGTON

Section: Index to Big Eddy
Location: Snohomish County near Gold Bar, western Washington
Distance: 8 miles (13 km)
Class: III–V; experience highly recommended
Trip Options: Paddle raft, oar raft; one day
Season: March–July
Outfitters: Blue Sky Outfitters
Downstream River Runners
North Cascades River Expeditions
Northern Wilderness River Riders
Orion Expeditions
Rapid Transit
River Recreation
Watershed
Wildwater River Tours

The exciting Skykomish, or "Sky," River is considered by many Washington outfitters to be the state's premier whitewater trip for thrill seekers. Starting below Sunset Falls in the shadow of 5,000-foot Mt. Index, the Skykomish is respected for its Class V Boulder Drop Rapid. Numerous other Class III–IV rapids, such as Marbleshoot, Lunch Hole, and little and big Deja Vu, and the spectacular Cascade setting combine to make the Skykomish a spectacular river experience. The Sky is included in the state's Scenic River System.

Approximately 45 miles (72 km) east of Everett, the Skykomish flows adjacent to U.S. Highway 2 and the Great Northern Railway tracks. While both the river and the highway offer superb views of Mt. Index, Baring, Persis, and the Merchant Peak, it is best to take photographs from the highway.

Most Skykomish outfitters require rafters to be at least sixteen years old and to have had previous whitewater experience. Since the snowmelt water is always cold, outfitters also require wet suits and provide helmets.

34. GREEN RIVER, WASHINGTON

Section:	Palmer State Park to Flaming Geyser State Park
Location:	King County near Black Diamond, western Washington
Distance:	14 miles (22 km)
Class:	III–IV; rafting experience recommended
Trip Options:	Paddle raft; one day
Season:	February–April
Outfitters:	Downstream River Runners
	North Cascades River Expeditions
	Northern Wilderness River Riders
	River Recreation
	Wildwater River Tours

Western Washington's steep-walled Green River gorge is not only one of the Cascade Mountains' most beautiful whitewater stretches, but at high-water levels it rivals the Skykomish River as one of the state's most strenuous rafting trips. Because of several very technical Class IV boulder-filled rapids, such as Ledge Drop, Pipeline, Mercury, and Nozzle, on the upper section from Palmer State Park to the Green River Resort, outfitters prefer customers to have previous rafting experience. The Class II–III rapids of the lower Green, from the resort to Flaming Geyser State Park, are considerably more suitable for first-time rafters.

Rafting during the spring is made possible by infrequent water releases from the U.S. Army Corps of Engineers' Howard Hansen Dam, southeast of Palmer. The Palmer State Park put-in for the Green River gorge is slightly more than a one-hour drive from both Seattle and Tacoma.

35. CISPUS RIVER, WASHINGTON

Section: Route 28 Bridge to Cowlitz Falls
Location: Skamania and Lewis counties near Randle, southwest Washington
Distance: 14 miles (22 km)
Class: II–III
Trip Options: Paddle raft, oar raft; one day
Season: April–June
Outfitters: Northern Wilderness River Riders
                River Recreation
                Wildwater River Tours

The Cispus River, one of the newest whitewater rafting trips offered by Washington's outfitters, is in the forested canyons of the state's southern Cascades. Although not yet well known, the lower Cispus combines technical Class III whitewater with calmer stretches that are ideal for enjoying the forested wilderness environment. One of the most impressive features of the trip is spectacular Tower Rock, the plug of an old volcano, which rises abruptly several hundred feet above the river near the put-in.

The waters of the Cispus are always cold because it is fed by the snow and glacial melt from 12,276-foot Mt. Adams, just to the east.

36. TOUTLE RIVER, WASHINGTON

Section: Toutle to Tower Bridge
Location: Cowlitz County, west of Mt. St. Helens National Volcanic Monument, western Washington near Castle Rock
Distance: 11 miles (18 km)
Class: III–IV
Trip Options: Paddle raft, oar raft; one day
Season: February–April
Outfitters: Northern Wilderness River Riders
                River Recreation
                Shaull's Whitewater Experience

Southwest Washington's Toutle River offers one of the most interesting rafting experiences anywhere. Throughout the trip, you can still see the wrath of the 1980 volcanic eruption of Mount St. Helens, less than 40 miles (64 km) to the east. Its subsequent mud flow has created a river environment of twisted bridges, remnants of houses, and devastated hills and farmlands.

Rafters on the Toutle must not become too captivated by the intriguing river environment. The 11-mile (18 km) trip from Toutle to

Tower Bridge below Interstate 5 requires the teamwork of all paddlers. Powerful waves and currents caused by almost constantly moving sandbars are sometimes difficult to navigate. Because of the changing river currents, the Toutle's several Class III and its Class IV Teakettle and Hollywood Gorge Falls are sometimes more difficult to negotiate than they might appear.

The Toutle River, transformed by the volcanic eruptions of Mount St. Helens in 1980, now traverses one of America's most unusual river landscapes.
Photo by Verne Huser

37. OLYMPIC RAIN-FOREST RIVERS, WASHINGTON

Rivers:	Hoh, Queets, and Quinault
Location:	Jefferson and Clallum counties, between Forks and Aberdeen, western Washington
Distance:	14 miles (22 km) (Hoh)
	13 miles (21 km) (Queets)
	8 miles (13 km) (Quinault)
Class:	I–II
Trip Options:	Oar raft; one day
Season:	April–September
Outfitters:	Olympic Guide and Raft Service
	Wildwater River Tours

Three rivers, flowing westward from Olympic National Park to the scenic Pacific coastline, provide extraordinary opportunities to float quietly through portions of the famous Olympic Peninsula rain forest. The Hoh, Queets, and Quinault, which begin in the park's snowcapped mountains, increase their flows as they pass through the moss and fern-covered rain forest where annual rainfalls often exceed 120 inches.

Appropriately promoted by outfitters as a rain-forest float rather than a whitewater trip, the splendid flora and fauna of this forest environment and its mild waters will delight nature lovers of all ages.

38. ELWHA RIVER, WASHINGTON

Section: Altaire to Elwha Resort
Location: Clallam County, southeast of Port Angeles, northwest Washington
Distance: 6.5 miles (10 km)
Class: I–II
Trip Options: Paddle raft, oar raft; half-day
Season: May–September
Outfitter: Olympic Guide and Raft Service

The Elwha River, on the northern Olympic Peninsula, offers rafters an excellent opportunity to experience the thrill of whitewater rafting and enjoy the beauty and serenity of the northern Olympic Peninsula. The Elwha originates in the snowcapped mountains of Olympic National Park. In addition to the ferns and wild flowers that adorn the Elwha's forested environs, rafters may also see elk, eagles, hawks, osprey, mountain goat, black bears, and deer.

The easy Class I–II rapids on the 6.5-mile (10 km) Elwha raft trip may be enjoyed by almost anyone above the age of six.

39. ROGUE RIVER, OREGON

Section: Wild and Scenic
Location: Josephine and Curry counties, west of Grants Pass, southwest Oregon
Distance: 35 miles (56 km)
Class: III–IV
Trip Options: Paddle raft, oar raft, paddle/oar raft, dory, inflatable kayak; three to five days
Season: May–October
Outfitters: American River Touring Association
                Beaver State Adventures
                Brigg's Rogue River Guide Service
                Dave Helfrich River Outfitter

Dean Helfrich Guide Service
ECHO: The Wilderness Company
James Henry River Journeys
Lute Jerstad Adventures
Northwest Drifters
Northwest Whitewater Excursions
O.A.R.S.
Orange Torpedo Trips
Oregon River Experiences
Oregon River Outfitters
Outdoor Adventures
Ouzel Outfitters
River Adventure Float Trips
River Trips Unlimited
Rogue Excursions
Rogue River Raft Trips
Sierra Whitewater Expeditions
Sundance Expeditions
Whitewater Voyages
Wilderness Waterways
Wilderness World
Wild Water Adventures

It is little wonder that when Congress began protecting the nation's rivers under the Wild and Scenic Rivers Act in 1968, they started with southern Oregon's Rogue River. The Rogue includes not just first-class whitewater, but heavily forested canyons with abundant wildlife, wildflowers, and fascinating folklore.

The Rogue River originates near Crater Lake National Park, and along its 140-mile (224 km) course cuts through numerous coastal range canyons to the Pacific Coast at Gold Beach. Most three- to five-day raft trips are run through the Siskiyou Mountains between Grave Creek, 5 miles north of Galice, and Foster Bar. This 35-mile (56 km) stretch includes the famed Mule Creek Canyon and most of the better Class III–III + rapids, such as Grave Creek and Black Bar Falls, Tyee, Wildcat, Slim Pickins, Coffee Pot, Blossom Bar, and Devil Stairs. These canyons are also home to deer, bears, otters, mink, ospreys, bald eagles, and dozens of bird species. Along with the thrill of whitewater rapids, there is sufficient time for rafters to hike and explore abandoned gold mines, cabins, and Indian grounds.

In an effort to preserve the wilderness experience of the Wild and Scenic Rogue, the Bureau of Land Management allows only four outfitters per day to begin trips at Grave Creek. Customers may choose between oar and paddle rafts, McKenzie-type drift boats, and dories; and even inflatable kayaks when water levels are low. On

Oarsman skillfully guides raft down Rainie Falls on the Wild and Scenic Rogue River in southern Oregon.
Photo by Nancy Jane Reid

multiday trips, the choice is between comfortable lodge accommodations and river-side tent camping. Finally, Rogue trips during the late summer and fall months are oriented to steelhead fishermen.

Although outfitters recommend early reservations to ensure the trip dates of your choice, it is often possible to book trips on fairly short notice.

Section:	Recreation
Location:	Josephine County near Grants Pass, southwest Oregon
Distance:	14 miles (22 km)
Class:	I–II
Trip Options:	Paddle raft, oar raft, inflatable kayak; half-day, one-day, multiday
Season:	May–October
Outfitters:	All Seasons Guide Service
	Eagle Sun
	ECHO: The Wilderness Company
	Galice Resort and Store
	Noah's World of Water
	Orange Torpedo Trips
	Otter River Trips
	Paul Brook's Raft Trips
	Pringle's Guide Service
	River Trips Unlimited
	Rogue Excursions
	Rogue–Klamath River Adventures
	Rogue River Raft Trips
	Tag Two Guide Service
	Wilderness World

Just upstream from the Wild and Scenic section, the "Recreation Section" of the Rogue offers an ideal introduction to whitewater rafting. With a guide-escorted trip, families, senior citizens, and inexperienced rafters can enjoy the impressive Hellgate Canyon between Hog Creek, some 15 miles (24 km) downstream from Grants Pass, and Grave Creek, the put-in for the Wild section.

Hellgate Canyon, with easy Class I–II rapids such as Dunn Riffle, Galice Chute, Rocky Riffle, Chair Riffle, Almeda, Argo, and Woolridge, can be enjoyed by oar or paddle raft, or inflatable kayak. One-half-day trips are also available. Either half- or one-day trips are excellent for those lacking either the time or money for the multiday Rogue trips. Vacationers can usually book both trips on short notice.

40. ILLINOIS RIVER, OREGON

Section:	Miami Bar to Oak Flat
Location:	Josephine County, west of Grants Pass, southwest Oregon
Distance:	40 miles (64 km)
Class:	III–V; experience recommended
Season:	March–May
Trip Options:	Paddle raft, oar raft; three to four days
Outfitters:	All Seasons Guide Service
	American River Touring Association
	Sundance Expeditions

The Illinois River, a seldom-run tributary of the Rogue River, is hidden in the remote canyons of southwest Oregon, less than 30 miles (48 km) from the Pacific Ocean and the California–Oregon border.

It is immediately apparent after put-in that the Illinois flows through a wilderness. There are no bridges, lodges, or roads. First growth coniferous forests, lush ferns, and abundant wildlife grace the rugged hills of the Siskiyou National Forest. Few persons will question that the river's 1984 inclusion into the National Wild and Scenic River System was long overdue.

The Illinois rapids are as exciting as the river is beautiful. Most of its Class IV rapids, Pine Flat, Prelude, Let's Make a Deal, Submarine Rock, and Green Wall (Class V), are in the canyon section, usually rafted on the second day of the three- to four-day, 35- to 40-mile (56–64 km) trip.

Rafting trips on the river normally last three or four days and include overnight tent camping. Trips are paced to allow sufficient time for short hikes to many of the scenic waterfalls.

The Illinois' biggest drawback is its very short rafting season. Its watershed, though rugged and remote, lacks sufficient elevation to hold the winter snows required for late spring and early summer river running. Rafters should make early reservations for the limited number of spring trips.

41. NORTH UMPQUA RIVER, OREGON

Section:	Boulder Flat to Cable Crossing
Location:	Douglas County, east of Roseburg, southern Oregon
Distance:	30 miles (48 km)
Class:	II–III +
Trip Options:	Paddle raft, oar raft, inflatable kayak; half-day, one to three days
Season:	April–July
Outfitters:	Cimarron Outdoors

Jim's Oregon Whitewater
Noah's World of Water
North Umpqua Outfitters
Orange Torpedo Trips
Oregon River Adventures
Oregon River Experiences
Oregon Whitewater Adventures
Ouzel Outfitters
Prince River Outfitter
Rivers West Whitewater Specialists
Sierra Whitewater Expeditions
Wilderness River Outfitters–Oregon
Wild Water Adventures

The North Umpqua River, east of Roseburg, provides whitewater enthusiasts an excellent opportunity to challenge exciting Class II–III + rapids in the heart of southern Oregon's Umpqua National Forest. While Oregon Route 138 allows outfitters several options for raft trips along the North Umpqua, most run one-day 16-mile (26 km) trips, from Boulder Flat to Cable Crossing.

The North Umpqua's many Class III + pool-drop rapids, including Pinball, Bridged Rock, and Amazon Queen, are fairly steep and exciting, yet forgiving. Flat stretches between many of the rapids give ample time for relaxation and swimming. In addition to paddle-raft trips, inflatable-kayak trips are becoming increasingly popular during the low-water summer months.

The North Umpqua is one of Oregon's five most popular whitewater rivers. Its easy access to Roseburg and Interstate 5, and its excellent rapids contribute to its high percentage of repeat customers.

42. MCKENZIE RIVER, OREGON

Sections: Paradise Campground to Blue River (upper)
               Blue River to Leaburg Dam (lower)
Location: Lane County, east of Eugene, western Oregon
Distance: 14 miles (22 km) (upper)
               12 miles (19 km) (lower)
Class: III–IV (upper)
               II–III (lower)
Trip Options: Paddle raft, oar raft, McKenzie drift boat; one day
Season: May–October
Outfitters: Dean Helfrich Guide Service
               Dennis Brandsma Outfitters
               Dick Helfrich Outfitters
               Exodus Whitewater Adventures

Go-For-It Whitewater Adventures
Jim's Oregon Whitewater
Ken Helfrich
McCann's Northwest River Guides
McKenzie River Adventures
Northwest Outdoor Adventures
Northwest Whitewater Excursions
Oregon River Adventures
Oregon River Experiences
Oregon Whitewater Adventures
Outdoor Adventures Plus
Ouzel Outfitters
Prince River Outfitter
Rivers West Whitewater Specialists
Sierra Whitewater Expeditions
Wilderness River Outfitters–Oregon
Wilderness Waterways
Wild Water Adventures

The McKenzie, one of central Oregon's most beautiful rivers, is ideal for new river runners and experienced rafters wanting another great challenge. In addition to fine whitewater, it is also easily accessible along Oregon Route 126 for almost its entire 90-mile (144 km) course, which runs between Clear Lake in the western Cascades and its confluence with the Willamette River at Eugene.

Paddle raft runs through Martin's Rapid on Oregon's McKenzie River near Eugene.
Photo courtesy of Wild Water Adventures Oregon

Whitewater trips are available on both the upper and lower McKenzie. Between Paradise Campground and Blue Lake, the more demanding upper McKenzie courses at rates of up to 90 feet per mile through numerous Class III–IV rapids, highlighted by Horse Creek, Redsides, and Big Fish. The lower McKenzie's many Class II–III rapids, such as Bear Creek, Brown's Hole, Eagle Rock, and Martin's, blend nicely with the many miles of easy Class I–II waters, where you can enjoy the superb scenery of the Willamette National Forest.

In addition to standard paddle and oar rafts, some outfitters use a modern version of the century-old, wooden McKenzie drift boat.

43. NORTH SANTIAM RIVER, OREGON

Section:	Pack Saddle Campground to Mehama
Location:	Marion and Linn counties, southeast of Salem, western Oregon
Distance:	20 miles (32 km)
Class:	II–III
Trip Options:	Paddle raft, oar raft, McKenzie drift boat; one day
Season:	April–June, September–October
Outfitters:	Go-For-It Whitewater Adventures
	Leierer's Outdoors Limited
	McCann's Northwest River Guides
	Northwest Outdoor Adventures
	Oregon River Experiences
	Sierra Whitewater Expeditions
	Wilderness Waterways

The North Santiam River offers convenient and enjoyable rafting for families and large groups in the western foothills of the Cascades east of Salem. Its proximity to the urban centers of the Willamette Valley, as well as its easy access to Oregon Route 22, makes the North Santiam one of the state's most popular rivers for raft trips.

The North Santiam's mostly Class II + rapids are fun, but not intimidating. There is ample time for paddle rafters to sharpen their skills before the river's biggest rapids, the Class III Spencer's Hole and Mill City Bridge rapids. The North Santiam flows through the Mt. Hood and Willamette national forests.

Rafting on the North Santiam is dependent upon water releases from the U.S. Army Corps of Engineers' Detroit Dam; consequently, the river is usually run only on weekends and primarily in the spring and fall. While most whitewater trips use paddle rafts, outfitters also use oar rafts and McKenzie-type drift boats.

44. CLACKAMAS RIVER, OREGON

Sections: Three Lynx Power Station to North Fork Reservoir (upper)
                McIver Park, or Barton Park, to the Willamette River (lower)
Location: Clackamas County, east of Gladstone, western Oregon
Distance: 10 miles (16 km) (upper)
                13 miles (21 km) (lower)
Class: III–IV (upper)
                I–II (lower)
Trip Options: Paddle raft, oar raft; one day
Season: March–June
Outfitters: Go-For-It Whitewater Adventures
                McCann's Northwest River Guides
                North Cascades River Expeditions
                Northwest Outdoor Adventures
                River Drifters Whitewater Tours
                Rivers West Whitewater Specialists
                Shaull's Whitewater Experience
                Wildwater River Tours

The Clackamas River provides rafters a choice between a fairly demanding 10-mile (16 km) upper section, beginning at the Three Lynx Power Station, and a float-type trip near the Portland suburb of Gladstone.

Trips on the Class III–IV upper Clackamas include challenging rapids, such as Carter Bridge, Hole-in-the-Wall, and Roaring Rapids, that offer excitement for both beginning and experienced paddlers.

The final stretch of the Clackamas River, from McIver Park to its confluence with the famed Willamette River, offers families and first-time rafters a relatively simple introduction to whitewater. The river's easy Class I–II waters give rafters ample time to relax and enjoy the Willamette Valley scenery, including its wildlife and beautiful Mt. Hood backdrop. Depending on the type of trip, rafters have the opportunity to perfect paddling skills or row the raft on some of the milder rapids. River take-out at Clackamette Park in Gladstone is convenient to Interstate 205.

While the snow- and rain-fed Clackamas has sufficient water to be run almost year-round, raft trips are normally available only during the spring.

45. DESCHUTES RIVER, OREGON

Sections:	Warm Springs to Maupin (upper)
	Columbia River to Columbia River (lower)
Location:	Wasco and Sherman counties, south of The Dalles, north-central Oregon
Distance:	110 miles (176 km)
Class:	II–III
Trip Options:	Paddle raft, oar raft, McKenzie drift boat; one to five days
Season:	April–October
Outfitters:	Canyon Outfitters
	Cooley River Expeditions
	Dennis Brandsma Outfitters
	Exodus Whitewater Adventures
	Go-For-It Whitewater Adventures
	Greenwood Outfitters
	Jim's Oregon Whitewater
	Ken Warren Outdoors
	Leierer's Outdoors Limited
	Lute Jerstad Adventures
	McCann's Northwest River Guides
	Mike Sallee Guide Service
	Northwest Outdoor Adventures
	Northwest River Outfitters
	Northwest Whitewater Excursions
	Northwest Whitewater Expeditions
	Oregon River Experiences
	Oregon Whitewater Adventures
	Orion Expeditions
	Outdoor Adventures Plus
	Ouzel Outfitters
	Prince River Outfitter
	Reachout Expeditions
	River Drifters Whitewater Tours
	Rivers West Whitewater Specialists
	Shaull's Whitewater Experience
	Sun Country Tours
	Wenatchee Whitewater and Scenic River Trips
	Whitewater USA
	Wilderness River Outfitters–Oregon
	Wilderness Waterways
	Wild Water Adventures
	Wildwater River Tours

The Deschutes, which offers Oregon's most popular whitewater trip, is the state's second longest river. Originating in the east Cascades between Crater Lake and Bend, it flows for nearly 240 miles (384 km) northward, providing much-needed water to adjacent central Oregon's farm and range lands. Normally raft- and drift-boat trips, which range from one to five days, are only run on portions of the last 110 miles (176 km) of the Deschutes, between the Warm Springs Indian Reservation and its confluence with the Columbia River near Biggs, some 15 miles (24 km) east of The Dalles.

While the Deschutes is best described as a desert-canyon float trip rather than a whitewater trip, one section between Warm Springs and Sherar's Falls is interrupted by more than a dozen exciting rapids. Both one-day as well as multiday rafters enjoy the lively splashes of Whitehorse, Buckskin Mary, Boxcar, Oak Springs, and many other challenging Class III rapids.

The Deschutes is a perfect multiday trip for first-time river runners, families, senior citizens, and outdoor lovers who want to enjoy a scenic river in an arid environment. In addition to the scenic river and the basalt canyons, there is usually ample time to enjoy the wildlife, hike, swim, or just relax.

46. JOHN DAY RIVER, OREGON

Sections:	Service Creek to Clarno (upper)
	Clarno to Cottonwood Bridge (lower)
Location:	Wasco, Wheeler, Sherman, and Gilliam counties, west of Fossil, central Oregon
Distance:	116 miles (185 km)
Class:	I–II +
Trip Options:	Paddle raft, oar raft; two to five days
Season:	April–June
Outfitters:	Go-For-It Whitewater Adventures
	Jim's Oregon Whitewater
	Leierer's Outdoors Limited
	Northwest Whitewater Expeditions
	Oregon River Experiences
	Prince River Outfitter
	Sierra Whitewater Expeditions
	Whitehorse Rafting
	Whitewater USA
	Wilderness River Outfitters–Oregon
	Wild Water Adventures

The John Day River, an Oregon Scenic Waterway, is the Pacific Northwest's longest free-flowing river. Outfitters and geologists call it a rock hound's paradise. It has many striking rock formations, including Hoot Owl Rock, Painted Hills, Cathedral Rock, Coffin, and the Great Basalt Canyon, in its desert environment. The John Day also passes through the colorful basalt rock formations of isolated river canyons, such as the John Day Fossil Beds National Monument and the Painted Hills National Monument.

Mostly sedate Class I–II + waters make it a perfect trip to enjoy the river's cool waters, relax in the sunshine or shade, or explore remote side canyons that are seen by no one but river runners.

Outfitters begin or end most river trips at Clarno, some 15 miles (24 km) west of Fossil. The 47-mile (75 km) upper John Day, above Clarno, is normally a three- or four-day trip; the 69-mile (110 km) trip below Clarno often runs four to six days. Both the upper and lower sections are designated parts of the Oregon Scenic Waterway.

47. GRANDE RONDE, OREGON-WASHINGTON

Sections: Minam to Troy
                  Troy to confluence with Snake River
Location: Wallowa County, northeast of La Grande, northeast
                  Oregon
                  Asotin County, south of Clarkston, southeast Wash-
                  ington
Distance: 44 miles (70 km) (Minam to Troy)
                  45 miles (72 km) (Troy to confluence of Snake River)
Class: I–II +
Trip Options: Paddle raft, oar raft, McKenzie drift boat, dory; three
                  to five days
Season: April–July
Outfitters: Anderson River Adventures
                  Barker River Trips
                  Downstream River Runners
                  Exodus Whitewater Adventures
                  Go-For-It Whitewater Adventures
                  Jim's Oregon Whitewater
                  Lower Salmon Express
                  Northwest Dories
                  Northwest Outdoor Adventures
                  Northwest Whitewater Excursions
                  Northwest Whitewater Expeditions

Oregon River Experiences
Oregon Whitewater Adventures
ROW (River Odysseys West)
Sierra Whitewater Expeditions
Steen's Wilderness Adventures
Wapiti River Guides
Wilderness River Outfitters–Oregon
Wild Water Adventures

The Grande Ronde River, which winds through the wild conifer canyons of northeastern Oregon's Blue Mountains to the Snake River in southeastern Washington, is a perfect multiday river trip for families. Its mostly Class I–II + waters are a lot of fun.

While the Grande Ronde's most popular raft, or float, excursion is normally the three-day 44-mile (70 km) section between Minam and Troy in northeast Oregon, many prefer the five-day trip that continues an additional 45 miles (72 km) to Heller's Bar near the river's confluence with the Snake River. Raft trips are usually run only between April and July when temperatures and water levels are at their best.

The Grande Ronde's diverse environs are rich in history, wildlife, and natural beauty. Chief Joseph and the Nez Percé Indians wintered on these lower stretches because of the mild winters and abundant wildlife. Even today, rafters commonly see Rocky Mountain elk, bighorn sheep, bears, deer, ospreys, and bald eagles in the river's spectacular geological gorges and forest habitat.

48. OWYHEE RIVER, OREGON

Sections: Three Forks to Rome (middle)
               Rome to Leslie Gulch (lower)
Location: Malheur County, southeast Oregon
Distance: 37 miles (59 km) (middle)
               64 miles (102 km) (lower)
Class: II–IV + (middle)
               II–III (lower)
Trip Options: Paddle raft, oar raft, McKenzie drift boat, dory; three
               to seven days
Season: April–June
Outfitters: Cooley River Expeditions
               Davis Whitewater Expeditions
               Dean Helfrich Guide Service
               Dick Helfrich Outfitters
               Downstream River Runners
               Exodus Whitewater Adventures

The relatively easy rapids of the Grande Ronde River make it an ideal multiday raft trip for families and senior citizens.
Photo by Lorrie North

Headwaters River Adventures
Hughes River Expeditions
Idaho Adventures River Trips
Idaho Guide Service
Ken Warren Outdoors
Leierer's Outdoors Limited
Lute Jerstad Adventures
Middle Fork River Company
Noah's World of Water
Northwest Dories
Northwest Voyaguers
Northwest Whitewater Excursions
Northwest Whitewater Expeditions
Orange Torpedo Trips
Oregon River Experiences
Oregon Whitewater Adventures
Ouzel Outfitters
Prince River Outfitter
ROW (River Odysseys West)
Sevy Guide Service
Sierra Whitewater Expeditions
Turtle River Rafting Company
Wapiti River Guides
Wilderness River Outfitters–Idaho
Wilderness World
Wild Water Adventures

The Owyhee River, a spectacular steep-walled tributary of the Snake, originates in the mountains of Nevada before cutting its way through the high-desert canyons of southwest Idaho and eastern Oregon. Its deep and remote canyons are as spectacular and beautiful as any in the world. Outfitters and rafters frequently compare portions of the Owyhee's multicolored basalt cliffs and bluffs to those of the Grand Canyon. Evidently the United States Congress agreed; in 1979 the middle and lower sections of the Owyhee were included in the National Wild and Scenic Rivers System.

The lower Owyhee extends from the small eastern Oregon town of Rome to Leslie Gulch on Lake Owyhee. During this 64-mile (102 km) stretch the varied scenery is superb and the rapids are fun, but fairly easy. This section of the Owyhee is preferred by families, senior citizens, and first-time rafters. There are also two excellent natural hot springs for relaxing in this stretch.

The middle Owyhee, between Three Forks—where the north and middle forks join the river—and Rome, is the section favored by whitewater enthusiasts. Major Class III–IV + technical rapids, including Ledge, Half-mile, Bomb Shelter Drop, Raft Flip Drop, and Widowmaker, challenge even those who consider themselves experienced rafters.

Owyhee rafting occurs during the spring when water levels, daytime temperatures, and desert wildflowers are best. The Owyhee is well known for the great variety of wildlife seen in the canyons. One outfitter has recorded more than sixty bird species, including golden eagles, Canada geese, teals, falcons, songbirds, and the rare Lazuli Bunting. Antelope, bighorn sheep, wild horses, deer, bobcats, coyotes, beavers, mink, and otters are also commonly seen.

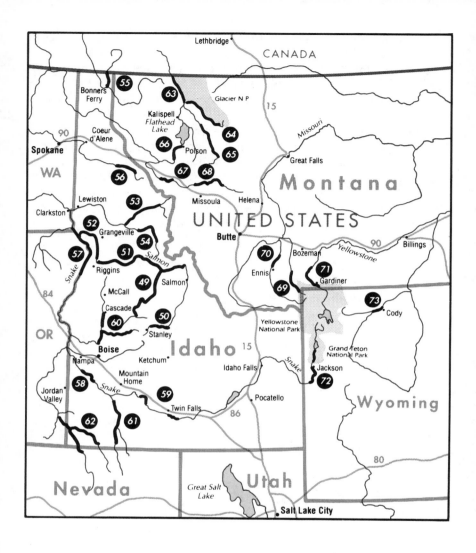

The Northern Rocky Mountain States

THE SPARSELY POPULATED STATES of Idaho, Montana, and Wyoming contain some of America's wildest and unspoiled wilderness areas. Prior to the popularization of whitewater rafting twenty years ago, only the hardiest of outdoor adventurers were able to enjoy the diverse wildlife and primitive mountain scenery in these states. Today, however, dozens of rafting outfitters provide easy and safe access to hundreds of miles of wilderness canyons in Idaho, Montana, and Wyoming.

In addition to spectacular alpine scenery, rafters of wilderness rivers are treated frequently to views of bears, whitetail deer, elk, moose, mule deer, Rocky Mountain bighorn sheep, mountain goats, cougars, coyotes, and fox.

The famed main Salmon River of central Idaho, its popular Middle Fork, and the lower Salmon, prior to its confluence with the Snake River, offer more than 230 miles (368 km) of exceptional wilderness rafting adventure through six national forests, the incredible Frank Church River of No Return Wilderness, and the Sawtooth National Recreation Area. In recent years the upper main Salmon near Sun Valley has become popular for half-day and one-day raft trips.

Other whitewater trips in northern and central Idaho include:

■ Lochsa, route of the early nineteenth century explorers Lewis and Clark, and the nearby Selway, of Nez Percé Indian fame, are becoming increasingly popular multiday wilderness river trips.

■ Two rivers in northern Idaho—the Moyie and St. Joe—while scenic and challenging, are infrequently rafted because of the short spring season.

■ On the Oregon–Idaho border, Hell's Canyon, the country's deepest canyon and the last major whitewater of the 1,500-mile (2,400 km) Snake, features a Class III–IV multiday trip.

Three additional rafting trips are offered on the Snake as it crosses Idaho to its confluence with the Columbia. A mostly Class I float trip, through the Snake's Bird of Prey Area south of Nampa, provides rafters with the opportunity to see many of nature's rare raptors in their spring nesting habitat. The Hagerman section has easy Class I–II rapids that can be enjoyed by anyone; the Murtaugh section, east of Twin Falls, has some of the Northwest's largest whitewater.

In southwest Idaho, less than an hour's drive from Boise, the three forks of the Payette River provide whitewater enthusiasts with nearly 80 miles (128 km) of Class II, III, and IV one-day rafting opportunities. South of Boise, the desert canyons of the Jarbidge and Bruneau rivers and the South and East forks of the upper Owyhee have Class III–V + whitewater in some of the west's longest and most remote desert canyons.

Montana's whitewater rafting activity is primarily located near two very popular national parks—Glacier and Yellowstone:

■ Near Glacier, the North, Middle, and South forks of the Flathead provide one-day and multiday rafting through the beautiful wilderness mountains of northwest Montana.

Oar-guided rafts negotiate Pistol Creek Rapid on the Middle Fork Salmon in Idaho.
Photo by Robert Winslow

■ Near Yellowstone, in southwest Montana, the Gallatin, Madison, and Yellowstone rivers provide summer visitors with excellent intermediate-level whitewater river trips. Half-day, family-type trips are available on the more moderate sections.

■ Elsewhere in western Montana, the Blackfoot River, east of Missoula; the Clark Fork, west of Missoula; and the lower Flathead, south of Polson, feature exciting Class II–III whitewater.

Float and whitewater trips on the upper Snake River, in Wyoming's Grand Teton National Park, and the canyons just below the Park, attract more than 100,000 rafters each year. The Shoshone River near Cody, east of Yellowstone National Park, has moderate Class II–III whitewater.

49. SALMON RIVER (Middle Fork), IDAHO

Section:	Boundary or Indian Creek to main Salmon River
Location:	Custer and Lemhi counties, east-central Idaho
Distance:	80 or 105 miles (128 or 168 km)
Class:	III–IV +
Trip Options:	Paddle raft, oar raft, drift boat, inflatable kayak; five and six days
Season:	May–mid-October
Outfitters:	Action Whitewater Adventures
	Aggipah River Trips
	American River Touring Association
	Canyons Incorporated
	Custom River Tours
	Dave Helfrich River Outfitter
	Dean Helfrich Guide Service
	Dick Helfrich Outfitters
	Don Hatch River Expeditions
	ECHO: The Wilderness Company
	Hughes River Expeditions
	Idaho Adventures River Trips
	MacKay Bar Corporation
	Middle Fork Rapid Transit
	Middle Fork River Company
	Middle Fork River Expeditions
	Middle Fork River Tours
	Middle Fork Wilderness Outfitters
	Norman H. Guth Company
	Orange Torpedo Trips
	Outdoor Adventures

Rocky Mountain River Tours
ROW (River Odysseys West)
Sawtooth River Expeditions
Sevy Guide Service
Solitude River Trips
Sun Valley Rivers
Triangle C Ranch Whitewater

The Middle Fork of the Salmon flows through the heart of the 2.4-million-acre River of No Return Wilderness. Between Boundary Creek, north of Stanley in east-central Idaho, and its confluence with the main Salmon near Cache Bar, the Middle Fork traverses portions of the Challis, Payette, and Salmon national forests, some 105 miles (168 km) and 250 side streams down river. Considered the "crown jewel" of Wild and Scenic Rivers by the U.S. Forest Service, the Middle Fork provides one of the world's best multiday river experiences.

More than eighty exciting rapids, including many Class III–IV rapids, such as Velvet Falls, Waterwheel, Pistol Creek, Tappan Falls, Haystack, Porcupine, Redside, Rubber, Hancock, and Jumpoff are in the Middle Fork. Although Middle Fork rafting begins in May, families and first-time rafters are advised to use the lower flows and warmer waters of July and August. The Middle Fork is graced with

Rocky Mountain bighorn sheep are often seen during early spring raft trips on the Middle Fork and main Salmon.
Photo courtesy of Aggipah River Trips

Wooden dories, similar to those used by explorer John Wesley Powell, are popular in the Grand Canyon and on Idaho's Middle Fork and lower Salmon rivers.
Photo courtesy of Northwest Dories

numerous excellent campsites, and most are adjacent to crystal-clear streams and rapids. Both mornings and evenings allow time to hike, visit, read, or relax.

The Middle Fork trip begins in an alpine environment about a two-hour drive north of Sun Valley. Its elevation, nearly 6,000 feet at the put-in, accounts for the variety of wildlife commonly seen. During spring and early summer trips, rafters commonly see deer, elk, bighorn sheep, mountain goats, and bears. Other wildlife sometimes seen are cougar, lynx, bobcats, coyotes, fox, porcupines, badgers, beavers, martens, mink, otters, muskrats, and skunks. Fishing for the fork's salmon, steelhead, and cutthroat, rainbow, and Dolly Varden trout is excellent.

Rafters use a segment of quiet waters on the main Salmon to enjoy the serene canyon beauty.

Photo courtesy of ECHO: The Wilderness Company/Charlie Patterson

50. SALMON RIVER (Upper Main), IDAHO

Section: Redfish Lake Creek to Slate Creek
Location: Custer County, north of Sun Valley, south-central Idaho
Distance: 35 miles (56 km) or less
Class: II–III + ; experience not required
Trip Options: Paddle raft, oar raft, inflatable kayak; half-day, one day
Season: May–mid-October
Outfitters: The River Company
Triangle C Ranch Whitewater
Two-M River Outfitters
White Otter Outdoor Adventures

Less than a one-hour drive north of Sun Valley, an alpine stretch of the upper main Salmon has recently become one of Idaho's most popular whitewater river sections. Here the Salmon's headwaters, although much smaller than the famed "River of No Return" section, provide summer visitors to Sun Valley-area resorts a very exciting, yet not difficult, opportunity to experience the thrills of rafting.

Outfitters specialize in various types of river trips. These include paddle trips where each guest helps control the raft under the direction of the licensed guide; oar-guided rafts for families with young children, fishermen, photo enthusiasts, senior citizens, and the disabled; and inflatable kayaks for the adventuresome where each guest follows the guide through the rapids. Outfitters welcome anyone above the age of four to share this exciting Salmon River adventure.

Trips begin near Stanley, Idaho, in the Sawtooth National Recreation Area. The Salmon's rapids and currents are ideal for practicing newly learned paddling techniques. Many first-time rafters catch "whitewater fever" and return year after year to enjoy the Salmon River's special allure.

51. SALMON RIVER (Main), Idaho

Section:	Main
Location:	Lemhi and Idaho counties, north-central Idaho
Distance:	80 miles (128 km)
Class:	III–IV; experience not required
Trip Options:	Paddle raft, oar raft, dory, inflatable kayak; four to five days
Season:	May–mid-October
Outfitters:	Action Whitewater Adventures
	Aggipah River Trips
	American River Touring Association
	Barker-Ewing Raft Trips
	Canyons Incorporated
	ECHO: The Wilderness Company
	Holiday River Expeditions–Idaho
	Idaho Adventure River Trips
	James Henry River Journeys
	Kingfisher Expeditions
	MacKay Bar Corporation
	Northwest Dories
	Northwest River Expeditions
	Orange Torpedo Trips
	Outdoor Adventures
	R & R Outdoors
	Salmon River Challenge
	Salmon River Lodge
	Salmon River Outfitters
	Silver Cloud Expeditions
	Tour West Whitewater Adventures
	Warren River Expeditions

White Water Adventures
Wilderness River Outfitters–Idaho
World Wide River Expeditions

The main Salmon or legendary "River of No Return," in its nearly 80-mile (128 km) trip through the remote granite canyons of central Idaho drops 1,000 feet creating more than 40 memorable rapids. Its most difficult and impressive rapids include Pine Creek, Ruby, Rainier, Salmon Falls, Bailey, Big and Little Mallard, Little Elk Horn, Johnson, Chittam, and Long Tom Creek.

Like the Middle Fork, the main Salmon offers a good chance to see big-game animals. Each spring and fall, deer, elk, bighorn sheep, mountain goats, and bears are commonly seen during their migrations between winter and summer ranges. There are also many interesting tributary side canyons to explore.

52. SALMON RIVER (Lower), IDAHO

Section: Whitebird to the confluence of the Snake River
Location: Idaho and Nez Percé counties, north-central Idaho
Distance: 52 miles (83 km)
Class: I–III
Season June–mid-October
Trip Options: Paddle raft, oar raft, paddle/oar raft, dory, inflatable kayak; three to five days
Outfitters: Barker River Trips
Dave Helfrich River Outfitter
Discovery River Expeditions
Epley's Whitewater Adventures
Holiday River Expeditions–Idaho
Hughes River Expeditions
Idaho Adventures River Trips
Idaho Guide Service
Ken Helfrich
Kingfisher Expeditions
Lower Salmon Express
Lyons Adventures
Nichols Expeditions
Northwest Dories
Northwest Voyageurs
Northwest Whitewater Excursions
Orange Torpedo Trips
Oregon River Experiences
Ouzel Outfitters
ROW (River Odysseys West)

R & R Outdoors
Salmon River Experience
Sawtooth River Expeditions
Wapiti River Guides
White Water Express
Wilderness River Outfitters–Oregon
Wild River Outfitters

The last 52 miles (83 km) of the Salmon, before its confluence with the Snake River, is known as the lower Salmon. While perhaps not as wild or remote as the Middle Fork or main Salmon, the lower Salmon does contain exciting whitewater and beautiful canyon scenery. The flatter stretches of the lower Salmon are excellent for hiking, relaxing, swimming, and fishing.

Four canyons—Green, Cougar, Snowhole, and Blue—hold the lower Salmon's best rapids. These include the Class III-rated Snowhole, Half and Half, China, Devil's Slide, Sluice Box, and Checkerboard the Needle. During July and August many families and senior citizens enjoy the whitewater and arid-canyon scenery.

Lower Salmon rafting trips also include an additional 20 miles (32 km), or more, of the Snake River below Hell's Canyon, along the Idaho–Oregon border. The take-out for the lower Salmon raft trip is Heller Bar, Washington.

53. LOCHSA RIVER, IDAHO

Section:	Lolo Pass to Lowell
Location:	Idaho County, northeast of Grangeville, north-central Idaho
Distance:	14–60 miles (22–96 km)
Class:	III–IV + ; experience recommended
Trip Options:	Paddle raft, oar raft; one, two, and three days
Season:	May–August
Outfitters:	Glacier Raft Company
	Holiday River Expeditions–Idaho
	Lochsa River Rafters
	ROW (River Odysseys West)
	Wilderness Trails

Historians record that it was the Shoshone who aptly named the river *Lochsa*, the Indian word for "rough water." Today these same turbid waters create one of the best multiday recreational challenges available to whitewater enthusiasts. More than twenty-five major rapids, such as Grim Reaper, Lochsa Falls, Bloody Mary, Horsetail Falls, and Ten Pin Alley, are rated Class III–IV + . The Lochsa is considerably more difficult than the Salmon River; it should be considered only by active paddlers in good physical shape.

Navigating the Lochsa's technical rapids requires a high degree of coordination and teamwork between guides and rafters. During high spring waters guides normally use a center- or rear-mounted oar frame and ask rafters to assist with paddling during the difficult rapids. As the water levels drop, and the river becomes even more technical, paddle raft trips become even more frequent.

The Lochsa, part of the Clearwater Wild and Scenic River System, parallels U.S. Highway 12 from just below Lolo Pass to Lowell, where it meets the Selway to form the Clearwater River. During years of average snow pack, commercial outfitters normally run two- and three-day trips between late May and late July. One-day trips are available on the lower Lochsa near Lowell.

Paddle rafters may choose between one- , two- , or three-day trips on north Idaho's beautiful Lochsa River.
Photo courtesy of ROW (River Odysseys West)

54. SELWAY RIVER, IDAHO

Section: Paradise Creek to Selway Falls
Location: Idaho County, east of Grangeville, north-central Idaho
Distance: 45 miles (72 km)
Class: III–IV + ; experience recommended
Trip Options: Paddle raft, oar raft, paddle/oar raft; three to five days
Season: June–July
Outfitters: American River Touring Association
              Elwood Masoner's Whitewater Adventures
              Lochsa River Rafters
              Northwest River Company
              White Water Adventures
              Wilderness Trails

The Selway River canyon, in the Selway–Bitterroot Wilderness Area near the Idaho/Montana border, is one of the most remote and secluded multiday river experiences in the northern Rockies. Unlike the Salmon River with numerous daily trips, rafting access to the Selway is very limited. The U.S. Forest Service issues only sixteen seasonal launch permits for all outfitters and limits the size of each party to just sixteen people, which includes the boatmen.

For those fortunate enough to raft the Selway, one of the first rivers protected by the Wild and Scenic Act, the river experience is unforgettable. For up to five days, rafters navigate exciting Class II–IV rapids, such as Galloping Gertie, Washer Woman, Ping Pong Alley, Goat Creek, Ham, Double Drop, Little Niagara, Puzzle Creek, Wolf Creek, and Tee Kem Falls. Take-out is just above the Class VI Selway Falls. In the quiet pools between the exciting whitewater, much time remains to enjoy the isolated wildlife and forest scenery.

55. MOYIE RIVER, IDAHO

Section: Copper Creek Campground
Location: Boundary County near Bonners Ferry, northern Idaho
Distance: 15 miles (24 km)
Class: II–III
Trip Options: Paddle raft; one day
Season: May–June
Outfitters: Moyie River Outfitters
              ROW (River Odysseys West)

Flowing south from the Rockies in adjacent British Columbia, northern Idaho's Moyie River is an excellent one-day river run. Its put-in is less than 20 miles (16 km) from both the Canadian and Montana borders. Few signs of civilization exist in the Moyie's 15-mile (24 km) stretch through the Kaniksu National Forest. You are more likely to see bears, deer, moose, ospreys, or eagles than other humans.

The fact that the Moyie is promoted as a river trip for beginners as well as experienced paddlers should not cause you to underestimate the difficulty of the whitewater. There are nearly two dozen Class II–III (IV during high water), rapids which will test the skills of each paddler. Outfitters have a minimum age requirement of fourteen years old.

The spring rafting season is short, the water is cold, and wet suits are required.

56. ST. JOE RIVER, IDAHO

Section:	Upper
Location:	Shoshone County, east of St. Maries, northern Idaho
Distance:	15–25 miles (24–40 km)
Class:	II–IV
Trip Options:	Paddle raft; one day
Season:	May–July
Outfitter:	ROW (River Odysseys West)

The St. Joe River begins high in the Continental Divide between Idaho and Montana, and flows west to St. Maries at the south end of Lake Coeur d'Alene. During this nearly 120-mile (192 km) journey through the vast St. Joe National Forest, there is much history, beauty, and whitewater. Early in the twentieth century, paddle steamers regularly moved some 15 miles (24 km) above St. Maries. In the years since, most of the St. Joe's river canyons escaped the wrath of northern Idaho's loggers and miners. The St. Joe was one of the first rivers to be included in the National Wild and Scenic River System.

St. Joe's outfitter offers one-day rafting trips. Depending upon water levels, put-ins and take-outs are often not determined until the day of the trip. The frequent Class III–IV rapids at medium- to high-water levels are still exciting and fun Class II–III when water levels are lower.

Skilled oarsman navigates the Class III–IV waters of the famed Hells Canyon of the Snake River between Idaho and Oregon.
Photo by Verne Huser

57. SNAKE RIVER (Hells Canyon), IDAHO

Section:	Hells Canyon Dam to Pittsburg Landing or Heller Bar
Location:	Idaho and Nez Percé counties, west of Grangeville, north-central Idaho
Distance:	32 or 83 miles (51 or 133 km)
Class:	III–IV; experience not required
Trip Options:	Paddle raft, oar raft, dory, inflatable kayak; three to six days
Season:	May–October
Outfitters:	Anderson River Adventures
	Barker River Tours
	Beamer's Hells Canyon Tours
	Canyon Outfitters
	Davis Whitewater Expeditions
	Hells Canyon Adventures
	Holiday River Expeditions–Idaho
	Hughes River Expeditions
	Idaho Adventures River Trips
	Idaho Afloat
	Ken Warren Outdoors
	Northwest Dories
	Northwest Voyageurs
	ROW (River Odysseys West)
	Steen's Wilderness Adventures

The Snake River's Hells Canyon provides a multiday rafting experience. It compares with the popular Grand Canyon and the Middle Fork and main Salmon rivers' trips. The Snake River carves North America's deepest canyon gorge in Hells Canyon. Averaging nearly 6,600 feet, the spectacular canyon creates a most impressive border between Oregon's Wallowa and Idaho's Seven Devils mountains.

Most of the Snake's largest rapids, including Wildsheep, Granite Falls, Waterspout, and Rush Creek, are during the first 30 miles (48 km) below Hells Canyon Dam. These rapids, while fairly difficult during early high-water levels, mellow during the summer. Many families and senior citizens safely enjoy the Snake River raft trip between July and September.

Hells Canyon is far more than a whitewater adventure. The canyon is rich is historic homesteads and cabins, ancient Indian ruins, and excellent petroglyphs and pictographs. It has abundant wildlife, which includes Rocky Mountain bighorn sheep, goats, mule deer, black bears, and numerous birds of prey. You can also fish its superb currents and holes for rainbow trout, smallmouth bass, steelhead, channel catfish, and white sturgeon.

In addition to the popular 83-mile (133 km) scenic trip between Hells Canyon Dam and Heller Bar, some 32 miles (51 km) above Lewiston, outfitters offer several shorter trips. It is possible to raft Hells Canyon from the dam to Pittsburg Landing, or put in at Pittsburg Landing and raft to Heller Bar.

Hells Canyon contains the last wild, free-flowing stretch of the Snake River. (Four hydro-electric dams harness the Snake between Lewiston, Idaho, and its confluence with the Columbia River, south of Pasco, Washington.) The Snake River in Hells Canyon is a National Wild and Scenic River. It is wild from Hells Canyon Dam to Pittsburg Landing, which is 32 miles (51 km), and scenic from Pittsburg Landing to Heller Bar, which is 51 miles (82 km). The entire trip is also included in the Hells Canyon National Recreation Area and the Wallowa–Whitman National Forest.

58. SNAKE RIVER (Birds of Prey), IDAHO

Section:	Swan Falls Dam to Walter's Ferry Bridge
Location:	Ada County, south of Boise, southwest Idaho
Distance:	16 miles (26 km)
Class:	I–II
Trip Option:	Oar raft; one day
Season:	April–June
Outfitters:	Idaho Guide Service

MacKay Bar Corporation
Middle Fork River Tours
Whitewater Shop River Tours

The Snake River's Birds of Prey Natural Area protects the nesting area of more than 700 pairs of raptors. Among the more frequently seen species are golden eagles, red-tailed hawks, ferruginous hawks, northern harriers, great horned owls, long-eared owls, Western screech owls, burring owls, and prairie falcons. Rafting is an ideal way to see these raptors and the impressive Snake River canyon scenery.

Other than two Class II rapids near the Swan Falls Dam put-in, this portion of the Snake is a very easy Class I float trip, providing plenty of time to use binoculars, spotting scopes, and cameras. Telephoto lenses are essential for photographing the birds of prey.

First-timers, senior citizens, families with young children, and the disabled may enjoy this trip. The best time for viewing raptors is from mid-March to mid-June. After June, the canyon becomes quite hot and most raptors seek cooler, higher elevations.

59. SNAKE RIVER (Middle), IDAHO

Section:	Lower Salmon Falls Dam to Bliss Bridge (Hagerman)
Location:	Gooding County near Gooding, southern Idaho
Distance:	8 miles (13 km)
Trip Options:	Paddle raft, oar raft; one day
Class:	I–II, III
Season:	April–September
Outfitters:	High Adventure River Tours
	Idaho Guide Service
	Middle Fork Rapid Transit
	White Otter Outdoor Adventures

Quite unlike the upstream Murtaugh section of the Snake, Hagerman's relatively calm waters shouldn't frighten anyone. The 8-mile (13 km) Hagerman trip, from the Lower Salmon Falls Dam to Bliss Bridge, has mostly easy Class I–II rapids, which are ideal for first-time rafters and families with children as young as five years old. Paddle rafters have ample time to sharpen raft control skills before Pillar Rapids, Hagerman's only Class III rapids.

Section:	Murtaugh Bridge to Twin Falls Park (Murtaugh)
Location:	Jerome County, east of Twin Falls, southern Idaho
Distance:	15 miles (24 km)

Class:	III–V; experience required for paddle-raft trips
Trip Options:	Paddle raft, oar raft; one day
Season:	March–June
Outfitters:	High Adventure River Tours
	Idaho Guide Service
	White Otter Outdoor Adventures

The Murtaugh section of the Snake, which cuts through southern Idaho's plateau country, has some of the state's biggest whitewater. Rafters who desire more demanding whitewater should be delighted. Murtaugh's waters are big, exciting, and demand respect.

At higher spring-water levels, Murtaugh has ten Class IV rapids, including Basalt Falls, Troll, Mabeline, and Misty; Class V Let's Make a Deal; and Class VI Pair of Dice.

During the calm stretches between Murtaugh's powerful rapids, rafters can enjoy the beautiful basalt canyon walls and picturesque waterfalls and often get glimpses of many birds of prey.

60. PAYETTE RIVER, IDAHO

Three forks of southwest Idaho's Payette River—the North, South, and Main—provide whitewater enthusiasts nearly 80 miles (128 km) of superb Class II–IV rafting opportunities within a one-hour drive of Boise. Commercially rafted are a 10-mile (16 km) section of the North Fork, some 60 miles (96 km) of the South Fork, and immediately after the confluence of the two forks, 9 miles (14 km) of the main Payette. While the Payette's half- and one-day whitewater trips are some of Idaho's most popular river runs, outfitters also offer multiday raft trips on the South Fork.

Section:	North Fork: Cabarton to Smith Ferry
Location:	Valley County, south of McCall, southwest Idaho
Distance:	10 miles (16 km)
Class:	III–IV; experience not required
Trip Options:	Paddle raft, oar raft; one day
Season:	May–September
Outfitters:	Bear Valley River Company
	Canyons Incorporated
	Cascade Raft Company
	Lyons Adventures

Rafting on the Cabarton section of the North Fork, a very popular summertime Class III–IV trip adjacent to Idaho Route 55, is made possible by controlled-water releases from Cascade Reservoir by

Idaho Power. There are several easy rapids on which first-time rafters can perfect newly learned paddling skills before the North Fork's biggest whitewaters: the Class III–IV Tressel Rapid and Howard's Plunge. Unfortunately, because of its deep canyon and steep gradient, the North Fork Payette is currently being studied as a potential hydro power site.

Section:	South Fork (canyon and lower)
Location:	Boise County, north of Boise, southwest Idaho
Distance:	15 miles (24 km) (upper South Fork)
	14 miles (22 km) (Old Swirley Canyon)
	7 miles (11 km) (lower South Fork Canyon)
Class:	III–IV (upper)
	III (Old Swirley)
	II–III + (lower canyon)
Trip Options:	Paddle raft, oar raft, multiday (upper), one day (Old Swirley), one-half day (lower canyon)
Season:	May–September
Outfitters:	Bear Valley River Company
	Cascade Raft Company
	Lyons Adventures

The Payette's premier whitewater challenges are in the canyons and gorges of its South Fork. The narrow, steep-walled canyon run has mostly Class III pool-drop rapids, but it does have four technical Class IV rapids—S-turn, Blackadar's Drop, Little Falls, and Surprise, as well as a mandatory portage around the 40-foot, Class VI Big Falls. Although an adjacent county road allows take-out just below Little Falls, some one-day and all multiday South Fork rafting trips continue through the breathtaking Class III Old Swirley Canyon. The South Fork also has several refreshing hot springs.

Downstream, the last 5 miles (8 km) of the lower South Fork before its confluence with the North Fork, is one of Idaho's most popular whitewater runs. Well known as the site of the annual Payette Whitewater Rodeo, the lower run has fairly continuous and exciting Class II–III + rapids. Rafters frequently take advantage of the relatively short length of the whitewater trip and run the Staircase section twice in one day. Prior to the South Fork's confluence with the Main Payette, Staircase Rapid (a long Class IV rapid) will adequately test the skills of paddle rafters.

Section:	Main
Location:	Boise County, north of Boise, southwest Idaho

Distance:	9–14 miles (4–22 km)
Class:	I–III
Trip Options:	Paddle raft, oar raft; one-half, one day
Season:	May–September
Outfitters:	Bear Valley River Company
	Cascade Raft Company
	Lyons Adventures

The very popular main Payette, created by the confluence of the river's North and South forks, offers an excellent introduction to whitewater rafting for families and inexperienced paddlers. This beautiful whitewater river is also a favorite with large groups. Guide-escorted half- and one-day raft trips start at the town of Banks. Nearly 4 (6 km) miles of easy Class I–II rapids at the beginning of the trip give paddle rafters ample time to practice their skills before Class III-rated Mike's Hole. The main Payette's two other Class III rapids, Mixmaster and AMF, are located just prior to the Beehive Bend take-out for half-day trips.

On morning and afternoon trips, outfitters allow time for swimming and relaxing. For those wishing to scout the river prior to their trip, Idaho Route 55 parallels the main Payette's entire whitewater run.

61. JARBIDGE–BRUNEAU RIVERS, IDAHO

Section:	Murphy Hot Springs to Bruneau River (Jarbidge)
	Confluence of Jarbidge to Bruneau (Bruneau)
Location:	Owyhee County, south of Mountain Home, southwest Idaho
Distance:	30 miles (48 km) (Jarbidge)
	45 miles (72 km) (Bruneau)
Class:	III–VI (Jarbidge)
	III–IV + (Bruneau)
Trip Options:	Paddle raft, oar raft, inflatable kayak; six to seven days (Jarbidge–Bruneau)
	Oar raft; three to four days (Bruneau)
Season:	May–June
Outfitters:	Hughes River Expeditions
	Middle Fork River Company
	Sevy Guide Service
	Wilderness River Outfitters–Idaho

The Jarbidge–Bruneau rivers, scenic tributaries of the Snake River in southwest Idaho, offer 75 (120 km) miles of exciting, small-stream whitewater combined with some of the Northwest's most dramatic and varied desert scenery. Juniper and cedar trees are dwarfed by towering rock spires and basalt cliffs that rise up to 2,000 feet above the river.

Jarbidge's dramatic Class III–VI whitewater, created by narrow chutes and steep drops, necessitates one of the highest guide-to-guest ratios of any multiday river trip in the West. One of the West's longest rapids, Five Mile is nearly continuous Class III–IV whitewater action for several miles.

While spring raft trips on the Jarbidge–Bruneau are normally six to seven days long, outfitters do run shorter three-to-four-day trips on the Bruneau River. The canyons of the Bruneau are great for exploring. In addition to many spectacular caves and rock arches, the canyon's abundant wildlife includes mule deer, otter, chukar partridge, Canada geese, ducks, eagles, and other migratory birds.

62. OWYHEE RIVER, IDAHO

Sections: South Fork and upper canyons
                 East Fork and upper canyons
Location: Owyhee County, south of Mountain Home, southwest
                 Idaho
Distance: 105 miles (168 km) (South Fork)
                 98 miles (157 km) (East Fork)
Class: III–IV + (South Fork); III–VI (East Fork)
Trip Options: Paddle raft, oar raft, inflatable kayak; six to nine days
Season: April–June
Outfitters: Hughes River Expeditions
                 Middle Fork River Company
                 ROW (River Odysseys West)
                 Sevy Guide Service
                 Wilderness River Outfitters–Idaho

Whitewater and desert lovers who want to escape civilization and explore remote river canyons should head for the little-known and seldom-run Owyhee River. Though advertised as southwest Idaho's Owyhee trip, there are actually two river sections: South Fork and the upper section of the Owyhee canyon, and the East Fork and the upper canyon.

Owyhee's East Fork, the most difficult of the two forks, has several Class IV–V rapids and the normally portaged Class VI Owyhee Falls. The South Fork also has challenging Class III–IV + rapids, including Cabin or Thunder Egg and Cable Rapids. Depending upon water levels, Cable may have to be portaged.

Some of the West's most remote canyons are located on the Owyhee River near the Oregon, Idaho, and Nevada borders.
Photo courtesy of ROW (River Odysseys West)

Each fork has dramatic canyon scenery. The wildlife seen is similar to that in the Jarbidge–Bruneau and middle Owyhee. Outfitters offer six to nine day trips on both forks of the Owyhee. In addition to these trips, either of the Owyhee forks trips can be combined with a trip on the middle and lower Owyhee for a unique and memorable 16- or 17-day trip.

63. FLATHEAD RIVER (North Fork), MONTANA

Section: Canadian border to confluence with Middle Fork
Location: Flathead County, western border of Glacier National
                Park, northwest Montana
Distance: 60 miles (96 km)
Class: I–II
Trip Options: Paddle raft, oar raft; three and four days
Season: June–August
Outfitters: Glacier Raft Company
                Glacier Wilderness Guides
                Wild River Adventures

The North Fork of the Flathead River provides one of Montana's most scenic river trips. Flowing south from British Columbia, Canada, the North Fork creates the western boundary of Montana's Glacier National Park. For almost 60 miles (96 km), from the put-in near the Canadian–United States border to its confluence with the Middle Fork, North Fork rafters enjoy panoramic views of the park's impressive Livingston Mountains.

Although the North Fork Flathead attracts many rafters interested in Glacier National Park's remote western regions, it is also popular for fishing for cutthroat trout.

64. FLATHEAD RIVER (Middle Fork), MONTANA

Section: Essex to confluence with North Fork (lower)
                Shafer Meadows to Essex (upper)
Location: Flathead County, southern border of Glacier National
                Park, northwest Montana
Distance: 7–15 miles (11–24 km) (lower)
                35 miles (56 km) (upper)
Class: II–IV (lower)
                II–IV + (upper)
Trip Options: Paddle raft, oar raft; half-day, one to four days
Season: May–September

Outfitters: Glacier Raft Company
                   Glacier Wilderness Guides (lower)
                   Great Northern Whitewater (lower)
                   Wilderness River Outfitters–Idaho

The lower Middle Fork of the Flathead River, which marks Glacier National Park's southern border, is the river's most popular rafting trip among park visitors. Rafters enjoy the excellent combination of good whitewater and scenic mountains and forests in the park and the Flathead Range. U.S. Highway 2, which parallels the Middle Fork, can occasionally be seen from the river. Rafters may choose between half- and one-day trips, which end near Glacier's west entrance.

Outfitters also offer multiday raft trips on the 35-mile (56 km) upper stretches of the Middle Fork, from the Bob Marshall Wilderness Area northwest to the park. Rafters may enjoy some of the state's finest alpine wilderness. Immediately below the Schafer Meadows put-in, the run passes through the Great Bear Wilderness, home to grizzly bears, elk, deer, moose, mountain goats, waterfowl, and birds of prey. Outfitters normally run the upper Middle Fork in four days to allow rafters time to hike and fish.

65. FLATHEAD RIVER (South Fork), MONTANA

Section: South Fork
Location: Powell and Flathead counties, south of Glacier National Park, northwest Montana
Distance: 62 miles (99 km)
Class: II–IV; excellent physical condition mandatory
Trip Options: Paddle raft, oar raft; four to six days, including a 25-mile (40 km) hike or horseback ride
Season: June–August
Outfitters: Curtiss Outfitters
                Diamond R Guest Ranch
                Skyline Outfit–Roland Cheek
                Spotted Bear Ranch
                Wilderness Ranch and Lodge
                Wilderness River Outfitters–Idaho
                Wild River Adventures

The South Fork Flathead offers Montana's most remote and inaccessible river adventure. Reaching any of the river put-ins requires either a hiking or horse-pack trip over the Swan Mountain Range, a distance of at least 25 miles (40 km). The pace of hiking is slow so you can enjoy the beautiful lakes, glaciers, and wildflowers.

The Bob Marshall Wilderness Area is the main attraction of the South Fork hike-and-raft adventure. For much of the 62-mile (99 km) river journey from Big Prairie, the most frequently used river put-in, to the Spotted Bear Ranger Station, above Hungry Horse Reservoir, the river provides rafters with ample time to appreciate the area's wildlife, which includes mountain goats, elk, deer, bears, and moose.

The Meadow Creek Gorge, a narrow, 5-mile (8 km) canyon near the end of the South Fork trip, provides the river's most exciting whitewater. If the gorge cannot be run because of low water, however, trips will end at the head of the gorge with a short hike to the road.

66. FLATHEAD RIVER (Lower), MONTANA

Section: Lower
Location: Lake County, south of Polson, western Montana
Distance: 8 miles (13 km)
Class: II–III +
Trip Options: Paddle raft, oar raft; half-day
Season: June–August
Outfitters: Glacier Raft Company
                 Glacier Wilderness Guides
                 Great Northern Whitewater
                 Wild River Adventures

The lower Flathead River, which begins at the south end of Flathead Lake, provides an exciting, yet relatively easy, half-day introduction

Buffalo Rapids is one of several exciting Class II–III + rapids on Montana's lower Flathead River.
Photo by Tim Palmer

to whitewater rafting. While most of the lower Flathead is fairly easy Class I–II + whitewater, four of its rapids—The Ledge, Pinball, Eagle Wave, and Buffalo—are Class II–III + . The river gives novice and experienced paddlers a good opportunity to test paddling skills.

The lower Flathead, controlled by Montana Power's water releases from Kerr Dam, is usually raftable throughout the summer season. Trips on the lower Flathead normally take about three hours and are scheduled both mornings and afternoons. Reservations are recommended, but same-day raft trips are usually possible. Because of the intermediate nature of the whitewater, it is recommended that families and senior rafters consider only the summer oar trips.

Put-in for the lower Flathead is just a few minutes south of Polson. Located within the boundaries of the Flathead Indian Reservation, the scenic lower Flathead is home to many birds of prey and waterfowl.

67. CLARK FORK RIVER, MONTANA

Section:	Alberton Gorge
Location:	Mineral County, northwest of Missoula, western Montana
Distance:	12 miles (19 km)
Class:	II–III
Trip Options:	Paddle raft, oar raft, inflatable kayak; one day
Season:	July–September
Outfitters:	Montana River Outfitters
	Wild River Adventures

Alberton Gorge, on the Clark Fork, is one of western Montana's best whitewater rafting stretches during late summer. The later runoff of the eastern slopes of the Bitterroot Range provide the Clark Fork with water when most other rivers are nearing their water-level low.

During the summer, the gorge's exciting Class II–III rapids—Fang, Boateater, Tumbleweed, Trip Bridges, Cliffside, and Rest Stop—are ideal for both beginning and intermediate rafters.

Although Interstate 90 parallels the river for the entire gorge, the highway can seldom be seen. The Clark Fork's mountain canyons provide habitat to a variety of wildlife including deer, bears, ospreys, hawks, turkey vultures, and eagles. Its waters are well stocked with trout.

68. BLACKFOOT RIVER, MONTANA

Section: Middle
Location: Missoula County, east of Missoula, western Montana
Distance: 12–30 miles (19–48 km)
Class: II–III
Trip Options: Paddle raft, oar raft, inflatable kayak; one to three days
Season: May–July
Outfitter: Montana River Outfitters

Less than a half-hour-drive east of Missoula, the middle Blackfoot River provides an ideal introduction to whitewater rafting for families, senior citizens, and first-time rafters. The raft trip passes through beautiful pine-forested rocky gorges. Its relatively easy Class II–III rapids alternate with quiet river stretches that provide relaxing, fishing, and swimming.

Most one-day trips on the Blackfoot cover about 12 miles (19 km). Two- and three-day trips normally travel about 30 miles (48 km). They also leave plenty of time for fishing for the river's excellent trout.

69. GALLATIN RIVER, MONTANA

Section: Greek Creek to Squaw Creek
Location: Gallatin County, near Yellowstone National Park, southwest Montana
Distance: 8 miles (13 km)
Class: II–IV; experience not required
Trip Options: Paddle raft, oar raft; half-day, one day
Season: June–August
Outfitter: Yellowstone Raft Company

The put-in for whitewater rafting on the Gallatin is almost immediately outside Yellowstone National Park. Deep in the Gallatin canyon, alongside U.S. Highway 191, Class III + rapids, such as Show Stopper, House Rock, and The Mad Mile, highlight a stretch of almost continuous whitewater.

While most of the Gallatin's rafters are guests at Montana's Big Sky Resort, all visitors are welcome on half- and one-day raft trips. Half-day trips, which run three times a day, include most of the river's best whitewater. Full-day trips have a more leisurely pace, and lunch is served. Oar-guided raft trips during the summer are suggested for families. Scenic float trips on calmer stretches of the Gallatin are also available.

70. MADISON RIVER, MONTANA

Section: Bear Trap Canyon
Location: Madison County, west of Bozeman, southwest Montana
Distance: 9 miles (14 km)
Class: II–IV
Trip Options: Paddle raft, oar raft; one day
Season: July–August
Outfitter: Yellowstone Raft Company

The Madison River's majestic Bear Trap Canyon, about an hour's drive northwest of Yellowstone National Park, contains one of Montana's finest whitewater stretches. Unlike the Gallatin and Yellowstone raft trips, no roads and few signs of civilization are seen from the river. Raft trips, which begin near the Madison Dam powerhouse below Ennis Lake, are usually run at a leisurely pace so you can appreciate the beauty of the 1,500-foot canyon, its plentiful wildlife, and its challenging whitewater.

Bear Trap's whitewater includes four major rapids: Double Drop, White Horse, Kitchen Sink, and Green Wave. On warm summer days, outfitters permit swimming and tubing.

71. YELLOWSTONE RIVER, MONTANA

Sections: Paradise Valley and Yankee Jim Canyon
Location: Park County near Gardiner, north of Yellowstone National Park, southwest Montana
Distance: 8–21 miles (13–34 km)
Class: II–III; experience not required for oar-guided rafts
Trip Options: Paddle raft, oar raft, inflatable kayak; half-day, one day
Season: May–October
Outfitters: Crazy Mountain Raft
                Montana River Outfitters
                Yellowstone Raft Company

The historic Yellowstone River is an almost 680-mile (1,088 km) free-flowing tributary of the Missouri River. It is rafted just north of Yellowstone National Park in southwest Montana. For some 20 miles (32 km) below the Gardiner put-in, the exciting Class II–III waters of upper Paradise Valley and Yankee Jim Canyon attract thousands of rafters to the same canyons that were visited by early Indians and trappers.

Whitewater rafting on Montana's Gallatin River begins just outside Yellowstone National Park.
Photo courtesy of Yellowstone Rafting Company

Outfitters offer both half- and full-day trips on the Yellowstone. Full-day trips, which cover nearly 21 miles (34 km), still allow time for fishing or swimming. Visitors with less time can consider three- to four-hour trips. They have plenty of whitewater and still allow visitors time for other activities. Half-day paddle and oar-guided raft trips on the Yellowstone are an excellent introduction to whitewater for families, senior citizens, and first-time rafters. When requested, outfitters offer scenic float trips on calmer stretches of the Yellowstone River.

72. SNAKE RIVER (Upper), WYOMING

Section: Pacific Creek to Moose Village
Location: Grand Teton National Park, north of Jackson, northwest Wyoming
Distance: 5, 10, or 20 miles (8, 16, or 32 km)
Class: I–II
Trip Options: Oar raft; one hour, two hours, half-day, one day
Season: May–September
Outfitters: Barker-Ewing Scenic Tours
                   Flagg Ranch Float Trips
                   Fort Jackson Float Trips
                   Grand Teton Lodge Company
                   Heart Six Guest Ranch Float Trips
                   National Park Float Trips
                   Osprey Float Trips
                   Signal Mountain Lodge
                   Solitude Float Trips
                   Triangle X Float Trips

One of the more relaxing and enjoyable ways for visitors to enjoy the awesome beauty of Grand Teton National Park is a float trip on the Snake River. Beneath the majestic Grand Teton Mountains, the Snake's slow waters are the only avenue to see many of Jackson Hole's forests and meadows that provide secluded habitat to abundant wildlife, such as beavers, otters, bears, moose, eagles, and ospreys.

Below Jackson Lake, from mid-May until mid-September, the park's licensed rafting outfitters offer a wide variety of 5- and 10-mile (8 and 16 km) float trips that include sunrise and evening wildlife trips, deli or picnic lunch, supper floats, fishing trips, and overnight floats.

Snake River outfitters have few passenger restrictions. Almost anyone above the age of four can enjoy the river. Outfitters welcome families, senior citizens, the disabled, and first-timers. While it is almost always possible to join a raft trip on short notice, reservations a few days in advance are recommended.

Sections: Canyons
Location: Lincoln County, south of Jackson, northwest Wyoming
Distance: 8 and 16 miles (13 and 26 km)
Class: I–III
Trip Options: Paddle raft, oar raft; half-day, one day
Season: May–September

Outfitters: Barker–Ewing Raft Trips
Dave Hansen Whitewater
Jackson Hole Whitewater
Lewis and Clark River Expeditions
Lone Eagle Expeditions
Mad River Boat Trips
Sands Wildwater
Snake River Park

Just south of Grand Teton National Park, the Snake River affords vacationers two 8-mile (13 km) rafting choices in the Bridger–Teton National Forest. The first, near Hoback Junction, is a scenic float along the quiet waters of the Snake that enables you to relax and enjoy the beautiful mountain scenery. In addition to daytime float trips, several outfitters offer morning and evening floats so visitors can see much of the wildlife that are common to Grand Teton National Park.

The upper Snake River near Hoback Junction offers both a scenic float trip and Class II–III whitewater.
Photo by Robert Winslow

Photo by Robert Winslow

Downstream, from West Table Creek to Sheep Creek north of Alpine Junction, the upper Snake River canyon offers a more lively 8-mile (13 km) introduction to whitewater rafting. Class II–III rapids—Main Line, Three Oar-deal, Kahuna, Lunch Counter, Rope, Champagne, and Cottonwood—are not difficult and can be enjoyed by both families and tentative first-time rafters.

73. SHOSHONE RIVER, WYOMING

Section:	Red Rock Canyon
Location:	Park County, west of Cody, northwest Wyoming
Distance:	6 or 13 miles (9.5 km or 21 km)
Class:	II–III
Trip Options:	Paddle raft; two hours, half-day, one day
Season:	May–September
Outfitters:	Cody Rapid Transit
	River Runners of Cody
	Wyoming River Trips

Just one-hour-and-one-half east of Yellowstone National Park, the beautiful Shoshone River offers visitors an ideal introduction to whitewater rafting. Daily raft trips through the beautiful Red Rock Canyon adjacent to Wyoming routes 14/16 are the result of scheduled water releases from Buffalo River Reservoir.

Shoshone's Class II–III rapids are not difficult. First-timers may even want to try their skills with a paddle raft rather than an oar-guided raft trip.

Outfitters offer two- and four-hour trips on a 6-mile (9.5 km) section of the river. All-day trips are offered on a 13-mile (21 km) section. Both trips end in Cody.

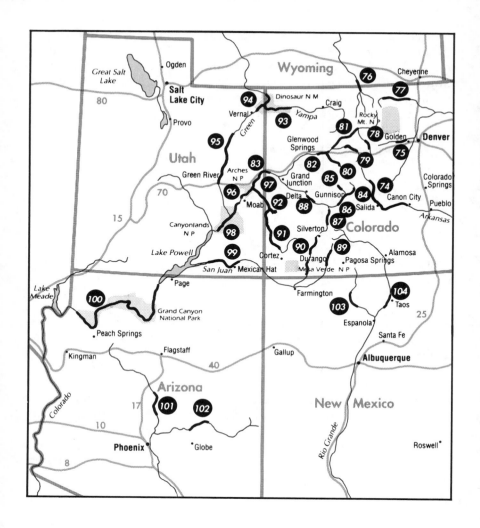

CHAPTER 5

The Southwest States

AMERICA'S SOUTHWEST STATES—Colorado, Utah, Arizona, New Mexico, and Texas—are famous for their unsurpassed mountain and canyon beauty. Whitewater rafting provides access to the region's sandstone canyons, granite and basalt gorges, and arid deserts that previously could only be seen from overlooks and aircraft. The Southwest's more than fifty rafting adventures include half-day, one-day, and multiday raft trips suitable for the adventurous, the timid, the old, and the young. Many of the more popular trips are also conveniently located near the region's well known parks, resorts, and other vacation centers.

Only four of Colorado's whitewater stretches are not part of the Colorado River drainage. The eastward flowing Arkansas, which is Colorado's and the West's most frequently rafted river, features daily trips for guests of all ages and experience levels. Clear Creek, a difficult Class IV–V + spring expedition, is just minutes west of Denver. The Cache la Poudre, an intermediate-level whitewater canyon northeast of Rocky Mountain National Park, can be easily reached from Fort Collins. The North Platte, a tributary of the South Platte, is a challenging and exciting alpine river running from Colorado into Wyoming.

Five of Colorado's popular whitewater stretches are in the central Rockies, less than a one-hour drive from Aspen and Vail. Near Kremmling, more than twenty-five outfitters provide half-day, one-day, and multiday raft trips for families and first-time rafters on the moderate waters of the upper Colorado. Two tributaries of the upper Colorado, the Eagle and the Blue, also have relatively easy whitewater sections for new paddlers. In the middle Colorado, Glenwood Canyon, near Glenwood Springs, allows visitors to experience whitewater thrills in a very scenic gorge. Spring and early summer visitors to Aspen, Snowmass, or Glenwood Springs who want to experience more challenging whitewater should not be disappointed with the Class II–IV Roaring Fork northwest of Aspen.

Rafting in southwest Colorado includes alpine streams and the rivers of the Colorado Plateau. The Gunnison River system, which joins the Colorado at Grand Junction, has rafting trips of varying difficulty on the Taylor, Slate, upper Gunnison, Lake Fork of the Gunnison, and the Gunnison Gorge. During spring, both the Piedra and upper Animas rivers in the San Juan Mountains provide some of the state's most exciting Class V waters. The moderate lower Animas at Durango provides daily rafting trips for families and first-time rafters throughout much of the summer. The Dolores River, which runs parallel to the Colorado–Utah border, offers several excellent multiday trip options. San Miguel, a Dolores tributary near Telluride, has half- and one-day trips for families.

In northwest Colorado, the Green and Yampa rivers unveil the majestic canyon splendor of Dinosaur National Monument on popular multiday raft trips. Two outfitters offer excellent one-day, family raft trips through Split Mountain Gorge, the last of Dinosaur's three spectacular canyons.

Utah's whitewater rafting is done on the middle Colorado and three of its tributaries: the Green, San Juan, and Dolores. Outfitters on the middle Colorado offer multiday excursions through spectacular Canyonlands National Park, one- or two-day trips through impressive Westwater Canyon, and a popular one-day trip through the Professor Valley–Fisher Towers canyons, which is adjacent to Arches National Park. On the Green, whitewater trips through Desolation Canyon traverse some of the most rugged and tortured landscaped in the United States. On the final stretches of the San Juan River in southeast Utah, rafters pass unusual and colorful geologic formations. The popular multiday Dolores River trip, although mostly in Colorado, meets the Colorado River just downriver from Westwater Canyon.

Arizona's Grand Canyon of the Colorado rafting excursion is one of the world's greatest wilderness river expeditions. Many of the canyon's twenty-one outfitters report that their trips are sold out a year or more in advance.

Some of the Southwest's lesser known rafting trips are in the semiarid and desert rivers of Arizona, New Mexico, and Texas. Central Arizona's Salt and Verde rivers offer late-winter and early-spring trips that often coincide with the northward bird migrations. New Mexico's Rio Chama and Rio Grande extend outstanding trip opportunities of varying difficulty in Wild and Scenic canyons near the charming old town of Taos and the state's capital of Santa Fe. In Texas, year-round rafting on the Rio Grande, through the towering canyons of Big Bend National Park, is possible for nearly 300 miles (480 km) along the United States–Mexico border.

74. ARKANSAS RIVER, COLORADO

The Arkansas River, from Twin Lakes below Independence Pass in south-central Colorado to Canon City, has a wide range of whitewater rafting. Both oar-raft and paddle-raft trips are available; families, first-timers, and experienced rafters will find some sections of the river—The Numbers, Browns Canyon, Salida–Cotapaxi, Cotapaxi–Parkdale, and Royal Gorge—to their liking. During a season with normal water flows, the Arkansas' forty-plus outfitters take more than 150,000 rafters down the river. Outfitters provide a number of one-day, half-day, and shorter trips on the Arkansas.

During winters of average, or better, snowpack in the Rocky Mountains, the Arkansas usually maintains sufficient water flows for rafting from May through early September. Outfitters, who prefer early trip reservations, can almost always accommodate same-day callers.

Sections: The Numbers, Browns Canyon, Salida–Cotapaxi, Cotapaxi–Parkdale, Royal Gorge

Location: Chaffee and Fremont counties adjacent to U.S. Highways 24 and 50, south-central Colorado

Distance: 12–19 miles (19–30 km) (the Numbers)
12–21 miles (19–34 km) (Browns Canyon)
11–23 miles (18–37 km) (Salida–Cotapaxi)
10–22 miles (16–35 km) (Cotapaxi–Parkdale)
9–19 miles (14–30 km) (Royal Gorge)

The Arkansas River's granite-walled Browns Canyon offers an exciting introduction to whitewater rafting.

Class:	III–IV + (the Numbers)
	II–III + (Browns Canyon)
	II–III (Salida–Cotapaxi–Parkdale)
	III–IV + , V in high water (Royal Gorge)
Trip Options:	Oar raft, paddle raft, inflatable kayak; half-day, one and two days
Season:	May–September
Outfitters:	Acquired Tastes
	Adrift Adventures
	Adventures in Rafting
	Adventures Unlimited
	American Adventure Expeditions
	Arkansas River Tours/OLTS
	Arkansas Valley Expeditions
	Bill Dvorak's Raft and Kayak Expeditions
	Blazing Paddles River Rafting
	Boulder Outdoor Center
	Browns Rafting
	Buffalo Joe River Trips
	Buggywhips Fish and Float Service
	Colorado Mountain Express
	Colorado Recreation Specialists
	Colorado Riff Raft
	Colorado River Runs
	Crested Butte Rafting
	Don Ferguson's Whitewater Rafting
	Eagle River Whitewater
	Echo Canyon River Expeditions
	Estes Park Adventures
	Far Flung Adventures
	Flexible Flyers
	Four Corners Expeditions
	GEO Tours
	Independent Whitewater
	Joni Ellis River Tours
	Keystone Resort
	KODI Whitewater Rafting
	Last Chance River Expeditions
	Lazy J Resort and Rafting Company
	Mad River Rafting
	Moondance River Expeditions
	New Wave Rafting
	Noah's Ark Whitewater Rafting
	Nova Guides
	Performance Tours

Families enjoy oar-guided raft trips on the Class I–III rapids of the Arkansas River.
Photo courtesy of Four Corners Expeditions/Colorado Whitewater Photography

Raftmeister
River Runners–Colorado
Roaring Fork River Company
Rocky Mountain Outdoor Center
Rocky Mountain River Expeditions
Rocky Mountain Tours
Royal Gorge River Adventures
Scenic River Tours
Sheri Griffith River Expeditions
Sierra Outfitters and Guides
Texas River Expeditions
The Adventure Company
Timber Rafting
Timberline Tours
Twin Lakes Expeditions
Whitewater Encounters
Whitewater Odyssey
Whitewater Voyageurs
Wilderness Aware
Wildwater

Rafters paddle under suspension footbridge in the Arkansas River's towering Royal Gorge.

The Numbers—One through Six—above Buena Vista, is the highest section of the Arkansas to be rafted by outfitters. Its continuous Class III–IV water—very popular with kayakers—is also considered some of the river's most technical and demanding rapids. Not all Arkansas outfitters run the Numbers, and it can only be rafted at certain water levels. Rafters must be in excellent physical condition and have had previous Class IV whitewater experience. Most outfitters require rafters to be at least eighteen years old.

The Arkansas River's most popular rafting trip is through the granite-walled Browns Canyon, a few miles south of Buena Vista. A relatively easy 12-mile (19 km) adventure has exciting, yet not intimidating, whitewater. Numerous large boulders and a gradient of almost 40 feet per mile create dozens of exciting and somewhat technical Class III + rapids such as Zoom Flume, Pinball, Big Drop, Staircase, Widowmaker, Siedell's Suckhole, and Twin Falls.

The Salida–Cotapaxi section of the Arkansas is a particular favorite of senior citizens and families with young children. Guided oar rafts allow these passengers to enjoy the impressive canyon scenery and beautiful views of the 14,000-foot Sangre de Cristo Mountains. Its exciting, but not difficult, Class II–III rapids—Bear and Badger creeks, Tin Cup, Red Rocks, and Cottonwood—should frighten no one. Outfitters offer two-hour, half-day, and all-day trips.

The Cotapaxi–Parkdale stretch of the Arkansas features a superb blend of canyon scenery and moderate whitewater. This section's Class III rapids—Maytag, Devils Hole, Wake Up, Three Rock Falls, and Spike Buck Falls—are not as difficult as those of the downstream Royal Gorge; they are nevertheless exciting and challenging for beginning and intermediate-level rafters. Cotapaxi–Parkdale, or Brown's Canyon, is a recommended prerequisite whitewater trip for the Class III–IV + Royal Gorge.

The Royal Gorge is the Arkansas River's most spectacular whitewater canyon trip. Nearly 1,000 feet below the world's highest suspension bridge, steep pool drops, large waves, and numerous demanding Class IV–IV + rapids—Sunshine Falls, Sledgehammer, the Narrows, Wall Slammer, Boateater, and Corner Pocket—create a truly extraordinary whitewater trip. The overall canyon river experience is made even more memorable by the historic river-level railroad, an inclined railway, and the remnants of the early century water flume. Most outfitters, who require previous whitewater experience for the Royal Gorge trip, are satisfied by beginning raft trips on the last few miles of the Cotapaxi–Parkdale section.

75. CLEAR CREEK, COLORADO

Section: Canyon
Location: Jefferson County, west of Golden, north-central Colo-
                   rado
Distance: 20 miles (32 km) or less
Class: IV–V + ; experience required
Trip Options: Paddle raft; one day
Season: May–July
Outfitter: Boulder Outdoor Center

Clear Creek, as it dashes and splashes down the Front Range into Golden and its confluence with the South Platte, is as exciting as any whitewater stretch in Colorado.

Clear Creek is a small river that requires paddle rafts. Fortunately, there are about 6 miles (9.5 km) of Class II–IV rapids before the serious whitewater begins. Three miles below the Colorado Route 119 junction with U.S. Highway 6, Class IV–V + rapids, including Double Knife, The Narrows, Black Rock, and Quiche, are part of a gradient that averages nearly 115 feet per mile. Many of the canyon's narrow chutes and steep drops are often barely wide enough to accommodate a raft.

Anyone who is considering rafting Clear Creek should scout the river's major rapids from the Highway 6 overlooks. Clear Creek rafters must have Class IV paddle rafting experience.

76. NORTH PLATTE RIVER, COLORADO–WYOMING

Section: Northgate Canyon
Location: Jackson County, northern Colorado; Carbon County,
                   southern Wyoming
Distance: 14–35 miles (22–56 km)
Class: III–IV; experience not required
Trip Options: Paddle raft, oar raft; one to three days
Season: May–mid-July
Outfitters: Adrift Adventures
                   Arkansas River Tours/OLTS
                   Bill Dvorak's Raft and Kayak Expeditions
                   Buggywhips Fish and Float Service
                   Highlands Rafting Company
                   The Old Baldy Club
                   Rocky Mountain River Expeditions
                   Whitewater Odyssey
                   Wilderness Aware
                   Wildwater

North Platte rafting is done in the high mountain valleys near the river's headwaters in north-central Colorado. About an hour's drive north of Steamboat Springs, the North Platte flows northwest through the scenic alpine wilderness of Northgate Canyon into southern Wyoming, creating a premier whitewater adventure.

Although Northgate Canyon is promoted as an intermediate-level raft trip, its narrow canyon, steep-gradient, and boulder-strewn channel creates exciting whitewater during spring. Several Class III–IV rapids, such as Windy Hole, the Narrows, and Stovepipe, can be very challenging to paddle rafters.

The North Platte's rafting season begins after the snowmelt, when outfitter vehicles can reach the 8,000-foot elevation put-in. The season normally lasts until mid-July. While outfitters run many two- and three-day raft trips through the canyon, a 14-mile (22 km), one-day trip is the most popular. As the mountain waters mellow in July, many outfitters offer leisurely fish-and-float trips through the Routt and Medicine Bow national forests in southern Wyoming.

77. CACHE LA POUDRE, COLORADO

Section:	Canyon
Location:	Larimer County, west of Fort Collins, north-central Colorado
Distance:	15 miles (24 km)
Class:	III–IV; experience not required
Trip Options:	Paddle raft, oar raft; one day
Season:	May–July
Outfitters:	Adrift Adventures
	Boulder Outdoor Center
	Estes Park Adventures
	National Outdoor Leadership School
	Wanderlust Adventures
	Wildwater

Colorado's Cache La Poudre, tumbling from the snowcapped peaks of Rocky Mountain National Park, is an exceptionally beautiful and exciting tributary of the North Platte. Long known for its scenic beauty, this historic Front Range river in Roosevelt National Forest became the state's first National Wild and Scenic River.

While the upper stretches of the Cache La Poudre are well known for their many fine kayak runs, whitewater trips begin less than 20 miles (32 km) west of Fort Collins. Adjacent to Colorado Route 14, almost continuous whitewater with numerous technical rapids, powerful hydraulics, and steep drops, such as the Class IV +

Mishawaka and Pineview Falls, leave little time to fully appreciate the river canyon's towering spires and sheer cliffs.

Depending upon the volume of winter snowpack, the Cache season can be short. Interested rafters should make early reservations with outfitters and call a few days prior to their trip to ensure water levels are ideal.

78. BLUE RIVER, COLORADO

Section:	Silverthorne to Columbine Landing or Green Mountain Reservoir
Location:	Summit County, northwest of Dillon, north-central Colorado
Distance:	8 miles (13 km)
Class:	II–III
Trip Options:	Paddle raft, oar raft; half-day, one day
Season:	May–July
Outfitters:	The Adventure Company
	Buggywhips Fish and Float Service
	Joni Ellis River Tours
	Keystone Resort
	KODI Whitewater Rafting
	Performance Tours

While much of the Blue River's flow, between its source near Breckenridge and its confluence with the upper Colorado River near Kremmling, has been quieted by the construction of Dillon Dam and Green Mountain Reservoir, rafting is possible from Silverthorne to the Green Mountain Reservoir during a few weeks each spring.

The most popular whitewater stretch is an 8-mile (13 km) run paralleling U.S. Highway 9 from Silverthorne to Columbine Landing about 8 miles (13 km) upriver from the Green Mountain Reservoir. This run features 6 miles (9.5 km) of rather easy Class I–II whitewater, which can be used as practice for new paddlers for the final 2 miles (3 km) of fairly continuous Class II–III waters.

Morning and afternoon trips on the Blue are convenient to those driving from Denver or the central-Colorado mountain resorts. Due to the short season and unpredictability of water flows, it is advisable to check with outfitters a day or two prior to scheduled trips.

79. EAGLE RIVER, COLORADO

Sections:	Upper, Lower, and Lower Wildlife
Location:	Eagle County, north-central Colorado, near Eagle
Distance:	15 miles (24 km) (upper)
	15 miles (24 km) (lower)
	10 miles (16 km) (lower wildlife)
Class:	III–IV + (upper)
	II–III + (lower)
	II (lower wildlife)
Trip Options:	Paddle raft, oar raft; half-day, one day
Season:	May–July
Outfitters:	The Adventure Company
	Adventures in Rafting
	Bill Dvorak's Raft and Kayak Expeditions
	Buggywhips Fish and Float Service
	Colorado Mountain Express
	Colorado Riff Raft
	Colorado River Runs
	Eagle River Whitewater
	High Times Rafting
	Keystone Resort
	Nova Guides
	Raftmeister
	Roaring Fork River Company
	Rock Gardens Rafting
	Timberline Tours
	Whitewater Rafting

The Eagle River, a free-flowing tributary of the upper Colorado, originates high in the central Rocky Mountain's Tennessee Pass, a few miles north of the historic mining town of Leadville. For most of its 60-mile (96 km) northwesterly journey to the Colorado at Dotsero, the Eagle parallels U.S. Highway 24. Its diverse course through narrow canyons, over steep drops, and through the popular Eagle Valley, features fine whitewater, peerless alpine scenery, and assorted high-elevation wildlife.

Two excellent whitewater rafting trips and a float trip are offered during the Eagle's short spring season. Beginning west of Minturn, the upper Eagle is a 15-mile (24 km) Class III–IV + whitewater ride for more adventurous rafters. The lower Eagle provides a more mellow, yet still exciting, 15-mile (24 km) Class II–III + family and first-time raft adventure; it ends just upriver from the town of Eagle.

Finally, at least two Eagle River outfitters promote early morning wildlife float trips when the bird and wildlife along the river are most active. The snow-covered Rocky Mountains provide an inspiring backdrop for this rare river adventure.

80. ROARING FORK RIVER, COLORADO

Sections:	Upper and lower
Location:	Pitkin, Eagle, and Garfield counties, northwest of Aspen, south-central Colorado
Distance:	12 miles (19 km) (upper)
	17 miles (27 km) or less (lower)
Class:	III–IV (upper)
	II–III (lower)
Trip Options:	Paddle raft, oar raft; half-day, one day
Season:	May–July
Outfitters:	Blazing Paddles River Rafting
	Buggywhips Fish and Float Service
	Colorado Recreation Specialist
	Colorado Riff Raft
	Roaring Fork River Company (lower)
	Rock Garden Rafting (lower)
	Rocky Mountain Tours
	Whitewater Rafting

The Roaring Fork gives late spring and early summer visitors to Aspen and Snowmass a convenient opportunity to experience challenging and exciting whitewater. The 60-mile (96 km) Roaring Fork, which starts near 12,000-foot Independence Pass, drops very quickly down the Rockies to the aspen-forested Roaring Fork valley. Almost 30 miles (48 km) of its length can be rafted between Aspen and its confluence with the Colorado River at Glenwood Springs.

Outfitters run trips on the upper and lower sections of the Roaring Fork. The more difficult upper fork trip, from Woody Creek, about 15 minutes northwest of Aspen, to the Frying Pan River, is a fast-flowing Class III–IV half-day run during normal spring runoff. Its numerous rocks and boulders create thrilling mazelike rapids and chutes, such as Toothache and Old Snowmass Hole. The milder lower fork, which includes Class III Cemetery Rapids, is a more relaxed trip. It is suitable to families and first-time rafters. Some outfitters may combine a portion of this trip with the Colorado at Glenwood Springs.

81. COLORADO RIVER (Upper), COLORADO

Section:	Gore Canyon to Dotsero
Location:	Grand and Eagle counties, between Kremmling and Dotsero, north-central Colorado
Distance:	14 miles (22 km) (Lower Gore Canyon to State Bridge)
	44 miles (70 km) (State Bridge to Dotsero)
Class:	II–III +
Trip Options:	Paddle raft, oar raft; half-day, one to three days
Season:	May–September
Outfitters:	Acquired Tastes
	Adrift Adventures
	The Adventure Company
	Adventures in Rafting
	American Adventure Expeditions
	Anderson Camps
	Arkansas River Tours/OLTS
	Colorado Adventures
	Colorado Mountain Express
	Colorado River Runs
	Eagle River Whitewater
	Estes Park Adventures
	GEO Tours
	High Times Rafting
	Joni Ellis River Tours
	Keystone Resort
	KODI Whitewater Rafting
	Lone Wolf Expeditions
	Mad River Rafting
	Nova Guides
	Performance Tours
	Raftmeister
	Rapid Transit Rafting
	Roaring Fork River Company
	Rocky Mountain River Expeditions
	Timberline Tours
	Timber Rafting
	Whitewater Odyssey
	Wilderness Aware

The upper stretches of the legendary Colorado River, west of its Rocky Mountain National Park source, feature some of the Colorado's finest and most popular beginning-level whitewater trips for families, first-time rafters, and large groups. In the beautiful high forests and steep canyons of the Gore Range just two and one-half hours from Denver, the upper Colorado is rafted and floated for nearly 58 miles (92 km) between Kremmling and Interstate 70 near Dotsero.

Upper Colorado outfitters offer a wide variety of relatively easy raft trips ranging in length from a half-day to three days. The most popular one-day trip is a 14-mile (22 km) Class I–II + run from the Pumphouse in Little Gore Canyon past Radium to State Bridge. Two-day trips with overnight camping continue downstream for an additional 14 miles (22 km) through scenic valleys and ranch lands. Any of the multiday trips have ample time for relaxing, swimming, hiking, and fishing.

A freight train and Colorado's Interstate 70 provide an interesting backdrop to the scenic Glenwood Canyon raft trip.

82. COLORADO RIVER (Glenwood), COLORADO

Sections: Glenwood Canyon and Shoshone Run
Location: Garfield County, near Glenwood Springs, north-central Colorado
Distance: 17 miles (27 km) or less
Class: I–II + (Glenwood Canyon)
              III–IV + (Shoshone Run)
Trip Options: Paddle raft, oar raft; half-day, one day (Glenwood Canyon); two hours (Shoshone Run)
Season: June–September
Outfitters: Adventures in Rafting
              Blazing Paddles River Rafting
              Blue Sky Adventures
              Colorado Recreation Specialist
              Colorado Riff Raft
              High Times Rafting
              Raftmeister
              Rock Gardens Rafting
              Timberline Tours
              Whitewater Rafting

The most frequently rafted section of the Colorado River is a 15- to 20-mile (24–32 km) stretch paralleled by Interstate 70 near Glenwood Springs in north-central Colorado. During normal, summer water levels, almost anyone older than six may enjoy fairly easy half- and one-day trips through the spectacular 5-mile (8 km) Class II + Glenwood Canyon above Glenwood Springs. Also available to rafters is all, or portions, of the even milder 10-mile (16 km) river trip from Glenwood Springs to New Castle.

While rafting the middle Colorado is very popular with summer visitors to Glenwood Springs, neither reservations nor rafting experience are necessary. Several of the outfitters have sales offices in the vicinity of the town's motels and the popular hot springs.

Above Glenwood Canyon's Grizzly Creek put-in, the Shoshone section of the Colorado provides more energetic rafters an extra two miles of action-packed whitewater. Six challenging Class III–IV rapids, including the Superstitions, The Wall, Tombstone, and Maneater, provide a dynamic preface to the easier rapids of the Glenwood Canyon trip.

83. COLORADO RIVER (Horsethief–Ruby), COLORADO

Section: Loma, Colorado to Westwater Canyon, Utah
Location: Mesa County, west of Grand Junction, western Colorado
Distance: 26 miles (42 km)
Class: I–II
Trip Options: Paddle raft, oar raft; two or three days
Season: April–September
Outfitters: Deer Hill Summer Expeditions
              Humpback Chub River Trips
              Scenic River Tours

The middle Colorado's Horsethief-and-Ruby canyons float trip is ideal for anyone wishing to enjoy a spectacular river canyon, a desert environment, and very mild waters. Near Loma, the middle Colorado turns south from Interstate 70 to flow through the two canyons that can only be enjoyed from the river.

On the multiday float trip, there is ample time to admire the river's spectacular sandstone canyon walls, explore its side canyons, or relax on its sandy beaches. The float trip is quite popular with families and the disabled.

Take-out for the Horsethief–Ruby canyons trip is at the Westwater Ranger Station in Utah. There are some Horsethief–Ruby–Westwater trips for those wishing to conclude their multiday canyon experience with more substantial and challenging whitewater.

84. TAYLOR RIVER, COLORADO

Section: Taylor Park Reservoir to Almont
Location: Gunnison County, northeast of Gunnison, south-central Colorado
Distance: 17 miles (27 km) or less
Class: III–IV
Trip Options: Paddle raft, oar raft; half-day, one day
Season: May–September
Outfitters: Crested Butte Rafting
              Scenic River Tours
              Three River Outfitting

The Taylor River, which meets the East River at Almont to create the upper Gunnison River, has carved one of Colorado's most impressive alpine canyons. Large herds of elk and bighorn sheep that winter in the Almont Triangle Game Refuge are often seen from the river during late spring and early summer.

Water releases from Taylor Park Reservoir generally permit sufficient water for rafting throughout the summer. The Class III–IV rapids of Taylor's forested upper section—The Slot, Sneaky Pete's, Generator Alley, The Squeeze, and Suckhole—start below Lottis, some 4 miles (6.5 km) below the dam. The narrow channel and regulated flow create an excellent whitewater run.

Downstream, the easier Class I–II lower Taylor, between Harmels and Almont, is an ideal river adventure for families and first-time rafters. Outfitters offering half-day trips on the lower Taylor will accommodate rafters of any age.

85. SLATE RIVER, COLORADO

Section:	Upper
Location:	Gunnison County, near Crested Butte, south-central Colorado
Distance:	3 miles (5 km)
Class:	V–V + ; experience required
Trip Options:	Paddle raft; half-day
Season:	May–June
Outfitter:	Crested Butte Rafting

The Slate River in south-central Colorado offers one of the state's newest and maybe liveliest whitewater runs. Just northwest of the Crested Butte ski community, the narrow Slate cascades dramatically down the mountainside. Slate's Class V–V + rapids—Tonar Falls, Juicy Lucy, Dead Man's Curve, and Wicked Wanda—are appropriately named.

First commercially rafted in 1988, the Slate is not a trip for beginners. Its 9,500-foot elevation should indicate the water's coldness. The more than two hours required to navigate the 3-mile (5 km) run results from the need to scout all major rapids. Without self-bailing rafts, this extraordinary run would be impossible.

86. GUNNISON RIVER, COLORADO

Section:	Almont to Gunnison or Blue Mesa Reservoir
Location:	Gunnison County, north of Gunnison, south-central Colorado

Distance:	25 miles (40 km) or less
Class:	I–II
Trip Options:	Paddle raft, oar raft; one and two days
Season:	May–September
Outfitters:	American Adventure Expeditions
	Crested Butte Rafting
	Scenic River Tours
	Three River Outfitting

The upper Gunnison River, created by the Taylor and East rivers, offers a number of very easy rafting trips between Almont and Blue Mesa Reservoir, downriver from Gunnison. Access points to the river from Colorado Route 135 and U.S. Highway 50 are numerous. Predominately Class I, there are a few Class II man-made drops in the 25-mile (40 km) river stretch.

Although outfitters promote the upper Gunnison as an easy trip for senior citizens or families with young children, anyone can enjoy the pastoral beauty of the Gunnison valley.

87. GUNNISON RIVER (Lake Fork), COLORADO

Section:	Upper and lower canyons
Location:	Hinsdale and Gunnison counties, north of Lake City, southwest Colorado
Distance:	10–24 miles (16–38 km)
Class:	III–IV + ; experience recommended on lower canyon
Trip Options:	Paddle raft, oar raft; half-day, one day
Season:	May–June
Outfitters:	Crested Butte Rafting
	Echo Canyon River Expeditions
	Peregrine River Outfitters
	Scenic River Tours
	Three River Outfitting

The Lake Fork of the Gunnison River, which flows north out of the San Juan Mountains, features two distinctly different whitewater rafting trips. Through its upper canyons, which begin a few miles south of Lake City, outfitters offer an easy Class I–II float trip suitable for families with young children and rafters who are interested in enjoying the geology of the box canyon.

The last half of the Lake Fork's final 10-miles (16 km) drop at a rate of more than 50 feet a mile and create superb Class III–IV + technical whitewater. As the Lake Fork makes it descent to Blue Mesa

Reservoir, one exciting rapid after another challenges whitewater enthusiasts. Outfitters recommend rafters have previous experience and that they be at least sixteen years old.

88. GUNNISON RIVER (Gorge), COLORADO

Section:	Gorge
Location:	Montrose and Delta counties, northwest of Black Canyon in the Gunnison National Monument, southwest Colorado
Distance:	14 miles (22 km)
Class:	II–III +
Trip Options:	Paddle raft, oar raft; one to three days
Season:	May–September
Outfitters:	Arkansas River Tours/OLTS
	Bill Dvorak's Raft and Kayak Expeditions
	Echo Canyon River Expeditions
	Far-Flung Adventures
	Gunnison River Expeditions
	Peregrine River Outfitters
	Telluride Whitewater
	Wilderness Aware

Southwest Colorado's Gunnison Gorge, immediately below the Black Canyon in the Gunnison National Monument, is one of the state's finest wilderness river trips. The mood for the remote river adventure is set before the trip begins. Access to the gorge put-in is a 1-mile (1.5 km) hike from the Chucker Trailhead down a side canyon. (Outfitters rent pack horses to carry the rafting equipment to the river.)

The outstanding characteristics of the gorge are its magnificent scenery, abundant wildlife, and fine whitewater. The canyon's sheer basalt and granite walls, although not as high as those of Black Canyon, are impressive. Peregrine falcons, bald eagles, bighorn sheep, ringtail cats, marmots, and river otters are just a few of the many wildlife species that inhabit Gunnison Gorge. The first 11 miles (18 km) of the 14-mile (22 km) gorge are interspersed with a number of fine Class III rapids, including Cable, The Squeeze, The Drops, and The Hall of the River King.

While the Gunnison Gorge can easily be rafted in a day, its pristine scenery, interesting side-canyon hiking, and excellent Gold Medal Trout fishing are good reasons to make it a two- or three-day trip.

89. PIEDRA RIVER, COLORADO

Sections:	Upper and lower box canyons
Location:	Hinsdale and Archuleta counties between Pagosa Springs and Durango, southwest Colorado
Distance:	22 miles (35 km)
Class:	III–V; Class IV experience highly recommended
Trip Options:	Paddle raft, oar raft; one and two days
Season:	May–July
Outfitters:	American Adventure Expeditions
	Echo Canyon River Expeditions
	Mountain Waters Rafting
	Pagosa Rafting Outfitters
	Peregrine River Outfitters

The Piedra River, in southwest Colorado's San Juan Mountains, is one of the state's finest alpine rivers. Historically referred to as the "River of the Rock Wall," the Piedra is a very demanding river adventure. It should be considered by only experienced, physically fit rafters.

The Piedra's very narrow and steep upper and lower box canyons create several very technical Class IV–V drops. Outfitters normally either run the 22–mile (35 km) raft trip in two days or a 14-mile (22 km) trip in one day. Its alpine mountain waters are always cold, and helmets and wet suits are required. Most trips include shuttles between the river and either Durango or Pagosa Springs.

Many wild animals, including elk, mule deer, black bears, river otters, and the endangered peregrine falcon, are frequently seen along the river's forested banks.

90. ANIMAS RIVER, COLORADO

The Animas River, high in the snowcapped San Juan Mountains of southwest Colorado between Silverton and Durango, provides a challenging alpine whitewater trip for advanced paddlers and a relatively easy stretch for families and first-time rafters.

Section:	Upper
Location:	San Juan County between Silverton and Durango, southwest Colorado
Distance:	26 miles (42 km)
Class:	IV–V, III–IV at low-water; experience required
Trip Options:	Paddle raft, two and three days
Season:	May–July

Outfitters: Le Grand Adventures
                Mountain Waters Rafting
                Pagosa Rafting Outfitters
                Peregrine River Outfitters
                Rivers West
                Telluride Whitewater

The upper Animas River provides an exceptional alpine raft experience that includes outstanding whitewater and mountain scenery adjacent to coal-powered narrow-gauge steam railway. While some persons describe it as one of the country's best whitewater runs, boating experts call it one of its more difficult.

    The river trip begins near Mineral Creek just outside the historic mining town of Silverton (elevation 9,230 feet) and parallels the Durango and Silverton Narrow Gauge Railroad south for 26 miles (42 km). During this exciting canyon course, the Animas drops an average of 85 feet per mile through dozens of Class III–IV and several Class V rapids. The intensity of the whitewater, however, does not give the paddler much time to fully appreciate all of the remnant foot bridges, abandoned cabins, and spectacular views of the 13,000-foot plus mountain peaks.

Raft trips on the lower Animas River in southwest Colorado begin in historic downtown Durango.

To provide access to the river's take-out downstream from Rockwood, outfitters have made arrangements with the Durango and Silverton Railroad to shuttle rafters and equipment to Durango on the afternoon train. Some outfitters also promote a three-day trip that includes a horseback trip through Cascade Canyon in the Weminuche Wilderness Area.

Normally, due to the high altitude, rafting on the upper Animas does not begin until late May or early June. All outfitters require rafters to have paddled Class IV technical whitewater. Wet suits and helmets are always mandatory, and rafters must be at least sixteen years old.

Section:	Lower
Location:	Durango, LaPlata County, southwest Colorado
Distance:	5–12 miles (8–19 km)
Class:	I–II, III
Trip Options:	Paddle raft, oar raft, half-day, one day
Season:	May–August
Outfitters:	American Adventure Expeditions
	Big Tujunga/Wild Goose River Tours
	Colorado Rivers-Tours
	Durango Rivertrippers
	Flexible Flyers
	Mountain Waters Rafting
	Peregrine River Outfitters
	Rivers West

The lower Animas River offers persons an easy introduction to whitewater rafting. Animas River trips begin in downtown Durango, just a few blocks from the Durango to Silverton railroad station.

Class III Smelter Rapids, the largest rapid on the Lower Animas, comes after a relaxing 2 miles (3 km) of Class I–II whitewater on the south side of Durango. As the raft trip proceeds south toward the Southern Ute Indian Reservation, old mine ruins, panoramic views of the southern Rockies, and occasional glimpses of wildlife add a memorable dimension to the family vacation.

Between Memorial Day and Labor Day outfitters generally operate one-day, half-day, and even two-hour excursions on the Animas. Outfitter brochures recommend advance reservations, but same-day reservations are almost always possible. (Many outfitters have kiosks in Durango.) During summer's low-water levels, families with young children are welcome.

91. DOLORES RIVER, COLORADO

Section: Desert canyons
Location: Montezuma, Dolores, San Miguel, Montrose, and Mesa counties in southwest Colorado; Grand County, eastern Utah
Distance: 185 miles (296 km) or less
Class: II–IV
Trip Options: Paddle raft, oar raft, inflatable kayak; three to six days
Season: April–June
Outfitters: Adrift Adventures
                 Arkansas River Tours/OLTS
                 Artemis Wilderness Tours
                 Bighorn Expeditions
                 Bill Dvorak's Raft and Kayak Expeditions
                 Blazing Paddles River Rafting
                 Boulder Outdoor Center
                 Buffalo Joe River Trips
                 Colorado Rivers-Tours
                 Deer Hill Summer Expeditions
                 Descent River Expeditions
                 Durango Rivertrippers
                 Echo Canyon River Expeditions
                 Four Corners Expeditions
                 Humpback Chub River Tours
                 Le Grande Adventures
                 Noah's Ark Whitewater Rafting
                 National Outdoor Leadership School
                 O.A.R.S.
                 Peregrine River Outfitters
                 Red Rock River Company
                 Roaring Fork River Company
                 Rocky Mountain River Expeditions
                 Sheri Griffith River Expeditions
                 Southwest Wilderness Center
                 Telluride Whitewater
                 Whitewater Odyssey
                 Wilderness Aware
                 Worldwide Explorations

In Colorado's southwest corner, the Dolores River flows in a southwest direction from the San Juan Mountains before meandering north through several impressive high-desert slickrock canyons before it meets the Colorado River near Moab, Utah. The 185-mile (296 km) Dolores trip is third only in length to the Colorado River's Grand Canyon and Texas Rio Grande River trips in the Lower 48 states. Each spring, outfitters run a variety of multiday oar- and paddle-raft trips through one or more of the four scenic desert-canyon sections.

Ponderosa Gorge and Dolores Canyon, the first two lower or desert canyons, start in a semialpine transition zone between the San Juan Mountains and the Colorado Plateau, below McPhee Dam. This 47-mile (75 km) section between Cahone and Slick Rock, Colorado, has numerous Class III–IV rapids, including the legendary Snaggletooth, which are difficult and require close attention.

Most outfitters agree that the 58-mile (93 km) slickrock canyon between Slick Rock and Bedrock is the most spectacular of all the river's canyons. Its easy Class II–III waters are overwhelmed by towering slickrock walls. Many grottos and side canyons are garnished with magnificent prehistoric Indian pictographs.

Between Bedrock and Gateway, Colorado, several Class II–III rapids provide ample time to relax and enjoy the diverse 45-mile (72 km) Paradox and Mesa canyons. After the river meets the San Miguel, the Dolores nearly doubles in size. At the rivers' confluences the remnants of a decades-old hanging flume, which was used to transport water to the Lone Tree placer mine, can be seen nearly 400 feet above the river.

Lower Gateway Canyon, the 30-mile (48 km) section of the Dolores before it meets the Colorado River in Utah, has both good whitewater and inspiring desert scenery. Stateline Rapid, a long and technical Class IV rapid, is the highlight stretch after many Class II–III rapids. Many Indian petroglyphs and pictographs adorn the canyon's walls.

92. SAN MIGUEL RIVER, COLORADO

Section: Placerville to Naturita Power Plant
Location: San Miguel and Montrose counties, northwest of Telluride, southwest Colorado
Distance: 6–35 miles (10–56 km)
Class: II–III
Trip Options: Paddle raft, oar raft; half-day, one day
Season: May–July
Outfitters: Echo Canyon River Expeditions
                 Telluride Whitewater

The Sam Miguel River, a major tributary of the Dolores, starts high in the San Juan Mountains near the popular resort town of Telluride and flows west, without any major falls or rapids, to the Dolores some 70 miles (112 km) downstream. The constant dropping, creates fairly continuous Class II–III whitewater action.

Most half- and one-day rafting trips begin near Norwood, some 30 miles (48 km) below Telluride. Each morning and afternoon from May to as long as the water lasts into summer, outfitters run an easy 6-mile (10 km) Class II–III trip that is suitable for families and first-time rafters. A 17-mile (27 km) trip through the wilderness of Norwood Canyon and a two-day 35-mile (56 km) trip are also available for those who wish longer and more difficult rafting adventures.

93. YAMPA RIVER, COLORADO

Section:	Canyon
Location:	Moffat County, within Dinosaur National Monument, northwest Colorado
Distance:	46 miles (74 km)
Class:	III–IV
Trip Options:	Paddle raft, oar raft; three to five days
Season:	May–June
Outfitters:	Adrift Adventures
	Adventure Bound
	American River Touring Association
	Anderson Camps
	Colorado Outward Bound School
	Don Hatch River Expeditions
	Don Neff River Company
	Holiday River Expeditions
	Le Grand Adventures
	Peak River Expeditions
	World Wide River Expeditions

The Yampa River rafting trip in Dinosaur National Monument is one of only two multiday trips that begin and end within a national park or monument. For 46 miles (74 km), from its put-in at Deerlodge Park to its confluence with the Green River near Echo Park, the free-flowing Yampa River carves its way through spectacular 2,000-foot-deep white Weber canyons.

Because of the premier beauty of the Dinosaur canyons, outfitters generally continue Yampa raft trips for 26 miles (42 km) onto the Green River and float an additional one to three days through Whirlpool Canyon and Split Mountain Gorge in the Utah portion of the national monument.

Guides and guests stop to scout Yampa River's Warm Springs Rapids in
Dinosaur National Monument.
Photo by Verne Huser

The Yampa is Colorado's last undamed major river. Its whitewater is best during May and June when its channel is swollen with the spring runoff from its upstream tributaries. During this time many Class III–IV rapids, such as Teepee, Big Joe, and the much-heralded Grand Canyon-size Warm Springs, are at their prime. In all, more than sixty notable rapids will challenge and delight Yampa rafters.

Rafters on the Yampa should allow an extra day to visit Dinosaur Quarry at the monument's southwest entrance.

94. GREEN RIVER (Dinosaur National Monument), COLORADO/UTAH

Sections:	Lodore Canyon, Whirlpool Canyon, and Split Mountain Gorge
Location:	Moffat County, northwest Colorado; and Uintah County near Vernal, northeast Utah
Distance:	45 miles (72 km)
Class:	II–III + (Lodore) II (Whirlpool) II–III (Split Mountain Gorge)
Trip Options:	Paddle raft, oar raft, inflatable kayak; three to five days, (one day at Split Mountain Gorge)
Season:	May–September
Outfitters:	Adrift Adventures Adventure Bound Colorado Outward Bound School Don Hatch River Expeditions Don Neff River Company Holiday River Expeditions Le Grand Adventures Peak River Expeditions S'Plore (Lodore Canyon) World Wide River Expeditions

Dinosaur National Monument's Green River provides 45 miles (72 km) of rafting through three magnificent canyons: Lodore, Whirlpool, and Split Mountain. Three- to five-day trips through the canyons afford rafters of almost any age the opportunity to enjoy the river's magnificent canyon scenery, its wildlife, and relatively easy whitewater.

Green River rafting begins at the Lodore Ranger Station at the monument's north boundary. Shortly after put-in, the brilliant precambrian red sandstone walls of Lodore Canyon, called the Gates of Lodore, rise to nearly 2,500 feet as the river dramatically cuts through the Uintah Mountains. Most of Lodore's exciting Class II–III + rapids—Disaster Falls, Triplet Falls, and Hells Half Mile—were named by John Wesley Powell and his brave explorers in 1869. Hikes into Lodore's interesting side canyons—Winnie Grotto, Rippling Brook, and Pot Creek—permit a close-up examination of Freemont Indian pictographs.

Immediately downriver from Lodore is Whirlpool Canyon, where the Green crosses from Colorado into Utah. Following Whirlpool is Split Mountain Gorge. In recent years the gorge has become a very popular one-day rafting adventure. The 9.5-mile (14.5 km) passage through the gorge near Vernal, Utah, gives families, first-timers, and experienced rafters an excellent occasion to enjoy relatively easy whitewater in one of the Southwest's most impressive canyons.

Water releases from Flaming Gorge Dam normally make it possible for outfitters to run trips through Dinosaur's canyons until late September. At most water levels outfitters allow teen-age and adult rafters to choose between oar and paddle rafts, or inflatable kayaks. Swimming in a few of the Green's rapids is also permitted.

Oar-guided raft provides a passage through the scenic Dinosaur National Monument's Split Mountain Gorge.

95. GREEN RIVER (Desolation), UTAH

Section:	Desolation and Gray canyons
Location:	Uintah and Grand counties, eastern Utah
Distance:	94 miles (150 km)
Class:	II–III
Trip Options:	Paddle raft, oar raft, motorized raft, inflatable kayak; three to six days
Season:	April–October
Outfitters:	Adventure Bound
	Adventure River Expeditions
	American River Touring Association
	Anderson Camps
	Bighorn Expeditions
	Bill Dvorak's Raft and Kayak Expeditions
	Colorado Outward Bound School
	Colorado River and Trail Expeditions
	Holiday River Expeditions
	Hondoo River and Trails
	Land Escape Expeditions
	Moki Mac River Expeditions
	National Outdoor Leadership School
	Peregrine Outfitters
	Rocky Mountain River Expeditions
	Sheri Griffith River Expeditions
	Tag-A-Long Expeditions
	Western River Expeditions
	Wild Rivers Expeditions
	World Wide River Expeditions

In east-central Utah, less than 100 miles (160 km) downriver from Dinosaur National Monument, the Green River traverses two remote and beautiful wildernesses: Desolation and Gray canyons. These canyons, rich in ancient Indian art and abandoned homesteads, are vividly described in the journals of John Wesley Powell. Desolation Canyon is the only western river canyon to be listed as a Registered National Historical Landmark.

The Green is one of the Southwest's best rivers on which to learn basic boating skills in rafts or inflatable kayaks. None of its more than sixty Class II–III rapids are technically difficult. The river's rapids gradually increase in difficulty from rolling waves to rapids, such as Three Fords, Steer Ridge, and Coal Creek.

The relaxed pace of the Green River itinerary, and its enchanting environment, has prompted a number of special excursions, which include professional instructional seminars, gourmet meals, and music concerts. Its relatively easy waters and sandy beaches have also made the Green a popular river stretch for disabled rafters.

Several outfitters begin the Green River trip with a plane flight from the town of Green River, Utah, or Grand Junction, Colorado, to the put-in at Sand Wash, Utah. The flight gives rafters a spectacular view of Desolation's and Gray's majestic canyons, which are deeper than those in the Grand Canyon.

96. COLORADO RIVER (Professor Valley), UTAH

Section:	Professor Valley
Location:	Grand County, north of Moab, eastern Utah
Distance:	30 miles (48 km) or less
Class:	I–II
Trip Options:	Paddle raft, oar raft, inflatable kayak; half-day, one and two days
Season:	May–October
Outfitters:	Adrift Adventures
	Adventure River Expeditions
	Red Rock River Company
	Sheri Griffith River Expeditions
	S'Plore
	Tag-A-Long Expeditions
	Tex's River Expeditions
	Western River Expeditions

One of the middle Colorado's more scenic stretches is also one of its easiest. Called the Professor Valley, or Fisher Towers section, its mild waters and proximity to Moab and Canyonlands and Arches national parks make it a favorite half-, one- or two-day raft trip for children's groups, families, senior citizens, and rafters who have special needs.

The beautiful Colorado flows gently through 30 miles (48 km) of red slickrock canyons, including the delicate spires and chimneys of Fisher Towers and the red buttes of Professor and Castle valleys, alongside the breathtaking Arches National Park. Rafters often see many eagles, red-tailed hawks, deer, coyotes, and desert fox.

97. COLORADO RIVER (Westwater), UTAH

Section:	Westwater Canyon
Location:	Grand County, northeast of Moab, eastern Utah
Distance:	17–40 miles (27–64 km)
Class:	III–IV +
Trip Options:	Paddle raft, oar raft, motorized raft; one or two days

Season: May–September
Outfitters: Adventure Bound
      Adventure River Expeditions
      Anderson Camps
      Bill Dvorak Raft and Kayak Expeditions
      Colorado River and Trail Expeditions
      Descent River Expeditions
      Holiday River Expeditions
      Humpback Chub River Tours
      Land Escape River Expeditions

The Colorado River's Westwater trip features Class IV + whitewater in one of the Southwest's most impressive river canyons.

Moki Mac River Expeditions
Rocky Mountain River Expeditions
Sheri Griffith River Expeditions
Tag-A-Long Expeditions
Western River Expeditions
World Wide River Expeditions

Utah vacationers who want to experience a big-water raft trip in a beautiful southwest canyon will find there is none better than the middle Colorado's Westwater. The diversity of Westwater's breathtaking sandstone and granite canyon walls and the challenge of its exciting whitewater make it one of the Southwest's classic short river trips.

At times the Colorado seems to roar within Westwater's spectacular canyon walls. Eleven Class III–IV+ (Class V in high-water) rapids, including Funnel Falls, The Steps, Last Chance, and Skull in the narrow Black Granite Gorge, will excite novice and experienced rafters.

Two-day trips are the most common Westwater excursion. However, the Bureau of Land Management does issue permits for a 17-mile (27 km) one-day trip to a limited number of outfitters. Westwater Canyon is between Grand Junction, Colorado, and Moab, Utah.

Guests enjoy whitewater opera alongside the Colorado River in Canyonlands National Park.
Photo courtesy of Tag-A-Long Expeditions

98. COLORADO RIVER (Cataract), UTAH

Section:	Cataract Canyon
Location:	Garfield, Wayne, and San Juan counties, Canyonlands National Park, southeast Utah
Distance:	96 miles (154 km) or less
Trip Options:	Paddle raft, oar raft, motorized raft; three to six days
Class:	III–V
Season:	April–October
Outfitters:	Adrift Adventures in Canyonlands
	Adventure Bound
	Adventure River Expeditions
	Colorado Outward Bound School
	Colorado River and Trail Expeditions
	Descent River Expeditions
	Don Hatch River Expeditions
	Holiday River Expeditions
	Moki Mac River Expeditions
	North American River Expeditions
	Sheri Griffith River Expeditions
	Tag-A-Long Expeditions
	Tour West Whitewater Adventures
	Western River Expeditions
	World Wide River Expeditions

The Colorado River's Cataract Canyon is in spectacular Canyonlands National Park. It offers a combination of relaxed floating and awesome whitewater that has changed little since the canyon was first navigated and explored by John Wesley Powell in 1869.

While it is possible to reach Cataract through the scenic sandstone chasms of Labyrinth and Stillwater canyons on the Green River, most outfitters put in for the Cataract trip on the middle Colorado, a few miles downstream from Moab. Either route necessitates two or three days of quiet and relaxed floating to reach Cataract's whitewater action.

Cataract's whitewater begins 4 miles (6.5 km) downstream from the confluence of the Green and Colorado rivers, deep within Canyonlands National Park. Hereafter, 26 major rapids, including Brown Betty, Mile Long, Little Niagara, and Satan's Gut, will excite rafters before they reach the quiet waters of Lake Powell above Glen Canyon Dam. In the spring, some of Cataract's rapids are larger than those of the Grand Canyon.

The first two or three days of the Cataract trip provides ample leisure time to enjoy the many cliff dwellings and petroglyphs of the ancient Anasazi Indian culture. There also are opportunities to hike, swim, fish, photograph, stare at the impressive canyon walls, or just do nothing.

Although Canyonlands may not look hospitable to wildlife, desert bighorn sheep, mule deer, golden eagles, great horned owls, hawks, ravens, desert fox, coyotes, bobcats, whiptail lizards, and kangaroo rats flourish in the arid habitat.

99. SAN JUAN RIVER, UTAH

Section: Bluff to Lake Powell
Location: San Juan County near Bluff and Mexican Hat, southeast Utah
Distance: 84 miles (134 km) or less
Class: I–III
Trip Options: Paddle raft, oar raft, inflatable kayak; one, two, three, four and six days
Season: April–September
Outfitters: Adventure Discovery Tours
    Colorado Outward Bound School
    Holiday River Expeditions
    Lake Powell Tours
    O.A.R.S.
    Ross River Ed-Ventures
    Tag-A-Long Expeditions
    Wild and Scenic Expeditions
    Wild Rivers Expeditions
    Worldwide Explorations

The San Juan River, a major tributary of the Colorado, has some of the Southwest's most unusual and beautiful geological formations and some of its best Indian rock art and ruins. Its entire channel from Bluff to Lake Powell parallels the northern boundary of the huge Navajo Indian Reservation.

The first day or two of the four-to-six day San Juan trip are spent leisurely floating through the inspiring monoclines, anticlines, and synclines of the river's upper section between Bluff and Mexican Hat. After Mexican Hat, the lower San Juan passes through the incredible Goosenecks, a deep and narrow canyon with towering walls of limestone, shale, and colorful sandstone.

Many veteran river runners claim that mile-for-mile the San Juan has more geological diversity, more Indian rock art, more ancient ruins, and more fossil outcrops than any other river in the West. The river's banks and side canyons have long been a popular gathering place for anthropologists, archaeologists, geologists, photographers, and canyon lovers.

The San Juan's whitewater is fun, but not difficult. While oar and paddle rafts have long been the standard conveyance, many outfitters now encourage customers to independently navigate the river with inflatable kayaks and sportyaks.

San Juan rafting usually runs from April until September or October. In addition to the multiday Bluff to Lake Powell trip, outfitters also offer one- and two-day upper canyon trips from Bluff to Mexican Hat, and three- to four-day trips from Mexican Hat to Lake Powell.

100. COLORADO RIVER (Grand Canyon), ARIZONA

Section:	Lee's Ferry to Diamond Creek or Lake Mead
Location:	Marble Canyon National Monument and Grand Canyon National Park, northern Arizona
Distance:	87 to 225 miles (139–360 km)
Class:	II–V, I–X on International Rating Scale
Trip Options:	Paddle raft, oar raft, motorized raft, dory; four to eighteen days
Season:	April–October
Outfitters:	Adventures West
	Arizona Raft Adventures
	Arizona River Runners

Grand Canyon's Crystal is one of the largest and most memorable of all western rapids.

Canyoneers
Canyon Explorations
Colorado River and Trail Expeditions
Diamond River Adventures
Expeditions
Georgie's Royal River Rats
Grand Canyon Dories
Grand Canyon Expeditions
Hatch River Expeditions
Hualapai River Runners (below Diamond Creek)
Moki Mac River Expeditions
O.A.R.S.
Outdoors Unlimited River Trips
Sleight Expeditions
Sobek White Water Expeditions
Tour West Whitewater Adventures
Western River Expeditions
Wilderness River Adventures

Little has changed in the almost century and a quarter since John Wesley Powell and his brave and adventurous companions first floated the incredible Grand Canyon. Its sandstone and basalt canyon walls render their same gorgeous red, yellow, black, and brown hues; its turbulent waters, while less silt-laden because of the hydro-electric dams, are just as thrilling and exciting.

Between the placid waters of lakes Powell and Mead, the Grand Canyon has more than 200 exciting and wild Class II, III, IV, and V rapids. Its powerful and technical Lava Falls and Crystal rapids, rated two of the finest whitewater drops anywhere, capture the imagination of rafters and guides long before and after every river trip.

A Grand Canyon rafting trip includes much more than plunging through its rapids. On most trips only about four to five hours a day are spent on the river. Equal or greater time is available for exploring the beauty and fascination of its colorful side canyons. Stops of varying length normally include the famous Vasey's Paradise, Redwall Cavern, Unkar Indian Ruins, the Little Colorado, Shinumo Creek, Elves Chasm, Deer Creek Falls, Havasu Creek, and Fern Glen Grotto. While rafting and hiking there is time for quite meditation and for contemplating the magnificent canyon's rock formations, flora, and fauna.

Perhaps the most important decisions regarding a Grand Canyon adventure occur months before the rafting trip begins. Rafters must choose between oar and motorized rafts and between trips ranging

Passengers on motorized raft enjoy the big waters of the Colorado River's Crystal Rapids.
Photo courtesy of Canyoneers/Gaylord L. Stavely

from as few as four to as many as eighteen days. The classic Grand Canyon rafting trip is the seven to thirteen-day 225 mile (360 km) trip from Lee's Ferry, near Page, Arizona, to Diamond Creek, below the Havasu Indian Reservation. Shorter trips may be run on either the upper or lower canyon sections. The 87-mile (139 km) upper trip from Lee's Ferry to the Phantom Ranch requires a strenuous 9-mile (14 km) hike to the Canyon's south rim, while the 138-mile (221 km) trip from Phantom Ranch to Diamond Creek requires the same long but, fortunately, downhill trek.

Time for a refreshing pause under Deer Creek Falls in the Grand Canyon.

Multiday raft trips provide time to explore the geologic formations of many side canyons.

Commercial rafting trips through the Grand Canyon are normally run from early April until late October. Camping is required on all trips. The spring and fall months have comfortable daytime temperatures, but nighttime temperatures can drop into the forties or lower. Wet suits are normally worn during spring trips.

Rafting the Grand Canyon ranks as one of the world's truly outstanding wilderness experiences. The National Park Service, which regulates outfitters and launch dates, says approximately 20,000 customers are accommodated by the twenty-one outfitters. Few of these outfitters have difficulty filling all of their alloted spaces for each launch permit. Outfitters report that a surprising percentage of rafting customers come from as far away as Germany, France, Great Britain, Australia, and Canada. Little wonder that reservations a year or more in advance are recommended.

Guides serve breakfast on the Colorado's multiday Grand Canyon rafting trip.

101. VERDE RIVER, ARIZONA

Section:	Beasley Flats to Horseshoe Reservoir
Location:	Yavapai County between Flaggstaff and Phoenix, central Arizona
Distance:	60 miles (96 km)
Class:	II–III
Trip Options:	Paddle raft, oar raft, inflatable kayak; one to five days
Season:	January–April
Outfitters:	Desert Voyagers
	Worldwide Explorations

In 1984, the Verde River became Arizona's first river to be designated a Wild and Scenic River. Its refreshing waters and lush green vegetation, which serve as an oasis in the Sonoran desert for migratory birds, also make it a popular habitat for the bald eagle and other wildlife including beavers, otters, and deer. Verde's January-to-April rafting season is the perfect time for both birdwatching and relaxing in the Southwest sun.

Although the upper Verde contains several Class III–IV rapids during high water, most of the river's relatively moderate Class II–III waters are ideal for first-time rafters and senior citizens. In normal-water years, outfitters offer one-, two-, three-, and five-day rafting trips on the Verde. Inflatable kayaks make it possible to extend the rafting season until early May.

102. SALT RIVER, ARIZONA

Section:	Fort Apache Indian Reservation to Roosevelt Lake
Location:	Gila County, northeast of Phoenix, east-central Arizona
Distance:	54 miles (86 km) or less
Class:	III–IV +
Trip Options:	Paddle raft, oar raft, inflatable kayak; one to five days
Season:	February–May
Outfitters:	Desert Voyagers
	Far-Flung Adventures
	Saguaro Whitewater (Apache reservation)
	Salt River Canyon Raft Trips (Apache reservation)
	Worldwide Explorations

The Salt River is born at the confluence of the White and Black rivers, below their headwaters in Arizona's White Mountains. West of U.S. Highway 60, north of Globe, the upper Salt carves a tumbling 54-mile (86 km) course through the granite gorges of the pristine Sonoran

The Verde River in central Arizona's Sonoran Desert serves as an oasis for migratory birds during the winter.
Photo by B. Witzeman

Desert that includes the Fort Apache Indian Reservation, Tonto National Forest, and the Salt River Canyon Wilderness before reaching the quiet waters behind Theodore Roosevelt Dam. With the passage of the Arizona Wilderness Act in 1984, approximately 35 miles (56 km) of the upper Salt, between Gleason Flat and the mouth of Pinal Creek, was incorporated into the Salt River Wilderness Canyon.

During the early spring runoff, the upper Salt is more than just a scenic desert canyon river; Granite Gorge has several excellent Class III–IV+ rapids, including the exciting Eye of the Needle, Black Rock, Maze, and Quartzite Falls—a riverwide ledge that often requires lining or portaging. One- to five-day raft trips are run in the spring when the wildflowers of the Sonoran Desert are at their best.

103. RIO CHAMA, NEW MEXICO

Section: El Vado Dam to Big Eddy above Abiquiu Reservoir
Location: Rio Arriba County, northwest of Espanola, northern New Mexico
Distance: 24–32 miles (38–51 km) or less
Class: II–III
Trip Options: Paddle raft, oar raft; one and two days
Season: April–September
Outfitters: Artemis Wilderness Tours
Bill Dvorak's Raft and Kayak Expeditions
Far-Flung Adventures
Los Rios River Runners
New Wave Rafting
Rio Grande Rapid Transit
Santa Fe Rafting Company
Sierra Outfitters and Guides
Southwest Wilderness Center
Whitewater Odyssey
Wolf Whitewater

Originating in the high San Juan Mountains of south-central Colorado, northern New Mexico's Rio Chama becomes a major tributary of the famed Rio Grande north of Espanola. Long recognized for its pristine canyon beauty, Rio Chama, first protected by the state's Scenic and Pastoral Rivers System, recently was added to the National Wild and Scenic River System. Its red and yellow sandstone canyons, celebrated in the art of Georgia O'Keefe, are some of the Southwest's best gorges for hiking and photography.

Taos Box Canyon on the New Mexico Rio Grande River is one of America's original Wild and Scenic Rivers.
Photo by Nancy Jane Reid

Chama Canyon, the largest of Rio Chama's remaining canyons, runs nearly 33 miles (49 km) from El Vado Dam to Abiquiu Reservoir. Most of its Class III rapids—Dark Canyon, Little Bridge, Skull Bridge, Gage Station, and Screaming Left Turn—are within 3 miles (5 km) of the Big Eddy take-out.

Chama's dam-controlled water flow makes it a very popular one- or two-day trip for families as well as for anyone who desires a relaxing and scenic canyon trip. The canyon's campsites are either hidden among the ponderosa pines and fir or abut the beautiful sandstone walls. While the best rafting times are April through mid-June, the water releases from the dam permit weekend trips during late July and August.

104. RIO GRANDE, NEW MEXICO

Sections:	Taos Box and Lower Gorge
Location:	Rio Arriba and Taos counties, near Taos, northern New Mexico
Distance:	17 miles (27 km) (Taos Box)
	5–12 miles (8–19 km) (Lower Gorge)
Class:	III–IV (Taos Box)
	I–III (Lower Gorge)
Trip Options:	Paddle raft, oar raft; half-day, one to three days
Season:	April–August
Outfitters:	Arkansas River Tours/OLTS
	Artemis Wilderness Tours
	Big River Raft Trips
	Bill Dvorak's Raft and Kayak Expeditions
	Far-Flung Adventures
	Los Rios River Runners
	New Wave Rafting
	Rio Bravo River Tours
	Rio Grande Rapid Transit
	Santa Fe Rafting Company
	Sierra Outfitters and Guides
	Southwest Wilderness Center
	Texas River Expeditions
	Whitewater Adventures
	Whitewater Odyssey
	Wolf Whitewater

In 1968, a 48-mile (77 km) section of the Rio Grande in northern New Mexico was among the first rivers to be included in the National Wild and Scenic River System. Near the quaint, northern New Mexico town of Taos, much of this protected Rio Grande offers a variety of popular whitewater opportunities for seasoned as well as young and inexperienced rafters.

During normal spring and early summer water flows, the 17-mile (27 km) raft trip through the remote and majestic 800-foot deep volcanic Taos Box is promoted as New Mexico's wildest whitewater ride. Its many dynamic Class III–IV + rapids, which include Ski Jump, Powerline, and Rock Garden, provide a thrilling and wet day for adventurous rafters. In addition to splendid whitewater, the Taos Box is also noted for its natural hot springs and bird life, which includes eagles, geese, herons, and ducks.

Immediately below the Box and its confluence with the Rio Pueblo De Taos, Rio Grande outfitters offer very popular half- and one-day trips on the more moderate sections of the Lower Gorge. Commonly referred to as Pilar, or Racecourse, this trip has been the sight of the annual Rio Grande Whitewater Races for more than twenty-five years. After a 5-mile (8 km) scenic float trip through Rio Grande State Park, the canyon walls narrow to create nearly 6 miles (10 km) of fairly continuous Class II–III whitewater. The stretch includes the exciting Albert Falls, The Narrows, Big Rock, and Souse Hole Rapids. Trips include half-day runs on the scenic flatwater of the Bureau of Land Management's Orilla Verde section and the Racecourse rapids or a full-day Lower Gorge trip. Outfitters welcome families with children as young as six years old on paddle- and oar-guided raft trips in the Lower Gorge.

105. RIO GRANDE, TEXAS

For nearly 300 miles (480 km) from Redford in west Texas through Big Bend National Park to Langtry near the Amistad National Recreation Area, river rafting provides the easiest way to explore the Rio Grande's scenic and legendary canyons. Rafting in these southwest Texas sections of the Rio Grande is not the result of snowmelt in the river's Colorado high mountain origins, but rather from the waters of the equally large watershed of the Rio Conchos tributary that drains

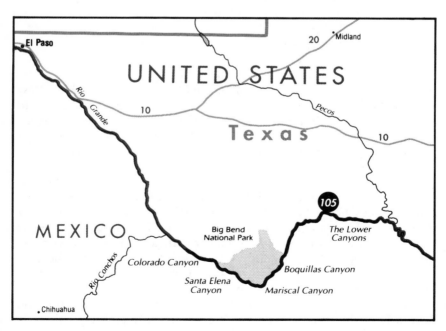

Guests enjoy a refreshing swim near the mouth of Rio Grande's St. Elena Canyon in Big Bend National Park.
Photo by Nancy Jane Reid

Several of the most remote canyons in the Southwest are found on the Texas Rio Grande River.
Photo by Nancy Jane Reid

from Chihuahua State in northern Mexico. Along part of the Big Bend National Park boundary and extending eastward below it, the Rio Grande is a Wild and Scenic River for 191 miles (306 km).

Sections:	Colorado Canyon
	Big Bend National Park canyons
Location:	Presidio and Brewster counties, Big Bend National Park, southwest Texas, United States–Mexico border
Distance:	14–25 miles (22–40 km) (Colorado Canyon)
	105 miles (168 km) (Big Bend)
Class:	I–II (Colorado Canyon)
	I–IV (Big Bend)
Trip Options:	Paddle raft, oar raft; half-day, one day, two days (Colorado Canyon); one to seven days (Big Bend)
Season:	Year-round
Outfitters:	Big Bend River Tours
	Far-Flung Adventures
	Outback Expeditions
	Rough Run Outfitters
	Texas River Expeditions

While the isolation of Rio Grande's spectacular canyons requires at least two or more days for most river adventures, one of the river's most popular trips is a one-day excursion near the western entrance to Big Bend National Park. Upstream from Lajitas, Colorado Canyon has relatively easy Class I–II whitewater that is ideal for families and park visitors. Oar-guided raft trips leave ample time to enjoy the vast beauty of the canyon.

Big Bend National Park's three best known river canyons—Santa Elena, Mariscal, and Boquillas—may be rafted individually during two- and three-day trips or as a continuous seven-day trip. Outfitters normally shuttle rafters between Lajitas and the put-in and take-out points for each trip.

Santa Elena, the park's first and most popular canyon, is known for its picturesque waterfalls, outstanding flora and fauna, and Rock Slide Rapids—a long and technical maze created by numerous large boulders. Hikes into Santa Elena's side canyons offer a close-up look at fossils, bat caves, and desert wildflowers. Its towering canyon walls are home to numerous bird species, including eagles and the endangered peregrine Falcon. During high water, some outfitters may run the 20-mile (32 km) Santa Elena as a one-day trip.

In southernmost Big Bend, Mariscal, a 10-mile (16 km) canyon, is the park's most colorful and remote chasm. Its walls tower nearly 1,600 feet above Tight Squeeze, a 10-foot-wide rapids, and Rockpile, a technical swirling maze. Two other remote park canyons, San Vicente and Hot Springs, are usually run with the Mariscal trip.

Boquillas Canyon, the longest and most tranquil of Big Bend's canyons, carves a picturesque route through the Sierra del Carmen Mountains on the eastern edge of the park. Sheer walls over 4,000 feet high, numerous side canyons with striking rock formations, and secluded caves add to the intrigue of the Boquillas adventure. Because of the very easy Class I–II rapids, outfitters will normally take families with children as young as five years old on the Boquillas section.

Section:	Lower canyons
Location:	Brewster, Terrell and Val Verde counties, United States–Mexico border, southwest Texas
Distance:	86–125 miles (137–200 km)
Class:	I–IV
Trip Options:	Oar-guided rafts, inflatable kayaks; seven to ten days
Season:	Year-round (spring and fall are best)
Outfitters:	Big Bend River Tours
	Far-Flung Adventures
	Outback Expeditions
	Texas River Expeditions

From La Linda, just north of Big Bend, to Langtry, some 135 miles (216 km) downriver, the Rio Grande provides a solitary journey

through some of the most remote river desert canyons in the Southwest. On the second day, rafters enter a section of almost 60 miles (96 km) of continuous canyon. Promoted by outfitters as the Lower Canyons of the Rio Grande trip, its entire length is protected by Wild and Scenic River legislation and consists of almost one deep canyon after another. Because of the river's remoteness, difficult access, and seven- to ten-day length, it should be attempted only by physically fit and adventurous campers. Oar-guided raft trips, often accompanied by canoes and kayaks, provide an abundance of time to hike side canyons or relax in the shade or warm springs.

The most common run of the lower canyons, which is from La Linda to Dryden Crossing, is about 86 miles (137 km) long; it can be run in five to seven days. Many rafters add Martin Canyon to their run, which requires another 50 miles (80 km) and an additional two or three days to reach Langtry.

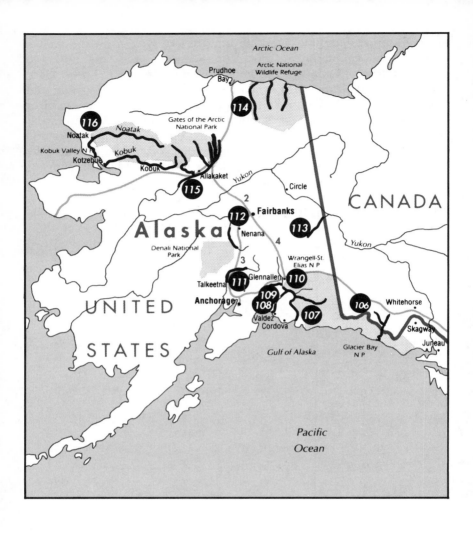

CHAPTER 6

Alaska

ALASKA, AMERICA'S LAST FRONTIER, offers adventure-spirited rafters more miles of wilderness waterways and more varied environments than does any other state or province. From the gently flowing wilderness rivers of the Brooks Range in the tundra north of the Arctic Circle to the sometimes gentle—and sometimes not so gentle—waters beneath towering mountains in south-central and southeast Alaska, there are dozens of river trips from which to choose. Outfitters provide half-day or less, one-day, multiday, and even multiweek river adventures. There are river trips suitable to persons of almost all ages and physical conditions.

Portions of forty-two Alaska rivers are protected from development by the National Wild and Scenic River System. In addition, many of the state's more frequently rafted rivers are all or partially included within boundaries of national parks or wildlife reserves, such as Glacier Bay, Wrangell–St. Elias, Denali, Gates of the Arctic, Kobuk Valley, Noatak Reserve, and Arctic Wildlife.

Continuous daylight during the short summer rafting season provides rafters with limitless opportunities to photograph Alaska's breathtaking scenery and its incredible wildlife. Rafters often find it difficult to record the towering mountains and massive glaciers on film. Photographs of Alaska's caribou, moose, bears, deer, countless species of waterfowl, birds of prey, and other wildlife will be greatly enhanced if you use a telephoto lens.

Access to many of Alaska's rivers is so remote that small aircraft transport guests and rafting equipment to and from put-in or take-out points. During many of these wilderness trips, rafting groups may be weeks from the nearest telephone or civilization. Rafters planning to participate in any of Alaska's wilderness river trips should be properly prepared for the Far North. Glacier-fed rivers are always cold, and wet suits are almost always required. Unpredictable weather can make Alaska summer days very chilly. Despite any discomforts during the long wilderness trips, almost everyone calls their Alaska river trip one of life's greatest experiences.

Alaska's long list of multiday wilderness trips includes:

■ Southeast Alaska, British Columbia and the Yukon's incredibly beautiful Alsek and Tatshenshini rivers. Their whitewater and scenery provide one of the best rafting trips available.

■ The Chitina and Copper rivers in the beautiful Wrangell–St. Elias Mountains rank a close second to the Alsek–Tatshenshini for mountain wilderness beauty.

■ Tazlina, from Tazlina Lake to the Copper River confluence and the Wrangell Mountains, offers relatively easy paddle rafting east of Anchorage.

■ The Talkeetna, from the Talkeetna Glacier to the mighty Susitna, provides Class III–IV + whitewater, placid waters, and outstanding mountain scenery northeast of Anchorage.

■ Fortymile River provides an interesting float trip through the early century gold country of eastern Alaska.

■ Northern Alaska's Brooks Mountain Range, the source of hundreds of rivers and streams, offers more than a dozen rafting opportunities in its many national parks and wildlife reserves north of the Arctic Circle.

The professional outfitters of Alaska also operate at least three rafting trips for residents and guests who want a brief introduction to whitewater:

■ The Nenana River, along the eastern boundary of Denali National Park, is Alaska's most popular whitewater trip. Several times a day throughout the summer rafting season, outfitters offer both two- and four-hour raft trips on Nenana's Class III–IV waters.

■ The Lowe River just east of Valdez has one-hour trips through Keystone Canyon.

■ Tonsina's 35-mile (56 km) excursion, from the Tonsina Lodge to the Copper River, may be the longest one-day raft trip in North America.

Guests marvel at massive icebergs on Alaska's Tatshenshini River.
Photo courtesy of Sobek Expeditions

106. ALSEK-TATSHENSHINI RIVERS, YUKON-BRITISH COLUMBIA-ALASKA

Sections: Haines Junction, Yukon to Dry Bay, Alaska (Alsek)
Dalton Post, Yukon to Alsek confluence of Alsek River,
British Columbia (Tatshenshini–Alsek)

Location: Southwest Yukon, northwest British Columbia, southeast Alaska

Distance: 140 miles (224 km) (Alsek)
184 miles (294 km) (Tatshenshini–Alsek)

Class: III–IV (Alsek)
II–III (Tatshenshini–Alsek)

Trip Options: Oar raft, paddle/oar raft; nine to twelve days

Season: June–September

Outfitters: Alaska Discovery
Canadian River Expeditions
Chilkat Guides
Colorado River and Trail Expeditions
Ecosummer Yukon Expeditions

Interior Whitewater Expeditions
James Henry River Journeys
Sobek Expeditions
Suskwa Adventure Outfitters
Tatshenshini Expeditions
Wilderness River Outfitters—Idaho

The Alsek and Tatshenshini rivers provide two of the most incredible outdoor adventures imaginable. For as many as nine to twelve days, it is possible to get away from virtually all traces of civilization and enjoy the remote northern wilderness environment of the Yukon, British Columbia, and Alaska. Rafters will enjoy and long remember massive glaciers and large icebergs, pristine waterfalls, majestic mountains, primitive forests, grizzlies, moose, mountain goats, hawks, eagles, rare wildflowers, and whitewater.

The Tatshenshini and Alsek rivers in southeast Alaska and northwest British Columbia provide spectacular mountain vistas.
Photo courtesy of Sobek Expeditions/Bart Henderson

Prior to the lower Alsek's final journey between the towering glaciers and icebergs of Alaska's Glacier Bay National Park, rafters may run the Alsek River from Haines Junction, Yukon, to Dry Bay, Alaska, or the Tatshenshini from Dalton Post, Yukon, to its confluence with the Alsek. Until recently most outfitters offered only the Tatshenshini–Alsek river trip. Now several also run the entire Alsek, which has somewhat more challenging whitewater and more varied and grander scenery. One section of the Alsek, the 4-mile (6.5 km) Class VI Turnback Canyon, must be portaged by helicopter. Both river trips offer an unforgettable primitive wilderness experience. The Tatshenshini and Alsek are the only two rivers that cut through the lofty St. Elias Mountain Range.

107. CHITINA–COPPER RIVERS, ALASKA

Sections:	Kennecott, Nizina, and Chitina rivers to Chitina (Chitina River)
	Chitina to Flagg Point east of Cordova (Copper River)
Location:	Wrangell–St. Elias National Park, east of Valdez, southeast Alaska
Distance:	70 miles (112 km) (Chitina)
	110 miles (176 km) (Copper)
Class:	I–III
Trip Options:	Paddle raft, oar raft, six to twelve days
Season:	June–mid-September
Outfitters:	Alaska Float Trips
	Alaska River Adventures
	Alaska Wilderness Group
	Keystone Raft & Kayak Adventures
	Nabesna Whitewater Rafting
	Nichols Expeditions
	Osprey Expeditions
	St. Elias Alpine Guides

Alaska's most extensive and rugged glaciated wilderness is in the Wrangell–St. Elias Range. It is here in the massive icefields of the St. Elias Mountains that the Chitina River gets its start. This huge river bisects the Wrangells as it flows west toward the mighty Copper River. Most raft trips begin at McCarthy on the Kennecott River, which then flows into the Nizina, Chitina, and Copper. This seemingly circuitous route allows rafters time to visit the interesting ghost town of McCarthy and the abandoned Kennecott copper mine before the multiday wilderness river journey to the Copper River at the small town of Chitina.

The Copper River, below Chitina, flows swiftly through the beautiful Copper River Valley adjacent to the Wrangell–St. Elias National Park until it reaches the park's coastal Chugach Mountains. The Childs and Miles glaciers enter the Copper River creating Miles Lake. During summer, rafters frequently observe ice calving—large chunks of ice breaking away from the glacier.

108. LOWE RIVER, ALASKA

Section: Keystone Canyon
Location: Northeast of Valdez, south-central Alaska
Distance: 4 miles (6.5 km)
Class: II–III
Trip Options: Paddle raft, oar raft, one hour
Season: Mid-May–mid-September
Outfitter: Keystone Raft and Kayak Adventures

The Lowe River, through Keystone Canyon, gives rafters a brief and enjoyable introduction to whitewater less than 20 miles (32 km) northeast of Valdez. While the rafting trip is short—the 4-mile (6.5 km) distance takes an hour—the Keystone Canyon doesn't lack either spectacular scenery or exciting whitewater. Its easy Class II–III rapids can be run by anyone above the age of five.

The Keystone trip starts approximately 1 mile (1.6 km) above the canyon and proceeds 4 miles (6.5 km) downstream to the take-out. Rafters make a stop at Bridal Veil Falls where waters cascade 900 feet down sheer rock walls to the river bank.

Keystone's outfitter provides rainsuits, life jackets, and rubber boots for guests.

109. TONSINA RIVER, ALASKA

Section: Lower
Location: Near Chitina, east of Valdez, south-central Alaska
Distance: 35 miles (56 km)
Class: III–IV
Trip Options: Paddle raft, oar raft; one day
Season: Mid-May–mid-September
Outfitter: Keystone Raft and Kayak Adventures

North America's longest one-day whitewater rafting trip may be the Tonsina River in south-central Alaska. The swift-flowing waters of the lower Tonsina make it possible to raft the 35-mile (56 km) segment from Tonsina Lodge to the Copper River, north of Chitina, in less than six hours. The Tonsina also has many exciting Class III–IV rapids.

110. TAZLINA RIVER, ALASKA

Section:	Tazlina Lake to Copper River near Glennallen
Location:	West of Glennallen, south-central Alaska
Distance:	30 miles (48 km), up to 20 miles (32 km) on Tazlina Lake
Class:	I–II +
Trip Options:	Paddle raft, oar raft; four to five days
Season:	June–September
Outfitters:	Keystone Raft and Kayak Adventures
	Osprey Expeditions

Tazlina Lake, north of the Chugach Mountains in south-central Alaska, is the starting point for a very scenic raft trip about 200 miles (320 km) east of Anchorage. Tazlina Lake, best reached by float plane, lies at the end of the Tazlina Glacier. Its shoreline beauty boasts bleached driftwood and northern spruce and birch forests. The scenery makes it desirable to raft a few miles across the lake before beginning the 30-mile (48 km) raft trip to the Copper River confluence and the Wrangell Mountains, just south of Glennallen.

The easy to moderate Class I–II + waters of the Tazlina River are suitable for almost anyone. Its steady current moves rafts quickly downriver, and plenty of time is available for hiking, fishing, and photographing. The Tazlina area is known for its large moose and grizzly and black bear populations. Dall sheep are also sometimes seen in the adjacent hills.

111. TALKEETNA RIVER, ALASKA

Section:	Yellowjacket Creek to Talkeetna
Loction:	East of Talkeetna, south-central Alaska
Distance:	60 miles (96 km)
Class:	III–IV +
Trip Options:	Paddle raft, oar raft; four to five days
Season:	June–September
Outfitters:	Alaska Float Trips
	Alaska Rafting Adventures
	Alaska River Adventures
	Alaska Wilderness Group

Keystone Raft and Kayak Adventures
Nova River Runners
Osprey Expeditions
Ouzel Expeditions

The Talkeetna River, a tributary of the Susitna River north of Anchorage, flows out of the Talkeetna Mountains in south-central Alaska. Its headwaters, below Sovereign Mountain's Talkeetna Glacier, can only be reached by aircraft.

While the Class I–II waters of the upper Talkeetna raft trip allow plenty of time to enjoy pristine mountain wilderness beauty and wildlife, the river does not remain easy. The granite walls of Devil's Canyon, usually reached on the third day of the trip, dramatically change the river's profile. During a 14-mile (22 km) stretch of the canyon, Class III–IV + rapids, such as Toilet Bowl and Sluice Box, are almost non-stop. Thrill-seeking rafters may enjoy some of the state's finest wilderness whitewater.

Talkeetna's mountains are home to caribou, grizzly and black bears, and bald eagles.

112. NENANA RIVER, ALASKA

Section: Canyon
Location: Denali National Park near Healy, south-central Alaska
Distance: 15 miles (24 km)
Class: III–IV
Trip Options: Paddle raft, oar raft, dory; two-hour, half-day
Season: Mid-May–mid-September
Outfitters: Denali Raft Adventures
McKinley Raft Tours
Osprey Expeditions
Owl Rafting
Sundog Dories

The Nenana River, on the eastern boundary of Alaska's magnificent Denali National Park, is fed from the Yannert and Nenana glaciers of the park's 20,320-foot Mt. McKinley. Nenana's proximity to Anchorage and Fairbanks, its beautiful scenery, and its exciting whitewater make it Alaska's most popular rafting trip.

The most popular stretch of the Nenana is the canyon section. Here anyone above the age of twelve will enjoy the exciting waves and holes of the river's numerous rapids. Outfitters offer two-hour, half-day, and all-day trips ranging from 10 to 15 miles (16 to 24 km) long. Multiday trips of up to 60 miles (96 km) can also be arranged on the river.

Denali National park is known for its abundant wildlife. Dall sheep, moose, caribou, grizzly bears, wolves, and eagles are sometimes seen during raft trips.

The Nenana is located along the George Parks Highway between Anchorage and Fairbanks. There are a number of excellent hotels and lodging accommodations at the entrance to Denali National Park.

113. FORTYMILE RIVER, ALASKA

Section: Middle Fork
Location: East of Fairbanks near Tok, eastern Alaska
Distance: 90 miles (144 km)
Class: II–III
Trip Options: Paddle raft, oar raft; seven days
Season: June–September
Outfitter: Osprey Expeditions

The Fortymile River and its many forks drain a large area of eastern Alaska's early twentieth-century gold mining region. Almost due east of Fairbanks, this clear wilderness river flows east through gently rolling mountains and white marble bluffs to the Yukon River in the Yukon Territory. Fortymile got its name, not because of its length, but because of its confluence 40 miles (64 km) downriver from an old Hudson's Bay Company trading post.

Fortymile's scenery is interesting, and its waters are not difficult. Rafting begins on the Class I–II Middle Fork near the old mining camp of Joseph or at the historic mining town of Chicken. Once the North Fork meets the Middle Fork, the pace quickens, and The Chute, a Class III rapid, is encountered. Shortly afterwards, the Kink, a Class V mining sluice, must be portaged.

The Fortymile offers an excellent opportunity to see moose, bears, and other wildlife. In early September, large herds of migrating caribou are frequently seen.

114. BROOKS RANGE (East) RIVERS, ALASKA

Rivers: Canning, Hulahula, and Kongakut
Location: Arctic National Wildlife Refuge, northeast Alaska
Distance: 100–150 miles (160–240 km)
Class: I–II
Trip Options: Oar raft; five to twelve days

Season:	June–September
Outfitters:	ABEC's Adventure Paddle-Rafting
	Adventure Alaska–Mexico
	Alaska Discovery
	Alaska River Adventures
	Alaska Wilderness Group
	Arctic Treks
	Brooks Range Wilderness Trips
	Osprey Expeditions
	Sourdough Outfitters
	Wilderness Expeditions

The Arctic National Wildlife Refuge, adjacent to the Canadian border in northeast Alaska, is one of the world's largest nature preserves. Nowhere else in North America is the transition of biotic communities from the Arctic slopes to the adjacent mountains so abrupt. Flowing northward out of the valleys of the eastern Brooks Range across the Tundra to the Arctic Ocean are three rivers: the Canning, the Hulahula, and the Kongakut. They provide rare opportunities to see undisturbed plant and animal communities.

During late-summer trips on any of the Arctic National Wildlife Refuge rivers, it is not uncommon to see thousands of wildlife including caribou, moose, musk ox, Dall sheep, wolves, grizzly bears, and waterfowl. Polar bears may also be seen near the Arctic Ocean.

115. BROOKS RANGE (Central) RIVERS, ALASKA

Rivers:	Koyukuk (North Fork), Alatna, Killik, John, and Wild
Location:	Gates of the Arctic National Park, Brooks Range, north-central Alaska
Distance:	100–140 miles (160–224 km)
Class:	I–II
Trip Options:	Paddle raft, oar raft; seven to fourteen days
Season:	June–September
Outfitters:	ABEC's Adventure Paddle-Rafting
	Adventure Alaska–Mexico
	Alaska Fish and Trails Unlimited
	Alaska Float Trips
	Alaska River Adventures
	Arctic Treks
	Bettles Lodge Wilderness Trips

Alaska's outfitters offer expedition-type rafting trips in the Brooks Range and on other wilderness rivers.
Photo courtesy of Adventure Alaska/Mexico

Brooks Range Wilderness Trips
Nichols Expeditions
Sourdough Outfitters
Wilderness Expeditions

Gates of the Arctic National Park, in Alaska's central Brooks Mountain Range, is the source of dozens of wild rivers that are enjoyed by hikers and rafters each summer. Several Class I–II wild rivers, such as the North Fork of the Koyukuk, Alatna, Killik, John, and Wild, offer a relaxing way to enjoy the Brooks wilderness. Many of the outfitters organize day hikes into the scenic mountains and side valleys.

The Gates of the Arctic is a photographer's paradise. In addition to the primitive mountain wilderness scenery, Dall sheep, moose, grizzly bears, and wolves are frequently seen.

The small village of Bettles, just north of the Arctic Circle near the John and Wild rivers' confluence with the Koyukuk River, is the outfitting and travel center for central Books Range hiking and river expeditions.

116. BROOKS RANGE (West) RIVERS, ALASKA

Rivers:	Noatak and Kobuk
Location:	Gates of the Arctic National Park, Noatak National Park, Kobuk Valley National Park
Distance:	350 miles (560 km) or less (Noatak)
	300 miles (480 km) or less (Kobuk)
Class:	I–II
Trip Options:	Paddle raft, oar raft; ten to fifteen days
Season:	June–September
Outfitters:	ABEC's Adventure Paddle-Rafting
	Adventure Alaska–Mexico
	Alaska Fish and Trails Unlimited

Alaska Float Trips
Alaska River Adventures
Arctic Treks
Bettles Lodge Wilderness Trips
Nichols Expeditions
Wilderness Expeditions

The Noatak and Kobuk rivers, which begin in the Arrigetch Peaks in the Gates of the Arctic National Park, flow westward for more than 300 miles (480 km) to Kotzebue Sound in the Chukchi Sea. Noatak, the more northern of the two rivers, which are separated by the Baird Mountains in the western Brooks Range, flows for more than 200 miles (320 km) through the Noatak National Park with no signs of civilization. The Kobuk River trip, which begins at Walker Lake south of the Arrigetch Peaks, parallels the southern slopes of the Baird Mountains. The river passes a few remote Eskimo villages and runs through the southern edge of Kobuk Valley National Park.

Neither of the rivers is difficult. Their mellow Class I–II waters are even more popular with canoeists and kayakers. Fishing for salmon and trout is excellent. There is also ample time to observe and photograph the caribou, wolves, goats, sheep, fox, and abundant summer birdlife.

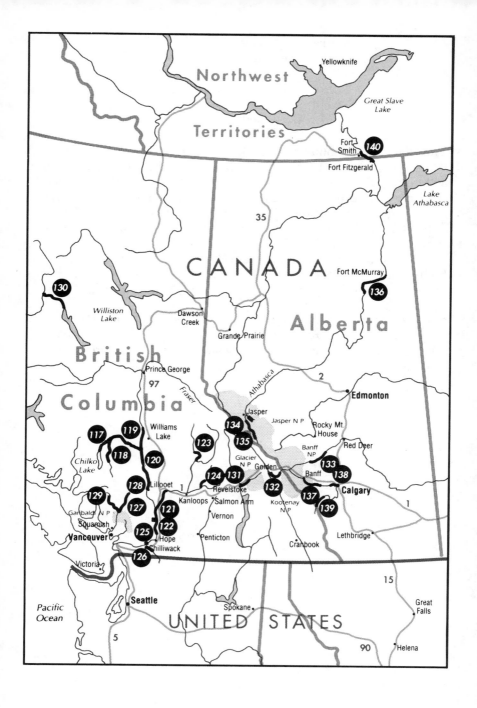

CHAPTER 7

Western Canada

FOR MORE THAN A CENTURY, the vast geographic regions of western Canada have become an increasingly valuable source of natural resources for the country's growing population. Its mountain glaciers, heavy winter snowfalls, and seasonal rains have provided water and electricity for Canada's factories, farms, and homes. Its expansive forests have supplied timber and wood products for domestic use and foreign trade. Countless miles (kilometers) of these mountain and forest wilderness canyons and gorges are also enjoyed by whitewater rafters.

Commercial whitewater rafting in western Canada, which began in British Columbia in 1973, has achieved widespread popularity in the coastal, the interior, and the Rocky Mountain ranges of British Columbia, and in the eastern Rocky Mountains in neighboring Alberta. More than three dozen outfitters provide a variety of half-day or less, one-day, and multiday rafting opportunities on almost two dozen rivers in the two provinces.

British Columbia's whitewater trips were first run on the mighty Fraser and Thompson rivers and their many tributaries: the Chilcotin, Chilko, Taseko, Nahatlatch, Adams, Clearwater, Chehalis, and Chilliwack. These waters remain summertime favorites for rafters. Rafting is also now popular on several coastal waters in the Whistler region north of Vancouver; these include the Squamish, Cheakamus, and Birkenhead rivers. In the Rocky Mountains in eastern British Columbia, the Illecillewaet is a favorite of visitors to Glacier National Park, as is the Kicking Horse River to visitors to Banff and Jasper national parks. In northern British Columbia, the Babine River offers a superb multiday rafting adventure.

Alberta's prime whitewater rivers and streams are nestled between the Rocky Mountains' eastern slope and Calgary, Red Deer, and Edmonton. The upper Red Deer River is the province's most popular raft trip. Rafting two rivers in Jasper National Park, the Maligne and the Athabasca, provides an excellent tour of the park's spectacular scenery. A quiet float trip on Banff National Park's Bow River enables visitors of all ages to take a relaxing look at Canada's most well-known national park. Near Canmore, site of the downhill ski events during the 1988 Winter Olympics, is the Kananaskis River, with Class I–III whitewater that is good for families. About an hour south of Calgary, the Highwood River offers some of Alberta's most continuous Class III–IV whitewater. Farther north, rafters may follow the water routes of early explorers on multiday raft trips on the Athabasca River north of House River or the Great Slave River near the border of Alberta and the Northwest Territories.

117. CHILKO RIVER, BRITISH COLUMBIA

Section: Chilko Lake to Taseko Junction
Location: West of Williams Lake, south-central British Columbia
Distance: 40 miles (64 km)
Class: I–V
Trip Options: Oar raft, paddle/oar raft; two to three days
Season: June–September
Outfitters: Action River Expeditions
                Canadian River Expeditions
                Clearwater Expeditions
                Clearwater Rafting Adventures
                Hyak Wilderness Adventures
                Kumsheen Raft Adventures
                Whistler River Adventures

Central British Columbia's Chilko River can be run singly or include the first segment of the popular 260-mile (416 km) Chilko–Chilcotin–Fraser multiday rafting expedition.

Access to the isolated Chilko is normally via seaplane to its source, 4,000-foot Chilko Lake. Below the lake, the easy first stretch of the river provides an ideal introduction to whitewater rafting. Its Class I–II waters give rafters an opportunity to test their whitewater skills and experience the pristine wilderness.

After 23 miles (37 km) of Class I–II whitewater, the river enters the spectacular Class IV–V Lava Canyon. Much of the anticipation (and anxiety) of the 17-mile (27 km) Lava Canyon is because several of its more difficult Class V rapids cannot be scouted. Immediately below Lava Canyon the Chilko joins the Taseko to form the Chilcotin River.

118. TASEKO RIVER, BRITISH COLUMBIA

Section: Taseko Lake to confluence with Chilko River
Location: Southwest of Williams Lake, central British Columbia
Distance: 70 miles (112 km)
Class: II–IV
Trip Options: Paddle raft, oar raft, paddle/oar raft; four days
Season: June–September
Outfitters: Action River Expeditions
    Clearwater Expeditions
    REO Rafting Adventures

The Taseko River, which joins the Chilko to form the Chilcotin, flows north from Taseko Lake near 10,043-foot Mt. Tatlow in central British Columbia. The 70-mile (112 km) Taseko raft trip takes four days and includes overnight camping along its scenic banks. Rafting begins at Taseko Falls below Taseko Lake.

Taseko whitewater, which starts out easy, gradually increases in difficulty. On the second and third days, several rather technical Class III–IV rapids must be navigated by paddle rafters. August is the preferred month for rafting the Taseko.

119. CHILCOTIN RIVER, BRITISH COLUMBIA

Section: Taseko Junction to Fraser River
Location: South Williams Lake, central British Columbia
Distance: 75 miles (120 km)
Class: III–V
Trip Options: Paddle/oar raft, oar raft, motorized raft; four to twelve days
Season: June–September
Outfitters: Action River Expeditions
    Canadian River Expeditions
    Clearwater Expeditions
    Hyak Wilderness Adventures
    Kumsheen Raft Adventures

The Chilcotin River, a tributary of the Fraser, is created at the confluence of the Chilko and Taseko rivers in central British Columbia. Its location between the Chilko, Taseko, and Fraser rivers offers rafters some of the longest multiday raft-and-camping trips in western Canada. In addition to four- and five-day raft trips on the Chilcotin, outfitters frequently run seven- to ten-day trips on the Chilcotin–Fraser rivers and twelve-day 230-mile (345 km) trips on the Chilko–Chilcotin–Fraser.

The Chilcotin River has a distinctive rafting environment. As the river carves its way through the Chilcotin Plateau, between the coastal mountains and the Canadian Rockies, rafters are impressed by the semiarid landscape that includes ridgetop forests, cacti in grass valleys, California bighorn sheep, and mule deer.

Chilcotin's rapids, which increase in size and number as the trip proceeds, get more difficult as the trip moves downriver. Its best Class III–IV rapids are in Farewell and Big John canyons, just prior to the Chilcotin's confluence with the Fraser.

120. FRASER RIVER, BRITISH COLUMBIA

Section: Soda Creek to Lillooet
Location: Near Williams Lake, central British Columbia
Distance: 120 miles (192 km)
Class: III–V
Trip Options: Motorized raft; six and seven days
Season: July–September
Outfitters: Canadian River Expeditions
                 Frontier River Adventures
                 Kumsheen Raft Adventures

The Fraser River, named after the nineteenth-century Canadian fur trapper and trader Simon Fraser, begins in the Canadian Rockies, just a few miles from the sources of the Thompson and Columbia rivers. During its nearly 850-mile (1360 km) course, it first flows north to the city of Prince George, and then south through countless mountains, canyons, and gorges, before reaching tidal waters near Vancouver.

Rafting on the central Fraser begins at the town of Soda Creek, north of Williams Lake. During its southward journey through isolated steep canyons, the most prominent features are the breathtaking hoodoos—rock spires capped with slate—and the 2,000-foot Moran Canyon, location of some of the Fraser's best whitewater. With the addition of the Chilcotin and countless other rivers and streams, the Fraser's volume is increased to nearly ten times the flow of the Colorado. Below the Chilcotin, rafters frequently see native Indians netting salmon.

Lillooet is the normal take-out for the Fraser and the Chilko–Chilcotin–Fraser trips

Section:	Lytton
Location:	North of Hope, south-central British Columbia
Distance:	43 miles (69 km) or less
Class:	III–V +
Trip Options:	Motorized raft; one to three days
Season:	July–September
Outfitters:	Fraser River Raft Expeditions
	Frontier River Adventures
	Kumsheen Raft Adventures

A motorized raft navigates the waters of southern British Columbia's powerful Fraser River.
Photo courtesy of Kumsheen Raft Adventures

The Fraser River, below its confluence with the Thompson at Lytton, provides 43 miles (69 km) of exciting whitewater. Many of the Thompson's multiday motorized raft trips also include the Lytton-to-Yale stretch of the Fraser.

The Fraser's most popular one-day trip is the 16-mile (26 km) stretch from Boston Bar to Yale, a few miles north of Hope. Paralleled by the Trans-Canada Highway, the Fraser passes through a steep canyon gorge containing exciting Class III–V rapids such as the infamous Hell's Gate, China Bar, Scuzzy Rock, and Sailor Bar.

The Fraser's best rafting season corresponds with the region's best weather, mid-July to mid-September.

The Thompson River in southern British Columbia offers exciting big water and beautiful scenery.
Photo courtesy of Kumsheen Raft Adventures

121. THOMPSON RIVER, BRITISH COLUMBIA

Section: Ashcroft to Lytton
Location: West of Kamloops, south-central British Columbia
Distance: 50 miles (80 km)
Class: III–IV
Trip Options: Paddle raft, oar raft, paddle/oar raft, motorized raft; half-day, one and two days
Season: May–September
Outfitters: Action River Expeditions
Clearwater Expeditions
Fraser River Raft Expeditions
Frontier River Adventures
Hyak Wilderness Adventures
Interior Whitewater Expeditions
Kumsheen Raft Adventures
Rapid Rafting
REO Rafting Adventures
River Rogues Adventures
Water and Outdoor Sports International
Whistler River Adventures

In 1973 the Thompson River became British Columbia's first white-water river to be commercially rafted. As word of its exciting rapids and magnificent canyon scenery spread, its numbers of guests have increased almost yearly. It is clearly the province's most popular river trip. Twelve outfitters offer half- and one-day raft trips on the Thompson.

While most outfitters run single-day trips on the lower Thompson between Ashcroft and its confluence with the Fraser at Lytton, the 25-mile (40 km) one-day trip through the lower Thompson Valley between Spences Bridge and Lytton has the river's best whitewater and most awesome scenery. This heavy-water section, containing more than thirty rapids, including The Frog, Devils Kitchen, Witch's Cauldron, Washing Machine, and everyone's favorite, Jaw's of Death will excite both first-timers and experienced rafters.

A few outfitters also offer an outstanding three-hour whitewater trip on the last 10 miles (16 km) of the Thompson. Although the trip is short, eighteen sets of exciting whitewater rapids will generate lasting memories. Outfitters also run two-day trips on the Thompson or multiday trips on the Thompson and Fraser.

While the demanding whitewater of the Thompson doesn't always permit full attention to the spectacular arid landscape, there is still plenty to enjoy during the more relaxing stretches. The Trans-Canada Highway and Canadian National and CP railways parallel the river.

122. NAHATLATCH RIVER, BRITISH COLUMBIA

Sections:	Nahatlatch, Hannah or Frances lakes to Acocymum Canyon
Location:	North of Hope, southwest British Columbia
Distance:	8–12 miles (13–19 km) (lakes–Acocymum)
	6 miles (9.5 km) (canyon)
Class:	III–IV (lakes–Acocymum)
	III–IV + (canyon)
Trip Options:	Paddle raft, oar raft, paddle/oar raft; one day
Season:	May–August
Outfitters:	Action River Expeditions
	Fraser River Raft Expeditions
	Rapid Rafting
	REO Rafting Adventures
	Water and Outdoor Sports International

The Nahatlatch, in southern British Columbia, offers rafters some of the province's most challenging and exhilarating paddle adventures. Paddle rafters may prepare for the Nahatlatch trip by running the half-mile or so stretch between Hannah and Frances lakes. Shortly below Frances Lake, the exciting whitewater action of the Nahatlatch begins. Many Class III–IV rapids such as Rose Garden, Meatgrinder, and Headwall, require active rafter participation and leave little time to enjoy the passing scenery.

The 6-mile (9.5 km) canyon section of the Nahatlatch is the most intense. Large boulders, giant waves, and a gradient dropping at a rate of nearly 100 feet per mile create more than a dozen technical Class III–IV + rapids. During high water, one Class V rapid may be portaged.

The canyon should only be attempted by experienced rafters in good physical condition who are at least eighteen years old. The best time for the canyon section is usually during the more moderate water of July and August.

123. CLEARWATER RIVER, BRITISH COLUMBIA

Sections:	Upper and lower
Location:	North of Kamloops, eastern British Columbia
Distance:	15 or 25 miles (24 or 40 km)
Class:	III–IV +
Trip Options:	Paddle/oar raft; one and two days
Season:	June–September
Outfitters:	Clearwater Expeditions
	Interior Whitewater Expeditions

British Columbia's Clearwater Valley and Wells Gray Provincial Park, popular areas for horseback riding, canoeing, fishing, hiking, and camping, offer visitors some of the province's most challenging whitewater rafting. The Clearwater, which flows south from Wells Gray Park to its confluence with the north Thompson at the town of Clearwater, is less than a ninety-minute drive north of Kamloops.

Clearwater rafters may choose between one-day trips on the popular 15-mile (24 km) lower section or 10-mile (16 km) upper section, a two-day trip that includes both sections, or a half-day trip on a portion of the lower river. All of these trips contain superb wilderness scenery, abundant wildlife, and spectacular Class III–IV + whitewater.

124. ADAMS RIVER, BRITISH COLUMBIA

Section:	Adams Lake to Highway Bridge above Shuswap Lake
Location:	Near Adams Lake, east of Kamloops, south-central British Columbia
Distance:	6 miles (9.5 km)
Class:	II–III +
Trip Options:	Paddle/oar raft; two hours
Season:	May–September
Outfitter:	Interior Whitewater Expeditions

The Adams River, in the scenic Shuswap country of south-central British Columbia, offers an easy introduction to whitewater rafting for the whole family. Class I–II rapids alternating with fast-moving flat water provide the perfect environment to learn the paddling and safety skills needed to maneuver and guide the raft.

The 6-mile (9.5 km) Adams rafting trip between Adams and Shuswap lakes takes less than two hours and is less than ten minutes from the Trans-Canada Highway. The Adams rafting season runs from late May through early September.

125. CHEHALIS RIVER, BRITISH COLUMBIA

Section: Statlu Creek to campground
Location: Near Harrison Hot Springs, southern British Columbia
Distance: 5 miles (8 km)
Class: II–III
Trip Options: Paddle rafts; one-half day
Season: April–June
Outfitters: REO Rafting Adventures
                Wild Sports

The beautiful Chehalis River is one of British Columbia's whitewater jewels. Located in the mist-covered canyons near Harrison Hot Springs, east of Vancouver, its lovely jade-green pools alternate with exciting stretches of Class II–III whitewater. During spring rains the environment seems almost tropical as numerous small waterfalls cascade into the river.

The 5-mile (8 km) Chehalis raft trip runs from Statlu Creek to a campground about 2 miles (3.5 km) north of Harrison Hot Springs. Access is easy, the two- to three-hour trip is exciting, and lush scenery is excellent.

126. CHILLIWACK RIVER, BRITISH COLUMBIA

Sections: Foley Bridge to Slesse Creek (canyon)
                Slesse Creek to Veddar Crossing (lower)
Location: Southeast of Vancouver, southern British Columbia
Distance: 6 miles (9.5 km) (canyon)
                12 miles (19 km) (lower)
Class: III–IV + (canyon)
                II–III (lower)
Trip Options: Paddle-raft, oar raft; one day
Season: April–early August
Outfitters: Action River Expeditions
                Fraser River Raft Expeditions
                Hyak Wilderness Adventures
                R.A.F.T.
                Rapid Rafting
                REO Rafting Adventures
                Water and Outdoor Sports International
                Wild Sports

The Chilliwack, British Columbia's southernmost commercial rafting river, is also one of the province's most popular whitewaters. About a one-hour drive east of Vancouver, the scenic Chilliwack valley is easily accessible from both southern British Columbia and Washington state.

Most outfitters offer raft trips on two stretches of the Chilliwack: the 8-mile (13 km) canyon section and the 12-mile (19 km) lower river from Slesse Creek to Vedder Crossing. The gradient of the canyon, the more difficult of the two sections, at times reaches 100 feet per mile. Almost non-stop Class III–IV + whitewater, including Picket Fence and Fish Hatchery Drop, demand the teamwork of all rafters. The Chilliwack below Slesse Creek, while featuring more moderate Class II–III rapids, is a very exciting river trip for both first-timers and experienced rafters.

The Chilliwack flows from the north Cascades in Washington state to its confluence with the Fraser east of Vancouver. While the Chilliwack can be run from April until early August, its best whitewater is during May and June when the water is high.

127. CHEAKAMUS RIVER, BRITISH COLUMBIA

Section: Garibaldi
Location: Garibaldi, southwest British Columbia
Distance: 3 miles (4.5 km)
Class: III–IV
Trip Options: Paddle raft, oar raft; two hours
Season: June–July
Outfitters: Action River Adventures
                 Sea to Sky Raft Tours
                 Whistler River Adventures

The Cheakamus River, in the Whistler region of southwest British Columbia, gives visitors to Garibaldi Provincial Park an opportunity to experience whitewater rafting and still have time to enjoy the park's attractions. The Class III–IV river is also very popular with guests of the Whistler Resort.

Cheakamus's Garibaldi Run, a favorite of kayakers, has numerous waves, drops, and chutes that will excite and challenge first-time rafters. The 3-mile (4.5 km) trip takes less than two hours to run.

128. BIRKENHEAD RIVER, BRITISH COLUMBIA

Section: Owl Creek
Location: Whistler area, north of Mount Currie, southwest British Columbia
Distance: 5 miles (8 km)
Class: II–III

Trip Options: Paddle raft; one-half day
Season: June–July
Outfitter: Sea to Sky Raft Tours
               Whistler River Adventures

The Birkenhead River is in the Whistler region, a few miles north of southwest British Columbia's Garibaldi Provincial Park. It offers a very enjoyable one-half-day rafting trip in less than a three-hour drive north of Vancouver.

The 5-mile (8 km) Birkenhead raft trip, with continuous, but not too difficult, Class II–III rapids, offers plenty of excitement for novice and experienced rafters. Paddle trips permit the maximum participation of rafters. Many guests choose to refine their newly learned paddling skills by running the river again during the afternoon.

129. SQUAMISH RIVER, BRITISH COLUMBIA

Sections: Lower Elaho and Squamish
Location: Near Brackendale, north of Vancouver, southwest British Columbia
Distance: 17 miles (27 km)
Class: III–IV
Trip Options: Paddle raft, oar raft, paddle/oar raft; one day
Season: June–September
Outfitters: Sea to Sky Raft Tours
               Whistler River Adventures

Two hours north of Vancouver, the Squamish River, west of Garibaldi Provincial Park, provides first-time and experienced rafters an opportunity to see many of the glacier-laden peaks of British Columbia's coastal mountains.

The upper Squamish raft trip, which usually includes the last 2 miles (3 km) of the Elaho River, features the dynamic Class III–IV Big Wave and Steamroller rapids for those who don't mind a few splashes.

A Class I float trip on the lower Squamish offers families with young children frequent glimpses of bears, deer, and eagles. Its quiet waters are perfect for photographing the wildlife and spectacular mountains.

130. BABINE RIVER, BRITISH COLUMBIA

Section:	Below Salmonoid Project Weir to Kispiox Village or Hazelton
Location:	North of Smithers Lake, northern British Columbia
Distance:	95 miles (152 km)
Class:	II–IV
Trip Options:	Paddle/oar raft; four and five days
Season:	August–September
Outfitters:	Action River Expeditions
	Interior Whitewater Expeditions
	Silver Hilton Lodge
	Suskwa Adventure Outfitters

Nestled in the majestic Pacific Coast mountain ranges of northern British Columbia, the Babine River offers a superb four-day adventure featuring hiking, camping, and river rafting in an isolated wilderness environment. Beginning at Nilkitkwa Lake, 60 miles (95 km) of the Babine flows in view of the Babine and Atna mountain ranges.

The first three days of Babine's multiday raft trips include several Class II–III rapids and numerous opportunities to photograph the unspoiled wilderness and its eagles, moose, and grizzly bears. On day four, rafters journey through a narrow steep-walled canyon that creates the Babine's most exciting Class IV whitewater. Guests frequently see grizzlies feeding on salmon during the stretch. The final day is spent floating the larger Skeena River to the take-out at Kispiox Indian Village.

The Babine is usually run during August and September.

131. ILLECILLEWAET RIVER, BRITISH COLUMBIA

Section:	Albert Canyon (upper)
Location:	East of Revelstoke, eastern British Columbia
Distance:	7 miles (11 km)
Class:	III–IV
Trip Options:	Paddle rafts, paddle/oar rafts; one-and-one-half hour
Season:	June–August
Outfitter:	Alpine Rafting Company

From eastern British Columbia's famous Glacier National Park and Rogers Pass come the mountain waters of the beautiful Illecillewaet River. Near Canyon Hot Springs, the Tangier River, which originates in the Selkirk Mountains, joins the Illecillewaet, nearly doubling its size. On its westward journey to the Columbia River at the town of

Revelstoke, the river flows amidst an impressive rain forest-like environment with giant cedar trees.

The most popular Illecillewaet trip is the one-and-one-half-hour trip down the narrow Albert Canyon along the boundary of Revelstoke National Park. This Class III + trip, which begins at Canyon Hot Springs, 22 miles (35 km) east of Revelstoke on the Trans-Canada Highway, is not recommended for children under ten. Because of the frequency of the Albert Canyon trips, advance reservations are normally not necessary.

132. KICKING HORSE, BRITISH COLUMBIA

Sections: Upper and lower
Location: Yoho National Park to Golden, southeast British Columbia
Distance: 12 miles (19 km) (upper)
                 5 miles (8 km) (lower)
Class: II–III (upper)
                 III–IV + (lower)
Trip Options: Paddle/oar raft; half-day, one day
Season: May–September (upper)
                 August (lower)
Outfitters: Alpine Rafting Company
                 Clearwater Rafting Adventures
                 Glacier Raft Company–British Columbia
                 Hydra River Guides
                 Kootenay River Runners
                 Selkirk Tangiers

One of the Canadian Rockies' most popular whitewater rafting trips is on the scenic Kicking Horse River, west of Banff National Park. Rafting on the Kicking Horse, a tributary of the upper Columbia River, is primarily done on the upper section of the river. The Class II–III rapids of the upper river are not for children or timid first-time rafters. Some outfitters, however, offer a half-day scenic float trip on the moderate stretches of the Kicking Horse.

When water levels are just right, usually in August, outfitters will offer experienced rafters an exciting adventure on the lower Kicking Horse. The lower trip is preceded by a morning run of the upper Kicking Horse and the portage of an unrunnable Class V–VI rapid.

133. RED DEER RIVER, ALBERTA

Section: Upper
Location: Near Sundre, west-central Alberta
Distance: 36 miles (60 km) or less
Class: II–III
Trip Options: Paddle raft, oar raft, one and two days
Season: Mid-May–mid-September
Outfitters: Chinook River Sports
                   Hunter Valley Recreational Enterprises
                   Mirage Adventure Tours
                   Mukwah and Associates Adventure Bound Tours
                   Otter Rafting Adventures
                   Outdoor Adventure Centre
                   River Adventure Float Trips–Alberta
                   Riverbend White Water Rafting
                   WB Adventures

The Red Deer, which flows through the forested eastern slopes of the Canadian Rockies, is Alberta's most popular whitewater rafting river. The Red Deer's attraction can be attributed to its location near Banff and Jasper national parks, its proximity to Alberta's largest cities, and its stable and exciting whitewater. The Red Deer was twice the site of the Canadian whitewater championships.

The Red Deer's exciting whitewater consists of both pool drops and continuous stairstep ledges. Many of its more technical Class III–IV + rapids—Big Rock, First Ledge, Gooseberry Ledge, Jimbo's Staircase, National's Site, Cache Hill, and Double Ledge—require precise maneuvering by rafters.

The Red Deer's rafting season is from mid-May until mid-September. Its waters are always cold, and wet suits are highly recommended. Some outfitters provide transportation from Calgary, Red Deer, and Edmonton.

134. MALIGNE RIVER, ALBERTA

Section: Maligne Lake to Big Bend Campground
Location: Jasper National Park, west–central Alberta
Distance: 6 miles (9.5 km)
Class: II–III
Trip Options: Paddle raft; half-day
Season: June–July
Outfitters: Maligne River Adventures
                   Whitewater Rafting (Jasper)

In Jasper National Park, the Maligne River offers a rousing challenge to visitors looking for exciting whitewater. The trip begins at Maligne Lake, a glacial lake in the park's eastern Maligne Mountains, and drops continuously for nearly 6 miles (9.5 km) to its take-out at Big Bend Campground.

Paddle rafters must learn to work together and make quick reactions to a number of Class III rapids. Rafters must be at least sixteen years old.

Depending upon winter snowpack in the Rockies, the Maligne is normally run from four to eight weeks during the late spring and early summer.

135. ATHABASCA RIVER (Upper), ALBERTA

Section:	Falls
Location:	Jasper National Park, south of Jasper, west-central Alberta
Distance:	6 and 10 miles (9.5 and 16 km)
Class:	II–III
Trip Options:	Paddle raft, oar raft; one-half day
Season:	June–September
Outfitters:	Jasper Raft Tours
	Whitewater Rafting (Jasper)

The Athabasca River, which originates at the Columbia Icefield of western Alberta's Jasper National Park, provides a unique opportunity for visitors to enjoy some of the park's finest scenery.

Half-day raft trips beginning immediately below Athabasca Falls run for either 6 or 10 miles (9.5 or 16 km) downstream. Six to eight sets of moderate Class II–II + rapids leave plenty of calm stretches for guests to view the inspiring park environment and its varied wildlife.

Athabasca's easy waters can be enjoyed by everyone. Outfitters welcome first-time rafters and families with children as young as six years old on paddle-raft trips. There is no age restriction on oar-guided trips.

136. ATHABASCA RIVER, ALBERTA

Section:	House River to Fort McMurray
Location:	North of Edmonton, eastern Alberta
Distance:	125 miles (200 km)
Class:	II–IV +
Trip Options:	Oar raft; eight days
Season:	July–August
Outfitter:	Hunter Valley Recreational Enterprises

Adventurous rafters in Alberta may now follow the routes of early explorers such as Alexander MacKenzie and Peter Pond—routes that opened the Canadian Northwest. It is possible to recapture the spirit of the voyageurs, fur traders, and gold seekers on this voyage into the past.

The eight-day trip across Alberta's fascinating northern wilderness also allows time to explore the river banks and environs. Rafters may visit old settlements and deserted gas wells, and maybe even meet some trappers.

137. BOW RIVER, ALBERTA

Section: Banff National Park
Location: Town of Banff within Banff National Park, southwest
                  Alberta
Distance: 3 and 6 miles (5 and 9.5 km)
Class: I +
Trip Options: Paddle raft, oar raft; one-half hour, two hours.
Season: June–August
Outfitter: Rocky Mountain Raft Tours

One of the more popular new attractions for visitors to Banff National Park is a quiet raft journey on the Bow River.

Scenic float trips on the Bow enable guests to relax and enjoy the panoramic views of Rundle and Tunnel mountains. One-half-hour and two-hour trips leave Banff during mornings and afternoons. The Bow trip is especially popular with senior citizens and families with young children.

Section: Banff National Park boundary to Historic Deadman's
                  Flats
Location: Near Canmore, southwest Alberta
Distance: 8 miles (14 km)
Class: I–II
Trip Options: Paddle raft, oar raft; two to three hours
Season: May–September
Outfitter: Outdoor Adventure Centre

A second scenic float trip on the Bow River begins just east of Banff National Park. Families, senior citizens, and visitors of all ages may enjoy the magnificent view of Three Sisters Mountain on the Bow's easy waters between the park boundary and Canmore. Canmore hosted the nordic ski events during the 1988 Winter Olympics. A camera is a must to capture the splendor of the Rockies.

138. KANANASKIS RIVER, ALBERTA

Section:	Barrier Dam to Seebe Dam
Location:	East of Canmore, southwest Alberta
Distance:	6 to 10 miles (9.5 to 16 km)
Class:	I–III
Trip Options:	Paddle raft; two hours
Season:	May–September
Outfitters:	Hunter Valley Recreational Enterprises
	Mirage Adventure Tours
	Outdoor Adventure Centre

The Kananaskis River, in southwest Alberta's Kananaskis Region, features a popular one-half-day whitewater trip for first-timers and families. Easy rafting begins at Lusk Creek, 1.5-miles (2.5 km) downstream of Barrier Lake, and provides a good introduction to Class I–III whitewater rapids.

The trip's highlight is going through the National Site of the 1988 Canadian Kayak Championships. This 1.5-mile (2.5 km) stretch of intense whitewater through a narrow canyon was redesigned in the early 1980s to accommodate the kayaking community.

Below the canyon the trip continues through the eastern Rockies' foothills to the take-out at Seebe Dam. The very scenic trip takes about two hours.

139. HIGHWOOD RIVER, ALBERTA

Sections:	Upper and lower
Location:	Kanaanaskis Region near Longview, southwestern Alberta
Distance:	14 and 25 miles (22 and 40 km)
Class:	III–IV
Trip Options:	Paddle raft; one day
Season:	May–early July
Outfitter:	Chinook River Sports

Each spring the Highwood River, in the Rocky Mountain foothills of southwestern Alberta, offers hardy rafters some of the province's most continuous whitewater.

Highwood rafting trips are scheduled to coincide with maximum runoff conditions, which normally take place between May and early July. Of Highwood's numerous Class III–IV rapids, the Horseshoe, Toilet Bowl, Highwood Falls, and Pin Ball, are considered the best.

Highwood rafters are expected to be physically fit and able to swim. Wet suits are required.

140. GREAT SLAVE RIVER, ALBERTA–NORTHWEST TERRITORIES

Section:	Center
Location:	Southern Northwest Territories, Northern Alberta
Distance:	45 miles (72 km)
Difficulty:	I–V; rafting experience desired on some sections
Trip Options:	Paddle/oar raft, oar raft; half-day to six days
Season:	June–August
Outfitter:	Subarctic Wilderness Adventures

Once a barrier to the birch-bark craft of the fur trade, the Great Slave River near the border of Alberta and the Northwest Territories has become an exciting passageway of adventure. Here, between Fort Fitzgerald in Alberta and Fort Smith in Northwest Territories, the age-old granite-sculptured waterway provides both calm waters and whitewaters suitable for everyone from novice to senior citizen.

Each summer, more and more people discover that running either the gentle or more rugged waters of the unspoiled Great Slave is an unusual way to experience an exciting sense of history in this gateway to the subarctic. Rafters may choose between very easy Class I–II flatwater one-half- and one-day trips or more difficult multiday whitewater trips. All four major raftable granite ledges, gorges, and chutes of the Great Slave—Cassette, Pelican, Mountain, and Drowned—are run and/or admired in awe.

The Great Slave has many picturesque waterfalls, thickly wooded inlets, and sandy beaches—idea for shoreline island camping. An exciting diversion from multiday river trips is a venture by vehicle and foot to Wood Buffalo National Park's Boreal Forest and the Interior (Salt) Plains.

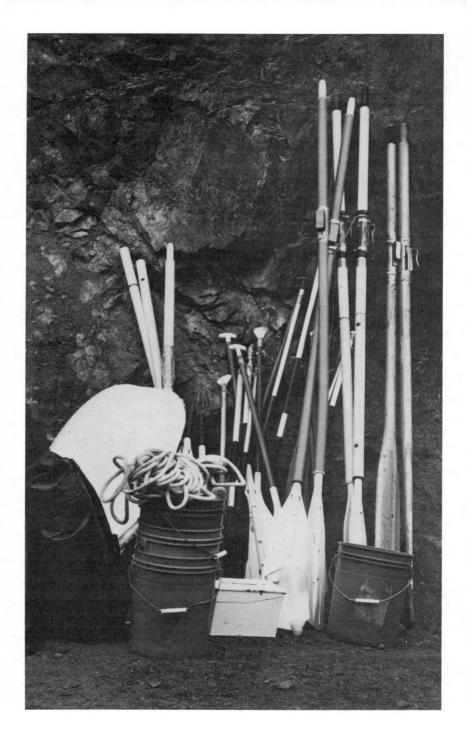

CHAPTER 8

Professional Outfitters

THE IMPORTANCE OF USING THE SERVICES of competent professional outfitters on swift-flowing whitewater rivers cannot be overemphasized.

Professional outfitters are experienced in whitewater rafting and should be completely familiar with the rivers they run. Some outfitters and guides are better prepared than others and extend a greater effort to provide enjoyable and safe rafting experiences. The safety record for commercial outfitters on western whitewater rivers is excellent. Other than occasional minor scrapes and bruises from rocks, injuries are rare during whitewater trips.

Outfitters must be licensed by states and provinces, the United States Forest Service, the Bureau of Land Management, the National Park Service, and even local authorities if there is a passage through such lands. Many outfitters also belong to various river safety and conservation associations and organizations.

Most outfitters in the western United States and Canada are members of both national and regional river organizations focused on promoting safety on rivers, maintaining the quality of the river trip experience, and preserving the wilderness and wildlife areas. The largest of these organizations is the Western River Guides Association, with more than two hundred members in the United States. In Canada the largest provincial rafting associations are the Professional River Outfitters Association of Alberta and the River Outfitters Association of British Columbia.

A brief description of the duties and responsibilities of professional whitewater rafting outfitters may be helpful in planning your upcoming rafting trip.

The outfitter is responsible for accurately advertising, promoting, and scheduling river trips. Outfitters must also ensure adequate guide preparation and safety training. They must maintain all equipment, including rafts, life jackets, paddles, helmets, and any company vehicles needed to transport rafters to or from the put-in or take-out. It is the outfitters who must decide when river water levels are either too high or too low to be run safely and who should or should not be permitted to participate in a trip because of age or physical limitations.

On the more popular rivers, rafters may choose from several outfitters. Write or call several of them. Study their brochures carefully. How quickly did they respond? How long have they been in business? Do they belong to river-safety and conservation organizations? Are they licensed? What aspects of river running do they emphasize? You also may wish to rely on the recommendations of friends who have rafted the river. Ask the outfitter for the names of people in your area to whom you can talk.

As you run a river, you may want to watch for a few points to help you evaluate the outfitter's performance: Was the orientation briefing informative and complete? Did the outfitter have an adequate number of responsible guides who were concerned about safety? Were the guides concerned about your personal comfort and enjoyment, or were the rafts overcrowded? Were swimming and horseplay permitted in or near rapids or unsafe areas? Was the transportation to or from the river carefully planned and executed to avoid unnecessary delays?

Outfitters appreciate receiving feedback from rafting customers. If the guides have done a good job, take time to write the outfitter a short note of appreciation. Likewise, if an essential part of a river trip was lacking or inadequate, politely bring this to the attention of the outfitter. Your comments, criticisms, and suggestions will help outfitters provide better river trips.

Although this book lists the names and addresses of nearly five hundred professional whitewater rafting outfitters in western America, it is not a complete list. The inclusion or omission of any outfitter should not be considered an endorsement or rejection.

ABEC'S ADVENTURE PADDLE-RAFTING
1304 Westwick Dr., Fairbanks, AK 99712
(907) 457–8907
Rivers: Brooks Range (east, central, west)

A.B.L.E. RAFTING COMPANY
P.O. Box 18, Coloma, CA 95613
(916) 626–6208
Rivers: American (South, Middle, North forks), California Salmon, Klamath (upper and lower), Merced, Scott, Stanislaus (North, Middle forks), Wooley

ACCESS TO ADVENTURE
P.O. Box 2014, Woodland, CA 95695
(800) 441-9463; (916) 662-7296
Rivers: American (South, Middle, North forks), Carson (East Fork)

ACQUIRED TASTES
2053 Yarmouth, Boulder, CO 80301
(303) 443-4120
Rivers: Arkansas, Colorado (upper)

ACTION ADVENTURES WET 'N WILD
P.O. Box 13846, Sacramento, CA 95853
(800) ADVENTU(re) (inside California); (916) 641-6676
Rivers: American (South, Middle, North forks), Carson (East
    Fork), Tuolumne

ACTION RIVER EXPEDITIONS
5389 S.E. Marine Dr., Burnaby, B.C. Canada V5J 3G7
(604) 437-6679
Rivers: Babine, Cheakamus, Chilko, Chilcotin, Chilliwack,
    Nahatlatch, Taseko, Thompson

ACTION WHITEWATER ADVENTURES
P.O. Box 1634, Provo, UT 84603
(800) 453-1482; (801) 375-4111
Rivers: American (South, Middle, North forks), Salmon (main,
    Middle Fork)

ADRIFT ADVENTURES
1816 Orchard Pl., Fort Collins, CO 80521
(800) 824-0150; (303) 493-4005
Rivers: Arkansas, Cache la Poudre, Colorado (upper, Professor
    Valley), Dolores, Green (Dinosaur), North Platte, Yampa

ADRIFT ADVENTURES IN CANYONLANDS
P.O. Box 577, Moab, UT 84532
(800) 874-4483; (801) 259-8594
Rivers: Colorado (Cataract)

ADVENTURE ALASKA-MEXICO
1231 Sundance Loop, Fairbanks, AK 99709
(907) 452-1821
Rivers: Brooks Range (east, central, west)

ADVENTURE BOUND
2392 H Rd. Grand Junction, CO 81505
(800) 423–4668; (303) 241–5633
Rivers: Colorado (Westwater, Cataract), Green (Dinosaur, Desolation), Yampa

THE ADVENTURE COMPANY
P.O. Box 3876, Breckenridge, CO 80424
(303) 453–0747
Rivers: Arkansas, Blue, Eagle, Colorado (upper)

ADVENTURE CONNECTION
P.O. Box 475, Coloma, CA 95613
(800) 556–6060 (outside California); (916) 626–7385
Rivers: American (South, Middle, North forks), Kaweah, Klamath (upper), Stanislaus (lower)

ADVENTURE DISCOVERY TOURS
319 N. Humphrey, Flagstaff, AZ 86001
(602) 774–1926; (602) 774–6828
River: San Juan

ADVENTURE RIVER EXPEDITIONS
P.O. Box 2133, Salt Lake City, UT 84110
(800) 331–3324; (801) 943–0320
Rivers: Colorado, (Professor Valley, Westwater, Cataract), Green (Desolation)

ADVENTURES IN RAFTING
P.O. Box 2447, Vail, CO 81658
(800) 247–7074; (303) 476–7576
Rivers: Arkansas, Colorado (upper, Glenwood), Eagle

ADVENTURES UNLIMITED
5201 S. Quebec St., Englewood, CO 81505
(719) 395–2468
River: Arkansas

ADVENTURES WEST
P.O. Box 2768, St. George, UT 84771
(801) 628–9378
River: Colorado (Grand Canyon)

ADVENTURES WHITEWATER
P.O. Box 321, Yreka, CA 96097
(916) 842–4667; (503) 482–0667
Rivers: California Salmon, Scott

AGGIPAH RIVER TRIPS
P.O. Box 425, Salmon, ID 83467
(208) 756–4167
Rivers: Salmon (Middle Fork, main)

ALASKA DISCOVERY
369 S. Franklin St., Juneau, AK 99801
(907) 586–1911
Rivers: Alsek–Tatshenshini, Brooks Range (east)

ALASKA FISH AND TRAILS UNLIMITED
1177 Shypoke Dr., Fairbanks, AK 99709
(907) 479-7630
Rivers: Brooks Range (central, west)

ALASKA FLOAT TRIPS
P.O. Box 140264, Anchorage, AK 99514
(907) 333–4442
Rivers: Brooks Range (central, west), Chitina–Copper, Talkeetna

ALASKA RAFTING ADVENTURES
P.O. Box 295, Talkeetna, AK 99676
(907) 733–2681
River: Talkeetna

ALASKA RIVER ADVENTURES
1831 Kuskokwim St., Anchorage, AK 99508
(907) 276–3418
Rivers: Brooks Range (east, central, west), Chitina–Copper, Talkeetna

ALASKA WILDERNESS GROUP
4341 MacAlister Dr., Anchorage, AK 99515
(907) 243-3068
Rivers: Brooks Range (east), Copper, Talkeetna

ALL-OUTDOORS ADVENTURE TRIPS
2151 San Miguel Dr., Walnut Creek, CA 94596
(415) 932-8993
Rivers: American (South, Middle, North forks), California Salmon, Klamath (upper, lower), Merced, Scott, Stanislaus, Tuolumne

ALL SEASONS GUIDE SERVICE
1360 Sunny Glen Way, Sunny Valley, OR 97526
(503) 479-1081
Rivers: Illinois, Rogue

ALPINE RAFTING COMPANY
P.O. Box 1409, Golden, BC, Canada V0A 1H0
(800) 663-7080 (USA); (604) 344-5016
Rivers: Illecillewaet, Kicking Horse

AMERICAN ADVENTURE EXPEDITIONS
P.O. Box 1549, Buena Vista, CA 81211
(800) 288-0675; (719) 539-6829 (Nov.–Mar.)
Rivers: Animas, Arkansas, Colorado (upper), Gunnison, Piedra

AMERICAN RIVER RECREATION
11257 South Bridge St., Rancho Cordova, CA 95670
(800) 333-7238; (916) 635-4479
Rivers: American (South, Middle, North forks), California Salmon, Carson (East Fork), Klamath (upper)

AMERICAN RIVER TOURING ASSOCIATION
Star Route 73, Groveland, CA 95321
(800) 323-2782; (209) 962-7873
Rivers: American (South, Middle, North forks), California Salmon, Green (Desolation), Illinois, Klamath (upper, lower), Merced, Rogue, Salmon (Middle Fork, main), Selway, Tuolumne, Yampa

ANDERSON CAMPS
7177 Colorado River Rd., Gypsum, CO 81637
(303) 524-7766
Rivers: Colorado (upper, Westwater), Green (Desolation), Yampa

ANDERSON RIVER ADVENTURES
Route 2, Box 192, Milton-Freewater, OR 97862
(800) 624–7583; (503) 558–3629
Rivers: Grande Ronde, Snake (Hells Canyon)

ARCTIC TREKS
P.O. Box 73452, Fairbanks, AK 99707
(907) 455–6502
Rivers: Brooks Range (east, central, west)

ARIZONA RAFT ADVENTURES
4050 E. Huntington Dr., Flagstaff, AZ 86004
(602) 526–8200
River: Colorado (Grand Canyon)

ARIZONA RIVER RUNNERS
P.O. Box 47788, Phoenix, AZ 85068
(602) 867–4866
River: Colorado (Grand Canyon)

ARKANSAS RIVER TOURS/OLTS
P.O. Box 20281, Denver, CO 80220
(800) 331–7238; (303) 333–7831
Rivers: Arkansas, Colorado (upper), Dolores, Gunnison (Gorge),
North Platte, Rio Grande–NM

ARKANSAS VALLEY EXPEDITIONS
P.O. Box 100, 944 East Hwy. 50, Salida, CO 81201
(800) 833–7238; (719) 539–6669
River: Arkansas

ARTEMIS WILDERNESS TOURS
P.O. Box 1178, Taos, NM 87571
(505) 758–2203
Rivers: Dolores, Rio Chama, Rio Grande–NM

BARKER-EWING RAFT TRIPS
P.O. Box 3032, Jackson, WY 83001
(307) 733–1000
Rivers: Salmon (main), Snake (upper)

BARKER-EWING SCENIC TOURS
P.O. Box 100, Moose, WY 83012
(307) 733–1800
River: Snake (upper)

BARKER RIVER TRIPS
2124 Grelle, Lewiston, ID 83501
(208) 743–7459
Rivers: Grande Ronde, Salmon (lower), Snake (Hells Canyon)

BEAMER'S HELLS CANYON TOURS
P.O. Box 1223, Lewiston, ID 83501
(208) 743–4800
River: Snake (Hells Canyon)

BEAR VALLEY RIVER COMPANY
3000 Lake Harbor, Boise, ID 83703
(208) 378–0615
River: Payette

BEAVER STATE ADVENTURES
4430 Laverne Ave., Klamath Falls, OR 97603
(503) 884-7587
River: Rogue

BETTLES LODGE WILDERNESS TRIPS
P.O. Box 27, Bettles, AK 99726
(907) 692–5111
Rivers: Brooks Range (central, west)

BEYOND LIMITS ADVENTURES
P.O. Box 4833, Davis, CA 95617
(916) 758–9270
Rivers: American (South, Middle, North forks), Carson (East
Fork), California Salmon, Klamath (upper, lower), Scott,
Stanislaus, Trinity, Yuba (North Fork)

BIG BEND RIVER TOURS
P.O. Box 317, Lajitas, TX 79852
(800) 545–4240; (915) 424–3219
River: Rio Grande–TX

BIGHORN EXPEDITIONS
P.O. Box 365, Bellvue, CO 80512
(303) 221–8110
Rivers: Dolores, Green (Desolation)

BIG RIVER RAFT TRIPS
Box 9B Pilar Route, Taos, NM 87571
(505) 471–5636
River: Rio Grande–NM

BIG TUJUNGA/WILD GOOSE RIVER TOURS
P.O. Box 2814, Durango, CO 81302
(303) 385–4675; (303) 259–4453
River: Animas

BILL DVORAK'S RAFT & KAYAK EXPEDITIONS
17921 Hwy. 285, Nathrop, CO 81236
(800) 824–3795 (inside Colorado); (303) 539–6851
Rivers: Arkansas, Colorado (Westwater), Dolores, Eagle, Green
(Desolation), Gunnison (Gorge), North Platte, Rio Chama,
Rio Grande–NM

BLAZING PADDLES RIVER RAFTING
Snowmass Whitewater
P.O. Box 5929, Snowmass Village, CO 81615
(303) 923–4544
Rivers: Arkansas, Colorado (Glenwood), Dolores, Roaring Fork

BLUE SKY ADVENTURES
P.O. Box 1566, Glenwood Springs, CO 81601
(303) 945–6605
River: Colorado (Glenwood)

BLUE SKY OUTFITTERS
740 Third Ave., S.E., Pacific, WA 98047
(206) 931–0637
Rivers: Klickitat, Methow, Nooksack, Skagit, Skykomish, Suiattle,
    Tieton, Wenatchee, White Salmon

BOULDER OUTDOOR CENTER
2510 N. 47th St., Boulder, CO 80301
(303) 444–8420
Rivers: Arkansas, Cache La Poudre, Clear Creek, Dolores

BRIGGS ROGUE RIVER GUIDE SERVICE
2750 Cloverlawn Dr., Grants Pass, OR 97527
(503) 476–2941; (503) 479–1504
River: Rogue

BROOKS RANGE WILDERNESS TRIPS
P.O. Box 48, Bettles, AK 99727
(907) 692–5312
Rivers: Brooks Range (east, central)

BROWN'S RAFTING
45045 U.S. Hwy. 50, Canon City, CO 81212
(719) 275–5161
River: Arkansas

BUFFALO JOE RIVER TRIPS
P.O. Box 1526, Buena Vista, CO 81211
(800) 356–7984; (719) 395–8757
Rivers: Arkansas, Dolores

BUGGYWHIPS FISH & FLOAT SERVICE
P.O. Box 770479, Steamboat Springs, CO 80477
(303) 879-8033; (303) 759-0343
Rivers: Arkansas, Blue, Eagle, North Platte, Roaring Fork

CACHE CANYON RIVER TRIPS
P.O. Box 34, Rumsey, CA 95679
(916) 796–3091
River: Cache Creek

CALIFORNIA ADVENTURES
2301 Bancroft Ave., Berkeley, CA 94720
(415) 642–4000
Rivers: American (South Fork), Carson (East Fork), Klamath
(lower)

CALIFORNIA RIVER TRIPS
P.O. Box 460, Lotus, CA 95651
(916) 626–8006
Rivers: American (South, Middle, North forks), Carson (East Fork)

CANADIAN RIVER EXPEDITIONS
845 Chilco St., Suite 401, Vancouver, BC, Canada V6G 2R2
(604) 738-4449
Rivers: Alsek–Tatshenshini, Chilcotin, Chilko, Fraser

CANYONEERS
P.O. Box 2997, Flagstaff, AZ 86003
(800) 525–0924 (outside Arizona); (602) 526–0924
River: Colorado (Grand Canyon)

CANYON EXPLORATIONS
P.O. Box 310, Flagstaff, AZ 86002
(602) 774–4559; (602) 774–4655
River: Colorado (Grand Canyon)

CANYON OUTFITTERS
519 S. 5th St., Jefferson, OR 97352
(503) 327–2016
Rivers: Deschutes, Snake (Hells Canyon)

CANYONS INCORPORATED
P.O. Box 823, McCall, ID 83638
(208) 634-4303
Rivers: Payette, Salmon (Middle Fork, main)

CASCADE RAFT COMPANY
P.O. Box 6, Garden Valley, ID 83622
(208) 462-3292
River: Payette

CHILI BAR OUTDOOR CENTER (CBOC)
P.O. Box 554, Coloma, CA 95613
(800) 356-CBOC; (916) 621-1236
Rivers: American (South, Middle, North forks)

CHILKAT GUIDES
P.O. Box 170, Haines, AK 99827
(907) 766-2409; (907) 766-2491
River: Alsek-Tatshenshini

CHINOOK RIVER SPORTS
341 10th Ave., S.W., Calgary, AB, Canada T2R 0A5
(403) 263-RAFT
Rivers: Highwood, Red Deer

CHUCK RICHARD'S WHITEWATER
Box W.W. Whitewater, Lake Isabella, CA 93240
(619) 379-4685
River: Kern

CIMARRON OUTDOORS
HC 60 Box 62, Idleyld Park, OR 97447
(503) 498-2235
River: North Umpqua

CLEARWATER EXPEDITIONS
613 Bissette Rd., Kamloops, BC, Canada V2B 6L3
(604) 579-8360
Rivers: Chilcotin, Chilko, Clearwater, Taseko, Thompson

CLEARWATER RAFTING ADVENTURES
116 Midridge Close, Calgary, AB, Canada T2X 1G1
(403) 256-6514
Rivers: Chilko, Kicking Horse

CODY RAPID TRANSIT
1370 Sheridan, Cody, WY 82414
(307) 587–3535
River: Shoshone

COLORADO ADVENTURES
P.O. Box 851, Steamboat Springs, CO 80477
(303) 879-2039
River: Colorado (upper)

COLORADO MOUNTAIN EXPRESS
P.O. Box 580, Vail, CO 81658
(800) 525–6363; (303) 949–4227
Rivers: Arkansas, Eagle, Colorado (upper)

COLORADO OUTWARD BOUND SCHOOL
945 Pennsylvania St., Denver, CO 80203
(303) 837–0880
Rivers: Colorado (Cataract), Green (Desolation), San Juan, Yampa

COLORADO RECREATION SPECIALISTS
2263 South Beech Way, Lakewood, CO 80228
(303) 986–2578
Rivers: Arkansas, Colorado (Glenwood), Eagle, Roaring Fork

COLORADO RIFF RAFT
P.O. Box 4949, Aspen, CO 81612
(303) 925–5405
Rivers: Arkansas, Eagle, Colorado (Glenwood), Roaring Fork

COLORADO RIVER & TRAIL EXPEDITIONS
P.O. Box 7575, Salt Lake City, UT 84157
(801) 261-1789
Rivers: Alsek–Tatshenshini, Colorado (Westwater, Cataract, Grand Canyon), Green (Desolation)

COLORADO RIVER RUNS
Star Route Box 32, Bond, CO 80423
(800) 826–1081 (inside Colorado); (303) 653–4292
Rivers: Arkansas, Colorado (upper), Eagle

COLORADO RIVERS-TOURS
P.O. Box 1386, Durango, CO 80301
(303) 259–0708; (303) 259–3493
Rivers: Animas, Dolores

COOLEY RIVER EXPEDITIONS
1230 Pulver Ln. N.W., Albany, OR 97321
(503) 967–8722
Rivers: Deschutes, Klamath (lower), Owyhee–OR, Salmon (Lower)

CRAZY MOUNTAIN RAFT
P.O. Box 216, Emigrant, MT 59027
(406) 333–4779
River: Yellowstone

CRESTED BUTTE RAFTING
309 6th St., Crested Butte, CO 81224
(800) 445–6639; (303) 349–7423
Rivers: Arkansas, Gunnison, Gunnison (Lake Fork), Slate, Taylor

CURTISS OUTFITTERS
326 Bench Dr., Kalispell, MT 59901
(406) 257–6215
River: Flathead (South Fork)

CUSTOM RIVER TOURS
P.O. Box 7071, Boise, ID 83707
(208) 343–3343
River: Salmon (Middle Fork)

DAVE HANSEN WHITEWATER
P.O. Box 328, Jackson, WY 83001
(307) 733–6295
River: Snake (upper)

DAVE HELFRICH RIVER OUTFITTER
47555 McKenzie Hwy., Vida, OR 97488
(503) 896–3786
Rivers: Rogue, Salmon (Middle Fork, main, lower)

DAVIS WHITEWATER EXPEDITIONS
P.O. Box 86, Winnemucca, NV 89445
(702) 623–2048
Rivers: Owyhee–OR, Snake (Hells Canyon)

DEAN HELFRICH GUIDE SERVICE
2415 N. 17th Pl., Springfield, OR 97477
(503) 747–8401
Rivers: McKenzie, Owyhee–OR, Rogue, Salmon (Middle Fork, main, lower)

DEER HILL SUMMER EXPEDITIONS
P.O. Box 180, Mancos, CO 81328
(303) 533–7492
Rivers: Dolores, Colorado (Horsethief)

DENALI RAFT ADVENTURES
Denali National Park, AK 99755
(907) 683–2234
River: Nenana

DENNIS BRANDSMA OUTFITTERS
P.O. Box 7052, Eugene, OR 97401
(503) 747–6487
Rivers: Deschutes, McKenzie

DESCENT RIVER EXPEDITIONS
321 North Main, Phoenix, AZ 85068
(800) 477–7238; (602) 867–4866
Rivers: Dolores, Colorado (Westwater, Cataract)

DESERT VOYAGERS
P.O. Box 9053, Scottsdale, AZ 85252
(800) 222–RAFT; (602) 998–RAFT
Rivers: Salt, Verde

DIAMOND R GUEST RANCH
P.O. Box 1419; Kalispell, MT 59903
(406) 752–4076
River: Flathead (South Fork)

DIAMOND RIVER ADVENTURES
P.O. Box 1316, Page, AZ 86040
(602) 645–8866
River: Colorado (Grand Canyon)

DICK HELFRICH OUTFITTERS
47611 McKenzie Hwy., Vida, OR 97488
(503) 896–0015
Rivers: McKenzie, Owyhee–OR, Salmon (Middle Fork)

DISCOVERY RIVER EXPEDITIONS
P.O. Box 465, Riggins, ID 83549
(208) 628–3319
River: Salmon (lower)

DON FERGUSON'S WHITEWATER RAFTING
1280 Ithaca Dr., Boulder, CO 80303
(303) 494–0824
River: Arkansas

DON HATCH RIVER EXPEDITIONS
P.O. Box 1150, 219 N. 400 E., Vernal, UT 84078
(800) 342–8243 (outside Utah); (801) 789–4316
Rivers: Green (Dinosaur), Colorado (Cataract), Salmon (Middle
Fork), Yampa

DON NEFF RIVER COMPANY
2021 North White Circle, Salt Lake City, UT 84109
(801) 467–5356
Rivers: Green (Dinosaur, Desolation), Yampa

DOWNSTREAM RIVER RUNNERS
12112 N.E. 195th, Bothell, WA 98011
(800) 732–RAFT; (206) 483–0335
Rivers: Grande Ronde, Green–WA, Klickitat, Methow, Nooksack,
Owyhee–OR, Sauk, Skagit, Skykomish, Suiattle, Tieton,
Wenatchee, White Salmon

DURANGO RIVERTRIPPERS
720 Main Ave., Durango, CO 81301
(303) 259–0289
Rivers: Animas, Dolores

EAGLE RIVER WHITEWATER
P.O. Box 3481, Vail, CO 81658
(303) 476–7487
Rivers: Arkansas, Colorado (upper), Eagle

EAGLE SUN
P.O. Box 611, Ashland, OR 97520
(503) 482–5139
Rivers: California Salmon, Klamath (upper), Rogue, Scott

EARTHTREK EXPEDITIONS
1534 E. Edinger, Suite 6, Santa Ana, CA 92705
(800) 544–TREK (inside California); (714) 547–5864
Rivers: American (South, Middle, North forks), Merced

ECHO CANYON RIVER EXPEDITIONS
45000 U.S. Hwy. 50, Canon City, CO 81212
(719) 275–3154; (719) 632–3684
Rivers: Arkansas, Dolores, Gunnison (Lake Fork, Gorge), Piedra,
    San Miguel

ECHO: THE WILDERNESS COMPANY
6529 Telegraph Ave., Oakland, CA 94609
(415) 652–1600
Rivers: American (South, North forks), California Salmon, Rogue,
    Salmon (Middle Fork, main), Tuolumne

ECOSUMMER YUKON EXPEDITIONS
P.O. Box 5095, Whitehorse, YK, Canada Y1A 4Z2
(403) 633–2742
Rivers: Alsek–Tatshenshini

ELECTRIC RAFTING COMPANY
P.O. Box 3456, Eureka, CA 95501
(707) 445-3456
Rivers: California Salmon, Klamath (lower), Trinity

ELWOOD MASONER'S WHITEWATER ADVENTURES
P.O. Box 184, Twin Falls, ID 83303
(208) 733–4548
River: Selway

ENVIRONMENTAL TRAVELLING COMPANIONS (E.T.C.)
Fort Mason Center, Building C, Room 360, San Francisco,
    CA 94123
(415) 474-7662
Rivers: American (South Fork), Carson (East Fork), Klamath
    (lower)

EPLEY'S WHITEWATER ADVENTURES
P.O. Box 987, McCall, ID 83638
(800) 233–1813 (inside Idaho); (208) 634–5173
River: Salmon (lower)

ESTES PARK ADVENTURES
P.O. Box 2924, Estes Park, CO 80517
(303) 586–2303
Rivers: Arkansas, Cache la Poudre, Colorado (upper)

EXODUS WHITEWATER ADVENTURES
3830 S.W. Country Club Dr., Corvallis, OR 97333
(503) 754–1010
Rivers: Deschutes, Grande Ronde, Klickitat, McKenzie,
  Owyhee–OR, White Salmon

EXPEDITIONS
625 North Beaver St., Flagstaff, AZ 86001
(602) 774–8176; (602) 779–3769
River: Colorado (Grand Canyon)

FAR-FLUNG ADVENTURES
P.O. Box 31, Terlingua, TX 79852
(800) 359–4138; (915) 371–2489
Rivers: Arkansas, Gunnison (Gorge), Rio Chama, Rio
  Grande–NM, Rio Grande–TX, Salt

FLAGG RANCH FLOAT TRIPS
South Gate of Yellowstone, P.O. Box 187, Moran, WY 83013
(800) 443–2311; (307) 543–2545
River: Snake (upper)

FLEXIBLE FLYERS
2344 CR 225, Durango, CO 81301
(303) 247–4628; (303) 385–7336
Rivers: Animas (lower), Arkansas

FORT JACKSON FLOAT TRIPS
310 West Broadway, Jackson WY 83001
(307) 733–2583
River: Snake (upper)

FOUR CORNERS EXPEDITIONS
P.O. Box 1032, Buena Vista, CO 81211
(800) 332–7238; (719) 395–8949 (Sept.–Apr.)
Rivers: Arkansas, Dolores

FRASER RIVER RAFT EXPEDITIONS
P.O. Box 10, Yale, BC, Canada V0K 2S0
(604) 863–2336
Rivers: Chilliwack, Fraser, Nahatlatch, Thompson

FRONTIER RIVER ADVENTURES
927 Fairfield Rd., North Vancouver, BC, Canada V7H 2J4
(604) 929–7612
Rivers: Fraser, Thompson

GALICE RESORT AND STORE
11744 Galice Rd., Galice, OR 97532
(503) 476–3818
River: Rogue

GEORGIE'S ROYAL RIVER RATS
P.O. Box 12057, Las Vegas, NV 89112
(702) 798–0602
River: Colorado (Grand Canyon)

GEO TOURS
2515 South Fillmore, Denver, CO 80210
(303) 756–6070
Rivers: Arkansas, Colorado (upper)

GLACIER RAFT COMPANY
P.O. Box 218, West Glacier, MT 59936
(406) 888–5454
Rivers: Flathead (North and Middle forks, lower), Lochsa

GLACIER RAFT COMPANY–BRITISH COLUMBIA
P.O. Box 428, Golden, BC, Canada V0A 1H0
(604) 344–6521
River: Kicking Horse

GLACIER WILDERNESS GUIDES
P.O. Box 535, West Glacier, MT 59936
(406) 888–5333
River: Flathead (North and Middle forks, lower)

GO-FOR-IT WHITEWATER ADVENTURES
P.O. Box 2625, Portland, OR 97208
(503) 645–4337; (503) 645–7768
Rivers: Clackamas, Deschutes, Grande Ronde, John Day,
　　　　McKenzie, North Santiam

Photo courtesy of ECHO: The Wilderness Company/Dick Linford

GOLD COUNTRY RIVER RUNNERS
P.O. Box 477, Coloma, CA 95613
(916) 626–7326
River: American (South Fork)

GOLD RUSH RIVER RUNNERS
P.O. Box 1013, Diamond Springs, CA 95619
(800) 344–1013; (916) 626–7631
River: American (South Fork)

GRAND CANYON DORIES
P.O. Box 216, Altaville, CA 95221
(209) 736–0805
River: Colorado (Grand Canyon)

GRAND CANYON EXPEDITIONS
P.O. Box O, Kanab, UT 84741
(800) 544–2691; (801) 644–2691
River: Colorado (Grand Canyon)

GRAND TETON LODGE COMPANY
P.O. Box 240, Moran, WY 83013
(307) 543–2811
River: Snake (upper)

GREAT NORTHERN WHITEWATER
P.O. Box 278, West Glacier, MT 59936
(800) 535–0303 (inside Montana); (406) 387–5340
River: Flathead (Middle Fork, lower)

GREAT OUT OF DOORS
Whitewater Rafting
16475 Julie Ln., Red Bluff, CA 96080
(916) 527–1417
Rivers: California Salmon, Sacramento (upper), Trinity

GREAT VALLEY CANOE AND RAFT TRIPS
3213 Sierra St., Riverbank, CA 95367
(209) 869–1235
Rivers: Mokelumne, Stanislaus (lower)

GREENWOOD OUTFITTERS
58214 E. Marmot Rd., Sandy, OR 97055
(503) 622–3385
River: Deschutes

GUNNISON RIVER EXPEDITIONS
P.O. Box 604, Montrose, CO 81419
(303) 249–4441
River: Gunnison (Gorge)

HATCH RIVER EXPEDITIONS
411 E. 2nd N., Vernal, UT 84078
(800) 433–8966; (801) 789–3813
River: Colorado (Grand Canyon)

HAULAPAI TRIBAL RIVER TRIPS
P.O. Box 246, Peach Springs, AZ 86434
(800) 622–4409 (outside Arizona); (602) 769–2209
River: Colorado (Grand Canyon below Diamond Creek)

HEADWATERS RIVER ADVENTURES
P.O. Box 1086, Ashland, OR 97520
(503) 488–0583
Rivers: Klamath (upper), Owyhee–OR, Trinity

HEART SIX GUEST RANCH FLOAT TRIPS
P.O. Box 70, Jackson Hole, WY 83013
(307) 543–2477
River: Snake (Upper)

HELLS CANYON ADVENTURES
P.O. Box 159, Oxbow, OR 97840
(800) HCA–FLOT (outside Oregon); (503) 785–3352
River: Snake (Hells Canyon)

HIGH ADVENTURE RIVER TOURS
P.O. Box 222, Twin Falls, ID 83303
(208) 733–0123
River: Snake (middle)

HIGHLANDS RAFTING COMPANY
4402 Cheyenne, Laramie, WY 82070
(307) 742–2294
River: North Platte

HIGH TIMES RAFTING
Baskin High Times Tours, P.O. Box 905, Steamboat Springs,
 CO 80488
(303) 879–8153
Rivers: Colorado (upper, Glenwood), Eagle

HOLIDAY RIVER EXPEDITIONS
544 East 3900 S., Salt Lake City, UT 84107
(800) 624–6323 (outside Utah); (801) 266–2087
Rivers: Colorado (Westwater, Cataract), Green (Dinosaur,
 Desolation), San Juan, Yampa

HOLIDAY RIVER EXPEDITIONS–IDAHO
P.O. Box 86, Grangeville, ID 83530
(208) 983–1518; (208) 983–2299
Rivers: Lochsa, Salmon (main, lower), Snake (Hells Canyon)

HONDOO RIVER & TRAILS
P.O. Box 98, Torrey, UT 84775
(801) 564–3369 (summer); (801) 425–3519
River: Green (Desolation)

HUGHES RIVER EXPEDITIONS
P.O. Box 217, Cambridge, ID 83610
(208) 257–3477
Rivers: Jarbidge–Bruneau, Owyhee–ID, Owyhee–OR, Salmon
(Middle Fork, lower), Snake (Hells Canyon)

HUMPBACK CHUB RIVER TOURS
P.O. Box 1109, Dolores, CO 81323
(303) 882–7940
Rivers: Colorado (Horsethief, Westwater), Dolores

HUNTER VALLEY RECREATIONAL ENTERPRISES
P.O. Box 1620, Canmore, AB, Canada T0L 0M0
(403) 678–2000
Rivers: Athabasca, Kananaskis, Red Deer

HYAK WILDERNESS ADVENTURES
1958 W. 4th Ave., Vancouver, BC, Canada V6J 2M5
(604) 734–8622
Rivers: Chilcotin, Chilko, Chilliwack, Thompson

HYDRA RIVER GUIDES
P.O. Box 2708, Banff, AB, Canada T0L 0C0
(403) 762–4554
River: Kicking Horse

IDAHO ADVENTURES RIVER TRIPS
P.O. Box 834, Salmon, ID 83467
(208) 756–2986
Rivers: Owyhee–OR, Salmon (Middle Fork, main, lower), Snake
(Hells Canyon)

IDAHO AFLOAT
P.O. Box 542, Grangeville, ID 83530
(208) 983–2414
River: Snake (Hells Canyon)

IDAHO GUIDE SERVICE
P.O. Box 1230, Sun Valley, ID 83303
(208) 734–8872
Rivers: Owyhee–ID, Salmon (lower), Snake (Birds of Prey, middle)

INDEPENDENT WHITEWATER
23850 South Hwy. 285, Buena Vista, CO 81211
(719) 395-2642
River: Arkansas

INTERIOR WHITEWATER EXPEDITIONS
P.O. Box 129, Celista, BC, Canada V0E 1L0
(604) 955-2447
Rivers: Adams, Alsek–Tatshenshini, Babine, Clearwater, Thompson

JACKSON HOLE WHITEWATER
650 W. Broadway, Jackson, WY 83001
(307) 733-1007
River: Snake (upper)

JAMES HENRY RIVER JOURNEYS
P.O. Box 807, Bolinas, CA 94924
(415) 868-1836
Rivers: Alsek–Tatshenshini, Rogue, Salmon (main)

JASPER RAFT TOURS
P.O. Box 398, Jasper, AB, Canada T0E 1E0
(403) 852-3613; (403) 852-3332
River: Athabasca (upper)

JIM'S OREGON WHITEWATER
56324 McKenzie Hwy., McKenzie Bridge, OR 97413
(503) 822-6003
Rivers: Deschutes, Grande Ronde, John Day, McKenzie, North
        Umpqua

JONI ELLIS RIVER TOURS
P.O. Box 764, Dillon, CO 80435
(303) 468-1028
Rivers: Arkansas, Blue, Colorado (upper)

KEN HELFRICH
378 S. 69th Pl., Springfield, OR 97478
(503) 741-1905
Rivers: McKenzie, Salmon (lower)

KEN WARREN OUTDOORS
4201 S.W. Borland, Tualatin, OR 97062
(503) 638–8803
Rivers: Deschutes, Klamath (upper), Owyhee–OR, Snake (Hells Canyon)

KERN RIVER TOURS
P.O. Box 3444, Lake Isabella, CA 93240
(805) 872–5792; (619) 379–4619
River: Kern

KEYSTONE RAFT AND KAYAK ADVENTURES
P.O. Box 1486, Valdez, AK 99686
(907) 835–2606
Rivers: Chitina–Copper, Lowe, Talkeetna, Tazlina, Tonsina

KEYSTONE RESORT
P.O. Box 38, Keystone, CO 80435
(303) 468–4108
Rivers: Arkansas, Blue, Eagle, Colorado (upper)

KINGFISHER EXPEDITIONS
P.O. Box 1095, Salmon, ID 83467
(208) 756–2255; (208) 865–2444
River: Salmon (main, lower)

KINGS RIVER EXPEDITIONS
211 N. Van Ness, Fresno, CA 93701
(209) 223–4881
River: Kings

KLAMATH RIVER OUTDOOR EXPERIENCES
P.O. Box 369, Orleans, CA 95556
(916) 469–3351
River: Klamath (lower)

KLAMATH RIVER OUTFITTERS
2033 Ti Bar Rd., Somes Bar, CA 95568
(916) 469–3349
Rivers: California Salmon, Klamath (lower)

KODI WHITEWATER RAFTING
P.O. Box 1215, Breckenridge, CO 80424
(800) 525–9624 (outside Colorado); (719) 395–2700
Rivers: Arkansas, Blue, Colorado (upper)

KOOTENAY RIVER RUNNERS
P.O. Box 81, Edgewater, BC, Canada V0A 1E0
(604) 347–9210
River: Kicking Horse

KUMSHEEN RAFT ADVENTURES
P.O. Box 30, 281 Main St., Lytton, BC, Canada V0K 1Z0
(604) 455–2296
Rivers: Chilko, Chilcotin, Fraser, Thompson

LAKE POWELL TOURS
P.O. Box 40, St. George, UT 84771
(801) 673–1733
River: San Juan

LAND ESCAPE EXPEDITIONS
112 E. Covecrest Dr., Price, UT 84501
(801) 637–0842
Rivers: Green (Desolation), Colorado (Westwater)

LAST CHANCE RIVER EXPEDITIONS
2925 Jay St., Denver, CO 80214
(303) 233–6061
River: Arkansas

LAZY J RESORT & RAFTING COMPANY
P.O. Box 109, Coaldale, CO 81222
(719) 942–4274
River: Arkansas

LEAVENWORTH OUTFITTERS
21588 Hwy. 207, Leavenworth, WA 98826
(509) 763–3733
Rivers: Tieton, Wenatchee

LEIERER'S OUTDOORS LIMITED
934 Hylo Rd. S.E., Salem, OR 97306
(503) 581-2803
Rivers: Deschutes, John Day, North Santiam, Owyhee–OR,
    Wenatchee, White Salmon

LE GRAND ADVENTURES
25 Elk Place, Blackhawk, CO 80422
(800) 548-2479; (303) 582-5826
Rivers: Animas, Dolores, Green (Dinosaur), Yampa

LEWIS AND CLARK RIVER EXPEDITIONS
P.O. Box 720, Jackson, WY 83001
(800) 824-5375; (307) 733-4022
River: Snake (upper)

LIBRA WHITEWATER EXPEDITIONS
P.O. Box 4280, Sunland, CA 91041
(800) 228-4121 (inside California); (818) 352-3205
Rivers: American (South, Middle, North forks), Kaweah

LOCHSA RIVER RAFTERS
c/o Powell Mtce. Station, Lolo, MT 59847
(208) 942-3333
Rivers: Lochsa, Selway

LONE EAGLE EXPEDITIONS
P.O. Box 17727, Holladay, UT 84117
(801) 485-2700
River: Snake (upper)

LONE WOLF EXPEDITIONS
1632 Osceola, Denver, CO 80204
(303) 825-2648
River: Colorado (upper)

LOS RIOS RIVER RUNNERS
100 E. San Francisco St., Santa Fe, NM 87501
(800) 338-6877; (505) 983-6565
Rivers: Rio Chama, Rio Grande–NM

LOWER SALMON EXPRESS
P.O. Box 1763, Lewiston, ID 83501
(208) 743-2997; (509) 758-0345
Rivers: Grande Ronde, Salmon (lower)

LUTE JERSTAD ADVENTURES
P.O. Box 19537, Portland OR 97219
(503) 244–4364
Rivers: Deschutes, Owyhee–OR, Rogue

LYONS ADVENTURES
4090 W. State St., Boise, ID 83703
(208) 345–4100
Rivers: Payette, Salmon (lower)

MACKAY BAR CORPORATION
3190 Airport Way, Boise, ID 83705
(800) 635–5336
Rivers: Salmon (Middle Fork, main), Snake (Birds of Prey)

MAD RIVER BOAT TRIPS
1060 South Hwy. 89, Jackson, WY 83001
(800) 458–RAFT (outside Wyoming); (800) 322–6008 (inside
    Wyoming)
River: Snake (upper)

MAD RIVER RAFTING
P.O. Box 650, Winter Park, CO 80482
(800) 451–4844; (303) 726–5290
Rivers: Arkansas, Colorado (upper)

MALIGNE RIVER ADVENTURES
P.O. Box 280, Jasper, AB, Canada T0E 1E0
(403) 852–3370
River: Maligne

MARIAH WILDERNESS EXPEDITIONS
P.O. Box 248, Point Richmond, CA 94807
(415) 233–2303
Rivers: American (South, Middle, North forks), Merced

MCCANN'S NORTHWEST RIVER GUIDES
12770 S.W. Daphne Ct., Beaverton, OR 97005
(503) 626–0829
Rivers: Deschutes, Clackamas, McKenzie, North Santiam, White
    Salmon

MCKENZIE RIVER ADVENTURES
P.O. Box 567, Sisters, OR 97759
(503) 549–1325
River: McKenzie

MCKINLEY RAFT TOURS
P.O. Box 138, Denali National Park, AK 99755
(907) 683–2392
River: Nenana

MERCED RIVER TRIPS
11257 South Bridge St., Rancho Cordova, CA 95670
(916) 635–4479
River: Merced

MG WHITEWATER ADVENTURES
P.O. Box 2472, Napa, CA 94558
(707) 255–0761
Rivers: Klamath (lower), Cache Creek

MIDDLE FORK RAPID TRANSIT
160 2nd St. W., Twin Falls, ID 83301
(208) 734–7890; (208) 774–3440
Rivers: Salmon (Middle Fork), Snake (middle)

MIDDLE FORK RIVER COMPANY
P.O. Box 54, Sun Valley, ID 83353
(208) 726–8888
Rivers: Bruneau–Jarbidge, Salmon (Middle Fork, upper main),
        Owyhee-ID, Owyhee–OR

MIDDLE FORK RIVER EXPEDITIONS
P.O. Box 199, Stanley, ID 83278
(208) 774–3659
River: Salmon (Middle Fork)

MIDDLE FORK RIVER TOURS
P.O. Box 2368, Ketchum, ID 83340
(208) 726–5666
Rivers: Salmon (Middle Fork), Snake (Birds of Prey)

MIDDLE FORK WILDERNESS OUTFITTERS
P.O. Box 4682, Ketchum, ID 83340
(208) 726–2467
River: Salmon (Middle Fork)

MIKE SALLEE GUIDE SERVICE
2245 S.W. Martha, Portland, OR 97201
(503) 245–9209
River: Deschutes

MIRAGE ADVENTURE TOURS
P.O. Box 2338, Canmore, AB, Canada T0L 0M0
(403) 678–4919
Rivers: Kananaskis, Red Deer

MOKI MAC RIVER EXPEDITIONS
P.O. Box 21242, Salt Lake City, UT 84121
(800) 284–7280; (801) 943–7607
Rivers: Colorado (Westwater, Cataract, Grand Canyon), Green
(Desolation)

MONTANA RIVER OUTFITTERS
1401 5th Ave. S., Great Falls, MT 59405
(406) 761–1677
Rivers: Blackfoot, Clark Fork, Yellowstone

MOONDANCE RIVER EXPEDITIONS
310 W. 1st St., Salida, CO 81201
(719) 539–2113
River: Arkansas

MOTHER LODE RIVER TRIPS
Scott-Free River Expeditions, P.O. Box 456, Coloma, CA 95613
(800) 367–2387 (northern California); (916) 626–4187
Rivers: American (South, Middle, North forks), California Salmon,
Klamath (lower), Sacramento (upper), Scott

MOUNTAIN WATERS RAFTING
P.O. Box 2681, Durango, CO 81302
(303) 259–4191
Rivers: Animas, Piedra

MOYIE RIVER OUTFITTERS
Hwy. 2, Bonners Ferry, ID 83805
(208) 267–2108
River: Moyie

MUKWAH AND ASSOCIATES ADVENTURE BOUND TOURS
#195, 601-10th Ave. S.W., Calgary, AB, Canada T2R 0B2
(403) 282–0509
River: Red Deer

MUNROE'S WILDERNESS ADVENTURES
P.O. Box 938, Redding, CA 96099
(916) 243–3091
Rivers: California Salmon, Klamath (upper, lower), Sacramento
(upper), Scott, Trinity, Wooley

NABESNA WHITEWATER RAFTING
Mile 42 Nabesna Rd., Star Route A, Box 1420, Slana, AK 99586
(907) 822-3426
Rivers: Chitina–Copper

NATIONAL OUTDOOR LEADERSHIP SCHOOL
P.O. Box AA, Lander, WY 82520
(307) 332–6973
Rivers: Dolores, Cache la Poudre, Green (Desolation)

NATIONAL PARK FLOAT TRIPS
Moose, WY 83012
(800) 733–6445; (307) 733–5500
River: Snake (upper)

NEW WAVE RAFTING
Route 5, Box 302A, Santa Fe, NM 87501
(505) 984–1444
Rivers: Arkansas, Rio Chama, Rio Grande–NM

NICHOLS EXPEDITIONS
590 N. 500 W., Moab, UT 84532
(800) 635–1792; (801) 259–7582
Rivers: Brooks Range (central, west), Chitina–Copper, Salmon
(lower)

NOAH'S ARK WHITEWATER RAFTING
P.O. Box 850, Buena Vista, CO 81211
(719) 395-2158
Rivers: Arkansas, Dolores

NOAH'S WORLD OF WATER
P.O. Box 11, Ashland, OR 97520
(503) 488-2811
Rivers: California Salmon, Klamath (upper, lower), North
Umpqua, Owyhee–OR, Rogue, Scott

NORMAN H. GUTH COMPANY
P.O. Box D, Salmon, ID 83467
(208) 756-3279
River: Salmon (Middle Fork)

NORTH AMERICAN RIVER EXPEDITIONS
543 N. Main St., Moab, UT 84532
(801) 259-5865
River: Colorado (Cataract)

NORTH CASCADES RIVER EXPEDITIONS
P.O. Box 116, Arlington, WA 98223
(800) 634-8433; (206) 435-9548
Rivers: Clackamas, Green, Klickitat, Methow, Nooksack, Skagit,
Skykomish, Suiattle, Tieton, Wenatchee, White Salmon

NORTHERN WILDERNESS RIVER RIDERS
23312 77th Ave., S.E., Woodinville, WA 98072
(206) 485-7238; (206) 448-7238
Rivers: Cispus, Green, Klickitat, Methow, Skykomish, Suiattle,
Tieton, Toutle, Wenatchee, White Salmon

NORTH UMPQUA OUTFITTERS
1659 N.E. Taylor, P.O. Box 1574, Roseburg, OR 97470
(503) 673-4599
River: North Umpqua

NORTHWEST DORIES
1127 B Airway Ave., Lewiston, ID 83501
(208) 743-4201
Rivers: Grande Ronde, Owyhee–OR, Salmon (main, lower), Snake
(Hells Canyon)

NORTHWEST DRIFTERS
4486 Campbell Rd., Medford, OR 95704
(503) 773-4782
River: Rogue

NORTHWEST OUTDOOR ADVENTURES
1575 S.E. 6th St., West Linn, OR 97068
(503) 655-4468
Rivers: Clackamas, Deschutes, Grande Ronde, McKenzie, North
Santiam

NORTHWEST RIVER COMPANY
P.O. Box 403, Boise, ID 83701
(208) 344-7119
River: Selway

NORTHWEST RIVER EXPEDITIONS
P.O. Box 824, North Fork, ID 83466
(208) 865-2534
River: Salmon (main)

NORTHWEST RIVER OUTFITTERS
P.O. Box 1481, Albany, OR 97321
(503) 928-4498
Rivers: Deschutes

NORTHWEST VOYAGEURS
P.O. Box 373, Lucille, ID 83549
(800) 727-9977; (208) 628-3700
Rivers: Owyhee–OR, Salmon (lower), Snake (Hells Canyon)

NORTHWEST WHITEWATER EXCURSIONS
P.O. Box 10754, Eugene, OR 97440
(503) 342-1222
Rivers: Deschutes, Grande Ronde, McKenzie, Owyhee–OR,
Rogue, Salmon (main, lower)

NORTHWEST WHITEWATER EXPEDITIONS
3411 S.E. 162nd Ave., Portland, OR 97236
(503) 760-8426
Rivers: Deschutes, Grande Ronde, John Day, Owyhee–OR

NOVA GUIDES
P.O. Box 2018, Vail, CO 81658
(303) 949–4232
Rivers: Arkansas, Eagle, Colorado (upper)

NOVA RIVER RUNNERS
Box 1120, Chickaloon, AK 99674
(907) 745–5753
River: Talkeetna

O.A.R.S.
P.O. Box 67, Angels Camp, CA 95222
(209) 736–4677
Rivers: American (South, North forks), California Salmon, Carson
(East Fork), Colorado (Grand Canyon), Dolores, Klamath
(lower), Merced, Mokelumne, Rogue, San Juan, Tuolumne

THE OLD BALDY CLUB
P.O. Box 707, Saratoga, WY 82331
(307) 326–5222
River: North Platte

OLYMPIC GUIDE AND RAFT SERVICE
P.O. Box 846, Port Angeles, WA 98362
(206) 457–7011
Rivers: Elwha, Olympic Rain Forest

OPERATION CHALLENGE
5946 Illinois Ave., Orangevale, CA 95662
(916) 989-0402
River: American (South Fork)

ORANGE TORPEDO TRIPS
P.O. Box 1111, Grants Pass, OR 97526
(800) 635–2925; (503) 479–5061
Rivers: Klamath (lower), North Umpqua, Owyhee–OR, Rogue,
Salmon (Middle Fork, main, lower)

OREGON RIVER ADVENTURES
P.O. Box 567, Sisters, OR 97759
(503) 549–1325
Rivers: McKenzie, North Umpqua

OREGON RIVER EXPERIENCES
18800 N.E. Trunk Rd., Dundee, OR 97115
(503) 538–3358
Rivers: Deschutes, Grande Ronde, John Day, Klamath (lower),
    McKenzie, North Santiam, North Umpqua, Owyhee–OR,
    Rogue, Salmon (lower)

OREGON RIVER OUTFITTERS
1715 Winter St., S.E., Salem, OR 97302
(503) 363–2074
River: Rogue

OREGON WHITEWATER ADVENTURES
660 Kelly Blvd., Springfield, OR 97477
(503) 726–8278
Rivers: Deschutes, Grande Ronde, Klamath (lower), McKenzie,
    North Umpqua, Owyhee–OR

ORION EXPEDITIONS
1516 11th Ave., Seattle, WA 98122
(800) 553–7466; (206) 322–9130
Rivers: Deschutes, Methow, Sauk, Skagit, Skykomish, Tieton,
    Wenatchee, White Salmon

OSPREY EXPEDITIONS
P.O. Box 209, Denali National Park, AK 99755
(907) 683–2734
Rivers: Brooks Range (east), Chitina–Copper, Fortymile, Nenana,
    Talkeetna, Tazlina

OSPREY FLOAT TRIPS
P.O. Box 120, Moose, WY 83012
(307) 733–5500
River: Snake (upper)

OTTER RAFTING ADVENTURES
4919–49 St., Red Deer, AB, Canada T4N 1V2
(403) 347–4280; (403) 295–1497
River: Red Deer

OTTER RIVER TRIPS
P.O. Box 338, Merlin, OR 97532
(503) 476–8590; (503) 479–1418
River: Rogue

OUTBACK EXPEDITIONS
P.O. Box 229, Terlingua, TX 79852
(915) 371-2490
River: Rio Grande-TX

OUTDOOR ADVENTURE CENTRE
P.O. Box 1620, Canmore, AB, Canada T0L 0M0
(403) 678-2000
Rivers: Bow, Kananaskis, Red Deer

OUTDOOR ADVENTURES
P.O. Box 1149, Pt. Reyes, CA 94956
(800) 323-4234; (415) 663-8300
Rivers: Kern, Rogue, Salmon (Middle Fork, main), Tuolumne

OUTDOOR ADVENTURES-MU RECREATION
University of California, Davis, CA 95616
(916) 752-2426
Rivers: American (South, North forks), California Salmon

OUTDOOR ADVENTURES PLUS
4030 W. Amazon Dr., Eugene, OR 97405
(503) 344-4499
Rivers: Deschutes, McKenzie

OUTDOORS UNLIMITED RIVER TRIPS
P.O. Box 854, Lotus, CA 95651
(916) 626-7668
Rivers: American (Middle Fork), Colorado (Grand Canyon),
    Klamath (lower)

OUZEL EXPEDITIONS
7540 E. 20th Ave., Anchorage, AK 99504
(907) 338-0620
River: Talkeetna

OUZEL OUTFITTERS
P.O. Box 827, Bend, OR 97709
(503) 385-5947
Rivers: California Salmon, Deschutes, Klamath (upper, lower),
    McKenzie, North Umpqua, Owyhee-OR, Rogue, Salmon
    (lower)

OWL RAFTING
P.O. Box 612, Denali National Park, AK 99755
(907) 683–2215 (May 15–Sept. 15)
River: Nenana

PACIFIC NORTHWEST FLOAT TRIPS
1039 Sterling Rd., Sedro Wooley, WA 98284
(206) 855–0535
River: Skagit

PAGOSA RAFTING OUTFITTERS
P.O. Box 222, Pagosa Springs, CO 81147
(303) 731–4081
Rivers: Animas, Piedra

PAUL BROOKS RAFT TRIPS
P.O. Box 638, 12221 Galice Rd., Merlin, OR 97532
(503) 476–8051
River: Rogue

PEAK RIVER EXPEDITIONS
475 8th Ave., Salt Lake City, UT 84103
(801) 364–9220
Rivers: Green (Desolation), Yampa

PEREGRINE RIVER OUTFITTERS
64 Ptarmigan Ln., Durango, CO 81301
(303) 385-7600
Rivers: Animas, Dolores, Green (Desolation), Gunnison (Lake Fork, Gorge), Piedra

PERFORMANCE TOURS
P.O. Box 7305, Breckenridge, CO 80424
(800) 328-RAFT; (303) 453-0661
Rivers: Arkansas, Blue, Colorado (upper)

PHIL'S GUIDE SERVICE
1244 Hwy. 141, BZ Corners, White Salmon, WA 98672
(509) 493-2641
Rivers: Klickitat, White Salmon

PRINCE RIVER OUTFITTER
41301 McKenzie Hwy., Springfield, OR 97478
(503) 896-3941
Rivers: Deschutes, John Day, McKenzie, North Umpqua, Owyhee-OR

R.A.F.T.
P.O. Box 34051, Sta. D, Vancouver, BC, Canada V6J 4M1
(800) 663-RAFT (Midwest USA); (604) 684-RAFT
River: Chilliwack

RAFTMEISTER
P.O. Box 1805, Vail, CO 81658
(800) 274-0636; (303) 476-7238
Rivers: Arkansas, Eagle, Colorado (upper, Glenwood)

RAM RIVER EXPEDITIONS
4050 Falling Water Dr., Reno, NV 89509
(702) 746-1400
Rivers: American (Middle, North forks), Carson (East Fork), Truckee

RAPID RAFTING
P.O. Box 600, 1755 Robson St., Vancouver, BC, Canada V6G 3B7
(604) 875-9745
Rivers: Chilliwack, Nahatlatch, Thompson

RAPID TRANSIT
P.O. Box 863, Gold Bar, WA 98251
(206) 793–2604
River: Skykomish

RAPID TRANSIT RAFTING
P.O. Box 4095, Estes Park, CO 80517
(800) 367–8523; (303) 586–8852
River: Colorado (upper)

REACHOUT EXPEDITIONS
P.O. Box 464, Anacortes, WA 98221
(206) 293–3788; (503) 244–0346
Rivers: Deschutes, Skagit, Suiattle, Wenatchee

RED ROCK RIVER COMPANY
2144 Highland Dr., Suite 150, Salt Lake City, UT 84106
(801) 484–9022
Rivers: Dolores, Colorado (Professor Valley)

REO RAFTING ADVENTURES
1199 West Pender St., Suite 390, Vancouver, BC, Canada V6E 2R1
(604) 684–4438; (604) 687–7611
Rivers: Chilliwack, Chehalis, Nahatlatch, Taseko, Thompson

RIO BRAVO RIVER TOURS
1412 Cerrillos Rd., Santa Fe, NM 87501
(800) 451–0708; (505) 988–1153
River: Rio Grande–NM

RIO GRANDE RAPID TRANSIT
P.O. Box A, Pilar, NM 87531
(800) 222–RAFT (inside New Mexico); (505) 758–9700
Rivers: Rio Chama, Rio Grande–NM

RIVER ADVENTURE FLOAT TRIPS
P.O. Box 841, Grants Pass, OR 97526
(503) 476–6493
Rivers: Rogue

RIVER ADVENTURE FLOAT TRIPS–ALBERTA
P.O. Box 518, Sta. G, Calgary, AB, Canada T2E 1Z4
(800) 661–1556 (inside Alberta); (403) 282–7238
River: Red Deer

RIVERBEND WHITE WATER RAFTING
P.O. Box 961, Red Deer, AB, Canada T4N 5H3
(403) 343–0429
River: Red Deer

THE RIVER COMPANY
380 Washington Ave., P.O. Box 233, Sun Valley, ID 83353
(208) 726–8890; (208) 774–2244 (summer)
River: Salmon (upper main)

RIVER COUNTRY RAFTING
P.O. Box 319, Happy Camp, CA 96039
(916) 493–2207
Rivers: Eel (middle), Klamath (lower)

RIVER DRIFTERS
324 N.W. 203rd, Seattle, WA 98177
(206) 546–3073
Rivers: Skagit, Suiattle, Wenatchee

RIVER DRIFTERS WHITEWATER TOURS
13570 N.W. Lakeview Dr., Portland, OR 97229
(503) 645–6264; (503) 224–9625
Rivers: Clackamas, Deschutes, White Salmon

RIVER JOURNEY
14842 Orange Blossom Rd., Oakdale, CA 95361
(800) 292–2938; (209) 847–4671
Rivers: Carson (East Fork), Stanislaus

RIVER MOUNTAIN ACTION
5916 West 77th Pl., Los Angeles, CA 90045
(818) 348–3727
River: American (South Fork)

RIVER RAT AND COMPANY
1669 Chili Bar Court, Placerville, CA 95667
(916) 622–6632
Rivers: American (South, Middle, North forks)

RIVER RECREATION
13-211th Pl. S.E., Redmond, WA 98053
(206) 392–5899
Rivers: Cispus, Green–WA, Klickitat, Methow, Nooksack, Skagit, Skykomish, Suiattle, Tieton, Toutle, Wenatchee, White Salmon

RIVER RIDERS WHITEWATER TOURS
P.O. Box 2229, North Highlands, CA 95660
(916) 334–8486
Rivers: American (South, North forks)

RIVER ROGUES ADVENTURES
P.O. Box 115, Spences Bridge, BC, Canada V0K 2L0
(604) 458–2252
River: Thompson

RIVER RUNNERS–CALIFORNIA
23801 Killion St., Woodland Hills, CA 91367
(916) 622–5110; (818) 340–1151
Rivers: American (South, North forks)

RIVER RUNNERS–COLORADO
11150 Hwy. 50, Salida, CO 81201
(800) 332–9100 (inside Colorado); (800) 525–2081 (outside Colorado)
River: Arkansas

RIVER RUNNERS OF CODY
P.O. Box 845, Cody, WY 82414
(307) 527–7238
River: Shoshone

RIVERS INCORPORATED
P.O. Box 2092, Kirkland, WA 98083
(206) 822–5296; (206) 524-8695
Rivers: Klickitat, Methow, Skagit, Suiattle, Wenatchee, White Salmon

RIVER TRIPS UNLIMITED
4140 Dry Creek Rd., Medford, OR 97504
(503) 779–3798
River: Rogue

RIVERS WEST WHITEWATER SPECIALISTS
1565 W. 7th St., Eugene, OR 97402
(503) 686-0798
Rivers: Clackamas, Deschutes, Klamath (lower), McKenzie, North
Umpqua

RIVERS WEST
P.O. Box 2974, Durango, CO 81302
(800) 622-0852; (303) 259-5077
River: Animas

ROARING FORK RIVER COMPANY
Bond River Ranch, 6805 E. Arizona Ave., Denver, CO 80224
(303) 759-1988
Rivers: Arkansas, Colorado (upper), Dolores, Eagle, Roaring Fork

ROCK GARDENS RAFTING
1308 Rd. 129, Glenwood Springs, CO 81601
(303) 945-6737
Rivers: Colorado (Glenwood), Eagle, Roaring Fork

ROCKY MOUNTAIN OUTDOOR CENTER
10281 Hwy. 50, Howard, CO 81233
(800) 255-5784; (303) 942-3214
River: Arkansas

ROCKY MOUNTAIN RAFT TOURS
P.O. Box 1771, Banff, AB, Canada T0L 0C0
(403) 762-3632
River: Bow

ROCKY MOUNTAIN RIVER EXPEDITIONS
P.O. Box 427, Westminster, CO 80030
(303) 430-8333
Rivers: Arkansas, Colorado (upper, Westwater), Dolores, Green
(Desolation), North Platte

ROCKY MOUNTAIN RIVER TOURS
P.O. Box 2552, Boise, ID 83701
(208) 344-6668
River: Salmon (Middle Fork)

ROCKY MOUNTAIN TOURS
P.O. Box 3031, Buena Vista, CO 80937
(800) 873–8008; (719) 395–4101
Rivers: Arkansas, Roaring Fork

ROGUE EXCURSIONS
P.O. Box 855, Medford, OR 97501
(503) 773–5983
River: Rogue

ROGUE–KLAMATH RIVER ADVENTURES
P.O. Box 4295, Medford, OR 97501
(503) 779–3708
Rivers: Rogue, Klamath (upper, lower)

ROGUE RIVER RAFT TRIPS
8500 Galice Rd., Merlin, OR 97532
(800) 826–1963; (503) 476–3825
River: Rogue

ROLLINSON RIVER RAFTING
P.O. Box 1156, Capitola, CA 95010
(800) 541–8551; (408) 688–8551
Rivers: American (South, Middle, North forks)

ROSS RIVER ED-VENTURES
East Route, Monticello, UT 84535
(800) 525–4456 (outside Utah); (801) 587–2859
River: San Juan

ROUGH RUN OUTFITTERS
General Delivery, Big Bend National Park, TX 79834
(800) USA–RAFT
River: Rio Grande–TX

ROW (RIVER ODYSSEYS WEST)
P.O. Box 579, Coeur d'Alene, ID 83814
(208) 765–0841
Rivers: Grande Ronde, Lochsa, Moyie, Owyhee–ID, Owhyee–OR,
St. Joe, Salmon (Middle Fork, lower), Snake (Hells
Canyon)

ROYAL GORGE RIVER ADVENTURES
P.O. Box 1359, Canon City, CO 81212
(719) 269–3700
River: Arkansas

R & R OUTDOORS
2755 Aspen Cove, Meridian, ID 83642
(800) 777–4676; (208) 888–4676
River: Salmon (main, lower)

RUBICON WHITEWATER ADVENTURES
P.O. Box 517, Forestville, CA 95436
(707) 887–2452
Rivers: American (South, North forks), California Salmon, Eel
(middle), Klamath (lower), Trinity

SAGUARO WHITEWATER
3223 E. Lee St., Tucson, AZ 85716
(602) 326–6206
River: Salt

ST. ELIAS ALPINE GUIDES
P.O. Box 111241, Anchorage, AK 99511
(907) 277–6867
River: Chitina–Copper

SALMON RIVER CHALLENGE
P.O. Box 1299, Riggins, ID 83549
(208) 628–3264
River: Salmon (main)

SALMON RIVER EXPERIENCE
812 Truman, Moscow, ID 83843
(208) 882–2385
River: Salmon (lower)

SALMON RIVER LODGE
P.O. Box 1843, Idaho Falls, ID 83403
(800) 635–4717; (208) 522–7756
River: Salmon (main)

SALMON RIVER OUTFITTERS
P.O. Box 307, Columbia, CA 95310
(209) 532–2766
River: Salmon (main)

SALT RIVER CANYON RAFT TRIPS
86 W. University Dr., Suite 101A, Mesa, AZ 85201
River: Salt

SANDS WILDWATER
P.O. Box 696, Wilson, WY 83041
(307) 733-4410
River: Snake (upper)

SANTA FE RAFTING COMPANY
P.O. Box 16255, Santa Fe, NM 87505
(800) 533-6980; (505) 988-4914
Rivers: Rio Chama, Rio Grande–NM

SAWTOOTH RIVER EXPEDITIONS
P.O. Box 1752, Boise, ID 83340
(208) 322-1052; (208) 726-4756
Rivers: Salmon (Middle Fork, lower)

SCENIC RIVER TOURS
703 West Tomichi, Gunnison, CO 81230
(303) 641-3131; (303) 641-1830
Rivers: Arkansas, Colorado (Horsethief), Gunnison, Gunnison
    (Lake Fork), Taylor

SEA TO SKY RAFT TOURS
P.O. Box 509, Squamish, BC, Canada V0N 3G0
(604) 932-2002
Rivers: Birkenhead, Cheakamus, Squamish

SELKIRK TANGIERS
P.O. Box 1409, Golden, BC, Canada V0A 1H0
(800) 663-7080 (USA only); (604) 344-5016
River: Kicking Horse

SEVY GUIDE SERVICE
P.O. Box 24, Stanley, ID 83278
(208) 744-2200
Rivers: Jarbidge–Bruneau, Owyhee–ID, Owyhee–OR, Salmon
    (Middle Fork)

SHAULL'S WHITEWATER EXPERIENCE
9327 N.E. Glisan St., Portland, OR 97220
(503) 252-2014
Rivers: Clackamus, Deschutes, Toutle, White Salmon

SHERI GRIFFITH RIVER EXPEDITIONS
P.O. Box 1324, Moab, UT 84532
(800) 332-2439; (801) 259-8229
Rivers: Arkansas, Colorado (Professor Valley, Westwater, Cataract), Dolores, Green (Desolation)

SIERRA MAC RIVER TRIPS
P.O. Box 366, Sonora, CA 95370
(209) 532-1327
River: Tuolumne

SIERRA OUTFITTERS AND GUIDES
P.O. Box 2756, Taos, NM 87571
(505) 758-1247
Rivers: Arkansas, Rio Chama, Rio Grande–NM

SIERRA SOUTH
11300 Kernville Rd., Kernville, CA 93238
(619) 376-3745
River: Kern

SIERRA WESTERN ADVENTURE TRIPS
P.O. Box 2967, Mission Viejo, CA 92690
(800) 367-8747; (714) 472-8623
River: American (South Fork)

SIERRA WHITEWATER EXPEDITIONS
P.O. Box 1330, Springfield, OR 97477
(800) 937-7300; (503) 741-2780
Rivers: California Salmon, Grande Ronde, John Day, Klamath (upper), Klickitat, McKenzie, North Santiam, North Umpqua, Owyhee–OR, Rogue

SIGNAL MOUNTAIN LODGE
P.O. Box 50, Grand Teton National Park, Moran, WY 83013
(307) 543-2831; (307) 733-5470
River: Snake (upper)

SILVER CLOUD EXPEDITIONS
P.O. Box 1006, Salmon, ID 83467
(208) 756–6215
River: Salmon (main)

SILVER HILTON LODGE
P.O. Box 3880, Smithers, BC, Canada V0J 2N0
(604) 852–6491
River: Babine

SKYLINE OUTFIT-ROLAND CHEEK
P.O. Box 1880, Columbia Falls, MT 59912
(406) 892–5560
River: Flathead (South Fork)

SLEIGHT EXPEDITIONS
P.O. Box 40, St. George, UT 84771
(801) 673–1200
River: Colorado (Grand Canyon)

SNAKE RIVER PARK
Star Route, Box 14A, Jackson, WY 83001
(307) 733–7078
River: Snake (upper)

SOBEK EXPEDITIONS
P.O. Box 1089, Angels Camp, CA 95222
(800) 777–7930; (209) 736–4524
Rivers: Alsek–Tatshenshini

SOBEK WHITE WATER EXPEDITIONS
P.O. Box 1359, Angels Camp, CA 95222
(209) 736-4524
River: Colorado (Grand Canyon)

SOLITUDE FLOAT TRIPS
P.O. Box 112, Moose, WY 83012
(307) 733–2871
River: Snake (upper)

SOLITUDE RIVER TRIPS
4258 Galice Road, Merlin, OR 97532
(503) 476–1876
River: Salmon (Middle Fork)

THE SOMES BAR LODGE
General Delivery, Somes Bar, CA 95568
(916) 469-3399
Rivers: California Salmon, Klamath (lower)

SOURDOUGH OUTFITTERS
P.O. Box 90, Bettles, AK 99726
(907) 692–5252
River: Brooks Range (east, central)

SOUTH BAY RIVER RAFTERS
P.O. Box 243, Hermosa Beach, CA 90254
(213) 545–8542
River: American (South Fork)

SOUTHWEST WILDERNESS CENTER
P.O. Box 9380, Santa Fe, NM 87504
(505) 983–7262; (505) 471–0589
Rivers: Dolores, Rio Chama, Rio Grande–NM

SPIRIT WHITEWATER
1001 Rose Ave., Penngrove, CA 94951
(707) 795–7305
River: Kings

S'PLORE
699 E.S. Temple, Suite 120, Salt Lake City, UT 84102
(801) 363–7130
Rivers: Colorado (Professor Valley), Green (Dinosaur)

SPOTTED BEAR RANCH
P.O. Box 28, Hungry Horse, MT 59919
(406) 755–3867
River: Flathead (South Fork)

STEEN'S WILDERNESS ADVENTURES
Route 1, Box 73, Joseph, OR 97846
(503) 432–5315
Rivers: Grande Ronde, Snake (Hells Canyon)

STEHEKIN ADVENTURE COMPANY
P.O. Box 36, Stehekin, WA 98852
(509) 682–4677
River: Stehekin

SUBARCTIC WILDERNESS ADVENTURES

P.O. Box 685, Fort Smith, NT, Canada X0E 0P0

(403) 872–2467

River: Great Slave

SUN COUNTRY TOURS

P.O. Box 771, Bend, OR 97709

(503) 593–2161; (503) 382–6277

River: Deschutes

SUNDANCE EXPEDITIONS

14894 Galice Rd., Merlin, OR 97532

(503) 479–8508

Rivers: Illinois, Rogue

SUNDOG DORIES

2532 Roland Rd., Fairbanks, AK 99708

(907) 479–3792

River: Nenana

SUNRISE EXPEDITIONS

P.O. Box 53, Woodacre, CA 94973

(415) 488–4590

Rivers: California Salmon, Klamath (lower)

SUNSHINE OUTDOOR CENTER

18341 Kennedy Rd., Knights Ferry, CA 95361

(800) 829–7238; (209) 881–3236

Rivers: Klamath (lower), Mokelumne, Stanislaus (lower)

SUN VALLEY RIVERS

P.O. Box 1776, Sun Valley, ID 83353

(208) 726–7404

River: Salmon (Middle Fork)

SUSKWA ADVENTURE OUTFITTERS

P.O. Box 3262, Smithers, BC, Canada V0J 2N0

(604) 847–2885

Rivers: Alsek–Tatshenshini, Babine

TAG-A-LONG EXPEDITIONS

452 N. Main St., Moab, UT 84532

(800) 453–3292 (outside Utah); (801) 259–8946

Rivers: Colorado (Professor Valley, Westwater, Cataract), Green
   (Desolation), San Juan

TAG TWO GUIDE SERVICE
606 Templin, Grants Pass, OR 97526
(503) 476–7962
River: Rogue

TATSHENSHINI EXPEDITIONS
1602 Alder St., Whitehorse, YK, Canada Y1A 3W8
(403) 633–2742
River: Tatshenshini

TELLURIDE WHITEWATER
666 Colorado Ave., P.O. Box 685, Telluride, CO 81435
(303) 728-3895
Rivers: Animas, Dolores, Gunnison (Gorge), San Miguel

TEXAS RIVER EXPEDITIONS
P.O. Box 301152, Houston, TX 77230
(800) 950–RAFT; (713) 242–1525
Rivers: Arkansas, Rio Grande–NM, Rio Grande–TX

TEX'S RIVER EXPEDITIONS
P.O. Box 336, Moab, UT 84532
(801) 259–5125
River: Colorado (Professor Valley)

THREE RIVER OUTFITTING
P.O. Box 339, Almont, CO 81210
(303) 641–1303
Rivers: Gunnison, Gunnison (Lake Fork), Taylor

TI BAR GUIDE SERVICE
2033 Ti Bar Rd., Somes Bar, CA 95568
(916) 469–3349
Rivers: California Salmon, Klamath (lower)

TIMBERLINE TOURS
P.O. Box 131, Vail, CO 81658
(303) 476–1414
Rivers: Arkansas, Eagle, Colorado (upper, Glenwood)

TIMBER RAFTING
Raven Adventure Trips, P.O. Box 108, Granby, CO 80446
(800) 332–3381; (303) 887-2141
Rivers: Arkansas, Colorado (upper)

TOUR WEST WHITEWATER ADVENTURES
P.O. Box 333, Orem, UT 84059
(800) 453–9107 (outside Utah), (801) 225–0755
Rivers: Colorado (Cataract, Grand Canyon), Salmon (main)

TRIANGLE C RANCH WHITEWATER
P.O. Box 69, Stanley, ID 83278
(208) 774–2266
Rivers: Salmon (Middle Fork, upper main)

TRIANGLE X FLOAT TRIPS
Moose, WY 83012
(307) 733–5500; (307) 733–6445
River: Snake (upper)

TRIBUTARY WHITEWATER TOURS
20480 Woodbury Dr., Grass Valley, CA 95949
(916) 346–6812
Rivers: American (South, Middle, North forks), California Salmon,
Carson (East Fork), Eel (middle), Kaweah, Klamath
(upper), Mokelumne, Sacramento (upper), Scott,
Stanislaus, Trinity, Yuba (North Fork)

TRINITY RIVER COMPANY
P.O. Box 572, Big Bar, CA 96010
(916) 243–6400; (505) 776–2481 (off-season)
River: Trinity

TRINITY RIVER RAFTING CENTER
Riverdale Park, Star Route 5, Willow Creek, CA 95573
(916) 629–3646
Rivers: Klamath (upper, lower), Trinity

TURTLE RIVER RAFTING COMPANY
507 McCloud Ave., Mount Shasta, CA 96067
(916) 926–3223
Rivers: American (South Fork), California Salmon, Eel (middle),
Klamath (upper, lower), Owyhee–OR, Sacramento (upper),
Scott, Trinity

TWIN LAKES EXPEDITIONS
P.O. Box 438, Twin Lakes, CO 81251
(800) 288–0497; (719) 486-3928
River: Arkansas

TWO-M RIVER OUTFITTERS
P.O. Box 163, Sun Valley, ID 83353
(208) 726–8844
River: Salmon (upper)

WANDERLUST ADVENTURES
3500 Bingham Hill Rd., Fort Collins, CO 80521
(303) 484–1219
River: Cache le Poudre

WAPITI RIVER GUIDES
P.O. Box 1125, Riggins, ID 83549
(800) 727–9998, then dial 8352; (208) 628–3523
Rivers: Grande Ronde, Owyhee–OR, Salmon (lower)

WARREN RIVER EXPEDITIONS
1219 E. Lewis, Pocatello, ID 83201
(208) 234–7361
River: Salmon (main)

WATER AND OUTDOOR SPORTS INTERNATIONAL
25458 125th Ave., Maple Ridge, BC, Canada V2X 4M2
(604) 467–6411
Rivers: Chilliwack, Nahatlatch, Thompson

WATERSHED
526 Central Way, Kirkland, WA 98033
(206) 822–1333
Rivers: Skykomish, Wenatchee

WB ADVENTURES
P.O. Box 3398, Sta. B, Calgary, AB, Canada T2M 4M1
(403) 637–2060
River: Red Deer

WENATCHEE WHITEWATER AND SCENIC RIVER TRIPS
P.O. Box 12, Cashmere, WA 98815
(509) 782-2254
Rivers: Deschutes, Methow, Tieton, Wenatchee, White Salmon

WESTERN RIVER EXPEDITIONS
7258 Racquet Club Dr., Salt Lake City, UT 84121
(800) 453–7450; (801) 942–6669
Rivers: Green (Desolation), Colorado (Professor Valley, Westwater, Cataract, Grand Canyon)

W.E.T. (WHITEWATER EXPEDITIONS AND TOURS)
P.O. 160024, Sacramento, CA 95816
(916) 451–3241
Rivers: American (South, Middle, North forks), California Salmon, Carson (East Fork), Klamath (upper, lower), Sacramento (upper), Scott

WHISTLER RIVER ADVENTURES
P.O. Box 202, Whistler, BC, Canada V0N 1B0
(604) 932–3532
Rivers: Birkenhead, Cheakamus, Chilko, Squamish, Thompson

WHITEHORSE RAFTING
P.O. Box 711, Condon, OR 97823
(503) 384–2303
River: John Day

WHITE OTTER OUTDOOR ADVENTURES
P.O. Box 2733, Ketchum, ID 83340
(208) 726–4331
Rivers: Salmon (upper main), Snake (Middle)

WHITE WATER ADVENTURES
P.O. Box 1126, North Fork, ID 83466
(208) 865–2474
Rivers: Salmon (main), Selway

WHITEWATER ADVENTURES
11311 Menaul N.E., Albuquerque, NM 87112
(505) 298–0000; (505) 293–4097
River: Rio Grande–NM

WHITEWATER CONNECTION
P.O. Box 270, Coloma, CA 95613
(916) 622–6446
Rivers: American (South, Middle, North forks), Klamath (upper)

WHITEWATER ENCOUNTERS
1422 S. Chambers Circle, Aurora, CO 80012
(303) 751–0161
River: Arkansas

WHITEWATER EXCITEMENT
P.O. Box 5992, Auburn, CA 95603
(800) 327-2386
Rivers: American (South, Middle, North forks), California Salmon,
   Merced

WHITE WATER EXPRESS
P.O. Box 1248, Riggins, ID 83549
(208) 628-3680
River: Salmon (lower)

WHITEWATER ODYSSEY
P.O. Box 2186, Evergreen, CO 80439
(303) 674-3637
Rivers: Arkansas, Colorado (upper), Dolores, North Platte, Rio
   Chama, Rio Grande-NM

WHITEWATER RAFTING
P.O. Box 2462, Glenwood Springs, CO 81601
(303) 945-8477
Rivers: Colorado (Glenwood), Eagle, Roaring Fork

WHITEWATER RAFTING (JASPER)
P.O. Box 362, Jasper, AB, Canada T0E 1E0
(403) 852-4721; (403) 852-7238
Rivers: Athabasca (upper), Maligne

WHITEWATER SHOP RIVER TOURS
8977 W. State St., Boise, ID 83706
(208) 342-0750
River: Snake (Birds of Prey)

WHITEWATER USA
1633 S.W. Sunset Blvd., Portland, OR 97201
(503) 245-1405
Rivers: Deschutes, John Day

WHITEWATER VOYAGES
P.O. Box 906, El Sobrante, CA 94803
(415) 222-5994
Rivers: American (South, Middle, North forks), Cache Creek,
   California Salmon, Carson (East Fork), Kern, Klamath
   (upper, lower), Merced, Rogue, Scott, Stanislaus, Trinity,
   Tuolumne, Yuba (North Fork)

WHITEWATER VOYAGEURS
P.O. Box 346, Poncha Springs, CO 81242
(800) 541–3395 (inside Colorado); (800) 255–2585 (outside
    Colorado)
River: Arkansas

WILD AND SCENIC EXPEDITIONS
P.O. Box 460, Flagstaff, AZ 86002
(602) 774–7343
River: San Juan

WILDERNESS AWARE
P.O. Box 1550, Buena Vista, CO 81211
(800) 462–7238; (719) 395–2112
Rivers: Arkansas, Colorado (upper), Dolores, Gunnison (Gorge),
    North Platte

WILDERNESS EXPEDITIONS
P.O. Box 83298, Fairbanks, AK 99708
(907) 479–8163
Rivers: Brooks Range (east central, west)

WILDERNESS RANCH AND LODGE
Hawkins Outfitters, P.O. Box 187, Eureka, MT 59917
(406) 296–2642
River: Flathead (South Fork)

WILDERNESS RIVER ADVENTURES
P.O. Box 717, Page, AZ 86040
(602) 645–3296
River: Colorado (Grand Canyon)

WILDERNESS RIVER OUTFITTERS–IDAHO
P.O. Box 871, Salmon, ID 83467
(208) 756–3959
Rivers: Alsek–Tatshenshini, Jarbidge–Bruneau, Flathead (Middle,
    South forks), Owyhee–ID, Owyhee–OR, Salmon (main)

WILDERNESS RIVER OUTFITTERS–OREGON
1567 Main St., Springfield, OR 97477
(503) 747–1470; (503) 726–9471
Rivers: Deschutes, Grande Ronde, John Day, McKenzie, North
    Umpqua, Salmon (lower)

WILDERNESS TRAILS
Three Rivers Resort, Kooskia, ID 83539
(208) 926–4430
Rivers: Lochsa, Selway

WILDERNESS WATERWAYS
625 N.W. Starker Ave., Corvallis, OR 97330
(503) 758–3150
Rivers: Deschutes, McKenzie, North Santiam, Rogue

WILDERNESS WORLD
P.O. Box 1647, Grants Pass, OR 97526
(800) 336–1647, (503) 479–9554
Rivers: Owyhee–OR, Rogue

WILD RIVER ADVENTURES
P.O. Box 272, West Glacier, MT 59936
(406) 442–7809; (406) 488–5539
Rivers: Clark Fork, Flathead (North and Middle forks, lower)

WILD RIVER OUTFITTERS
P.O. Box 232, Riggins, ID 83549
(800) 992–3484
River: Salmon (lower)

WILD RIVERS EXPEDITIONS
P.O. Box 118, Bluff, UT 84512
(800) 422–7654 (outside Utah); (801) 672–2244
Rivers: Green (Desolation), San Juan

WILD RIVER TOURS
P.O. Box 568, Columbia, CA 95310
(800) 821–0183; (209) 532–0160
Rivers: American (South, Middle, North forks), Carson (East
Fork), Klamath (lower), Merced

WILD SPORTS
808 Gatensbury St., Coquitlam, BC, Canada V3J 5H5
(604) 939–6217
Rivers: Chehalis, Chilliwack

WILDWATER
317 Stover St., Fort Collins, CO 80524
(303) 224–3379
Rivers: Arkansas, Cache La Poudre, North Platte

WILD WATER ADVENTURES
P.O. Box 249, Creswell, OR 97426
(503) 895-4465
Rivers: Deschutes, Grande Ronde, John Day, Klamath (lower), McKenzie, North Umpqua, Rogue

WILDWATER RIVER TOURS
P.O.Box 3623, Federal Way, WA 98063
(800) 522-WILD (inside Washington); (206) 939-2151
Rivers: Cispus, Clackamas, Deschutes, Green-WA, Klickitat, Methow, Olympic Rain Forest, Skagit, Skykomish, Suiattle, Tieton, Wenatchee, White Salmon

WOLF WHITEWATER
P.O. Box 666, Sandia Park, NM 87047
(505) 281-5042
Rivers: Rio Chama, Rio Grande-NM

WORLDWIDE EXPLORATIONS
P.O. Box 686, Flagstaff, AZ 86003
(602) 774-6462; (602) 774-0073
Rivers: Dolores, Salt, San Juan, Verde

WORLD WIDE RIVER EXPEDITIONS
942 East 7145, Suite A-202, Midvale, UT 84047
(800) 231-2769; (801) 566-2662
Rivers: Colorado (Westwater, Cataract), Green (Dinosaur, Desolation), Salmon (main), Yampa

WYOMING RIVER TRIPS
P.O. Box 1541, Cody, WY 82414
(307) 587-6661
River: Shoshone

YELLOWSTONE RAFT COMPANY
P.O. Box 608, Gardiner, MT 59030
(406) 848-7777
Rivers: Gallatin, Madison, Yellowstone

ZEPHYR RIVER EXPEDITIONS
P.O. Box 510, Columbia, CA 95310
(800) 431-3636 (inside California); (209) 532-6249
Rivers: American (South Fork), Carson (East Fork), Kings, Merced, Tuolumne

CHAPTER 9

Accommodations

THE FOLLOWING LIST OF SELECTED accommodations is for rafters who desire overnight lodging or campground facilities either prior to or following any river trip. Although most of these low and moderately priced accommodations have been recommended by the professional river outfitters, the inclusion or omission of any is not intended to be either an endorsement or disapproval of any specific lodging establishment or campground.

Since most western rivers flow through national parks, national forests, and other government lands, there are also countless public campgrounds available to rafting guests. Lists of these campgrounds can often be obtained from the river outfitters.

To avoid unnecessary morning driving time, rafters should check with outfitters regarding the time and location for their pre-trip meeting. While outfitters often meet guests at their base camp or business headquarters, the diverse geography of river trips necessitate that numerous rendezvous locations be used. While outfitters usually make shuttle arrangements, multiday trips may even require that someone shuttle a guest's automobile to or from river put-in or take-out points. In Alaska and western Canada, outfitters often arrange for pre- or post-rafting trip flights by charter aircraft.

CALIFORNIA

1. AMERICAN RIVER (South Fork), CALIFORNIA

Lodging

Best Western Cameron Park Inn
3361 Coach Ln., Cameron Park, CA 94803
(916) 677–2203

Best Western Placerville Inn
6850 Greenleaf Dr., Placerville, CA 95667
(916) 622-9100

Cameron Park Super 8 Motel
3444 Coach Ln., Cameron Park, CA 95682
(916) 677-7177

The Coloma Country Inn
P.O. Box 502, High St., Coloma, CA 95613
(916) 622-6919

Gold Trail Motor Lodge
1970 Broadway, Placerville, CA 95667
(916) 622-2906

Mother Lode Motel
1940 Broadway, Placerville, CA 95667
(916) 622-0895

Stage Coach Inn
5940 Pony Express Trail, Pollock Pines, CA 95726
(916) 644-2029

Campgrounds

Camp Coloma
P.O. Box 11, Coloma, CA 95613
(916) 622-6700

Camp Lotus
P.O. Box 578, Lotus, CA 95651
(916) 622-8672

Coloma Resort
6921 Mt. Murphy Rd., Coloma, CA 95613
(916) 622-5799

2. AMERICAN RIVER (Middle Fork), CALIFORNIA

Lodging

The Auburn Hotel
853 Lincoln Way, Auburn, CA 95603
(916) 885-8132

Auburn Inn
1875 Auburn Ravine Rd., Auburn, CA 95603
(916) 885-1800

Best Western Golden Key
13450 Lincoln Way, Auburn, CA 95603
(916) 885–8611

Dry Creek Inn (Bed & Breakfast)
13740 Dry Creek Rd., Auburn, CA 95603
(916) 878–0885

Foothills Motel
13431 Bowman Rd., Auburn, CA 95603
(916) 885–8444

Campground

Baxter Campground
P.O. Box 247, Baxter, CA 95704
(916) 389–2267

3. AMERICAN RIVER (North Fork), CALIFORNIA

See accommodations list for the American River (Middle Fork).

4. YUBA RIVER (North Fork), CALIFORNIA

Lodging

Annie Hooran's
415 W. Main St., Brass Valley, CA 95945
(916) 272–2418

Domike's Inn
20 Colfax Ave., Grass Valley, CA 95945
(916) 273–9010

Murphy's Inn
318 Neal St., Grass Valley, CA 95945
(916) 273–6873

Red Castle Inn
109 Prospect St., Nevada City, CA 95959
(916) 265–5135

Campgrounds

North Yuba Ranger Station
Star Rt., Box 1, Camptonville, CA 95922
(916) 288–3231

Willow Creek Campground
17548 Hwy. 49, Camptonville, CA 95922
(916) 288–3456

5. TRUCKEE RIVER, CALIFORNIA

Lodging

Motel 6
1400 Stardust St., Reno, NV 89503
(702) 747–7390

Travelodge–Tahoe City
455 N. Lake Blvd., Tahoe City, CA 95730
(916) 583–3766

Campground

Donner Memorial State Park
Donner Pass Rd., Truckee, CA 95734
(916) 587–3841

6. CARSON RIVER (East Fork), CALIFORNIA–NEVADA

Lodging

Carson Valley Inn
1627 U.S. 395, Minden, NV 89423
(702) 782–9711

Travelodge–South Tahoe
3489 Lake Tahoe Blvd., South Lake Tahoe, CA 95705
(916) 544–5266

Campground

Grover Hot Springs State Park
Hot Springs Rd., Markleeville, CA 96120
(916) 694–2248

7. MOKELUMNE RIVER, CALIFORNIA

Lodging

Best Western Amador Inn
200 S. Hwy. 49, Jackson, CA 95642
(209) 223–0211

Jackson Holiday Lodge
850 N. Hwys. 49 & 88, Jackson, CA 95642
(209) 223–0486

Campground

Lake Amador Resort
7500 Lake Amador Drive, Ione, CA 95640
(209) 274–4739

8. STANISLAUS RIVER, CALIFORNIA

Lodging

Avery Hotel
P.O. Box 321, Avery, CA 95224
(209) 795–9935

Dorrington Hotel
P.O. Box 4307, Dorrington, CA 95223
(209) 795–5800

Murphy's Hotel
457 Main St., Murphys, CA 95247
(209) 728–3444

Campgrounds

Calaveras Big Trees State Park
Hwy. 4, Arnold, CA 95223
(209) 795–2334

Golden Torch RV Resort and Campground
Hwy. 4, Arnold, CA 95223
(209) 795–2820

9. TUOLUMNE RIVER, CALIFORNIA

Lodging

The Berkshire Inn
P.O. Box 207, 19960 Hwy. 120, Groveland, CA 95321
(209) 962–6744

Hotel Charlotte
Hwy. 120, Groveland, CA 95321
(209) 962–6455

M & B Ranch (Bed & Breakfast)
9030 Smith Station Rd., Star Rt. Box 41, Groveland, CA
    95321
(209) 962–7257

Sugar Pine Ranch
Hwy. 120, Groveland, CA 95321
(209) 962–7823

Campground

Moccasin Point Campground
c/o Don Pedro Recreation Agency
P.O. Box 160, La Grange, CA 95329
(209) 852–2396

10. MERCED RIVER, CALIFORNIA

Lodging

Mariposa Lodge
5052 Hwy. 40, Mariposa, CA 95338
(209) 966–3607

Sierra Lodge
951 Motel Dr., Merced, CA 95340
(209) 722–3926

Sierra View Motel
7th & Bullion St., Mariposa, CA 95338
(209) 966–5793

Travelodge of Merced
2000 E. Childs Ave., Merced, CA 95340
(209) 723–3121

Campgrounds

Horseshoe Bend Campground
4240 Hwy. 132, Coulterville, CA 95311
(209) 878–3119

Yosemite–Mariposa KOA
Hwy. 140, Midpines, CA 95345
(209) 966–2201

11. KINGS RIVER, CALIFORNIA

Lodging

Best Western Village Inn
3110 N. Blackstone Ave., Fresno, CA 93703
(209) 226–2110

Economy Inn
2570 S. East St., Fresno, CA 93706
(209) 486–1188

Ramada Inn
324 E. Shaw, Fresno, CA 93710
(209) 224–4040

Campgrounds

Hume Lake Campground
Sequoia National Forest
Hume Lake, CA 93628
(209) 338–2251

Sierra Campground & RV Park
Mountain Rd. 453, Badger, CA 93603
(209) 337–2520

12. KERN RIVER, CALIFORNIA

Lodging

Kern Country Motel
32 Burlando Rd., Kernville, CA 93238
(619) 376–6733

Lake Isabella Motel (lower Kern)
Hwys. 155 & 178, P.O. Box 795, Lake Isabella, CA 93240
(619) 379–2800

Lazy River Lodge
Star Rt. 1, Kernville, CA 93238
(619) 376–2242

Pala Ranches Motel
11042 Kernville Rd., Kernville, CA 93238
(619) 376–2222

Sequoia Motor Lodge
Sierra Way, Kernville, CA 93238
(619) 376–2535

Sierra South Lodge
2 Sierretta St. & Kernville Rd., Kernville, CA 93238
(619) 376–6019

Valley Motel (lower Kern)
5328 Lake Isabella Blvd., Lake Isabella, CA 93240
(619) 379–8484

Whispering Pines Lodge
11781 Sierra Way, Kernville, CA 93238
(619) 376–2334

Campground

Rivernook Campground
14001 Sierra Way, Kernville, CA 93238
(619) 376–2705

13. KAWEAH RIVER, CALIFORNIA

Lodging

Giant Forest Lodge
P.O. Box 789, Three Rivers, CA 93271
(209) 561–3314

Three Rivers Motel
43365 Sierra Dr., Three Rivers, CA 93271
(209) 561–4413

Campground

Kaweah Park Resort
40457 Sierra Dr., Three Rivers, CA 93271
(209) 561–4424

14. KLAMATH RIVER (Upper), OREGON-CALIFORNIA

Lodging

Ben Bar Motel
1210 S. Main, Yreka, CA 96097
(916) 842–2791

Best Western Miner's Inn
122 E. Miner St., Yreka, CA 96097
(916) 842–4355

Klamath Motor Lodge
1111 S. Main St., Yreka, CA 96097
(916) 842–2751

Motel Orleans
1806 B Fort Jones, Yreka, CA 96097
(916) 842–1612

Thunderbird Lodge
526 S. Main, Yreka, CA 96097
(916) 842–4404

Wayside Inn
1235 S. Main, Yreka, CA 96097
(916) 842–4412

15. KLAMATH RIVER (Lower), CALIFORNIA

Lodging

Anglers Motel
Hwy. 96, P.O. Box 483, Happy Camp, CA 96039
(916) 493–2735

Best Western Miner's Inn
122 E. Miner, Yreka, CA 96097
(916) 842–4355

Forest Lodge Motel
Hwy. 96, Happy Camp, CA 96039
(916) 493–5424

Klamath Inn
Hwy. 96, 110 Nugget St., Happy Camp, CA 96039
(916) 493–2860

Rustic Inn Motel
Hwy. 96, P.O. Box 925, Happy Camp, CA 96039
(916) 493–2658

Campground

Elk Creek Campground
P.O. Box 785, 921 Elk Creek Rd., Happy Camp, CA 96039
(916) 493–2208

16. SCOTT RIVER, CALIFORNIA

See accommodations list for the Klamath River (lower).

17. SALMON RIVER, CALIFORNIA

Lodging

Somes Bar Lodge
Somes Bar, CA 95568
(916) 469–3399

Young's Ranch Resort
Somes Bar, CA 95568
(800) KLAMATH
(916) 469–3322

Campground

Oak Bottom Campground
Klamath National Forest
Salmon River Road, Somes Bar, CA 95568
(916) 469–3331

18. WOOLEY RIVER, CALIFORNIA

See accommodations list for the Salmon River, California.

19. TRINITY RIVER, CALIFORNIA

Lodging

49er Motel
P.O. Box 1608, Weaverville, CA 96093
(916) 623–4937

Granny's House
P.O. Box 31, Weaverville, CA 96093
(916) 623–2756

Motel Trinity
P.O. Box 1179, Weaverville, CA 96093
(916) 623–2129

Red Hill Motel
P.O. Box 234, Weaverville, CA 96093
(916) 623–4331

Weaverville Hotel
P.O. Box 537, Weaverville, CA 96093
(916) 623–3121

Campground

Big Foot Campground
P.O. Box 98, Junction City, CA 96048
(916) 623–6088

20. EEL RIVER (Middle), CALIFORNIA

Lodging

Best Western Inn
601 E. Talmage Rd., Ukiah, CA 95482
(707) 462–8862

Motel 6
1208 S. State St., Ukiah, CA 95482
(707) 468–5404

Travelodge
1070 S. State St., Ukiah, CA 95482
(707) 462–6657

Campground

MacKerricher State Park
Hwy. 1, Fort Bragg, CA 95437
(707) 937–5804

21. SACRAMENTO RIVER (Upper), CALIFORNIA

Lodging

Best Western Tree House
P.O. Box 236, Mt. Shasta, CA 96067
(916) 926–3101

Motel 6
1250 Twin View Blvd., Redding, CA 96003
(916) 246–4470

22. CACHE CREEK, CALIFORNIA

Lodging

Motel 6
1564 E. Main St., Woodland, CA 95695
(916) 666–6777

Campground

Clear Lake State Park
Soda Bay Rd., Kelseyville, CA 95451
(707) 279–4293

THE PACIFIC NORTHWEST STATES

23. WENATCHEE RIVER, WASHINGTON

Lodging

Best Western Rivers Inn
580 Valley Mall Pkwy., Wenatchee, WA 98801
(509) 884–1474

Holiday Lodge
610 N. Wenatchee Ave., Wenatchee, WA 98801
(509) 663–8167

River's Edge Lodge
8401 Hwy. 2, Leavenworth, WA 98826
(509) 548–7612

Scotty's AAA Motel
1004 N. Miller, Wenatchee, WA 98801
(509) 662–8165

Village Inn Motel
229 Cottage Ave., Cashmere, WA 98815
(509) 782–3522

Campground

Wenatchee River County Park
Hwy. 2, Wenatchee, WA 98801
(509) 662–2525

24. METHOW RIVER, WASHINGTON

Lodging

Idle-a-While Motel
Hwy. 120, Twisp, WA 98856
(509) 997–3222

Lake Pateros Motor Inn
P.O. Box 25, Jct. 97 & 153, Pateros, WA 98846
(509) 923–2203

Campgrounds

Alta Lake State Park
U.S. Hwy. 97, Pateros, WA 98846
(509) 923–2473

Methow River KOA
P.O. Box 305, Winthrop, WA 98862
(509) 996–2258

25. STEHEKIN RIVER, WASHINGTON

Lodging

Stehekin Valley Ranch
P.O. Box 36, Stehekin, WA 98852
(509) 682–4677

Campground

Harlequin Campground
Lake Chelan National Recreation Area
Main Valley Road, Stehekin, WA 98852
(206) 856–5700

26. TIETON RIVER, WASHINGTON

Lodging

Best Western Rio Miranda
1603 Terrace Heights Dr., Yakima, WA 98901
(509) 457–4444

Holiday Inn
9th St. and Yakima Ave., Yakima, WA 98901
(509) 452–6511

Campground

KOA Yakima
1500 Keyes Rd., Yakima, WA 98901
(509) 248–5882

27. KLICKITAT RIVER, WASHINGTON

Lodging

Hood River Village Resort
I-84N and Oregon 35, Hood River, OR 97031
(509) 386–2200

Ponderosa Motel
775 E. Broadway St., Goldendale, WA 98620
(509) 773–5842

28. WHITE SALMON RIVER, WASHINGTON

Lodging

Hood River Village Resort
I-84N and Oregon 35, Hood River, OR 97031
(509) 386–2200

Llama Ranch Bed & Breakfast
1980 Hwy. 141, Trout Lake, WA 98650
(509) 395–2786

29. NOOKSACK RIVER (North Fork), WASHINGTON

Lodging

Best Western Heritage Inn
151 E. McLeod Rd., Bellingham, WA 98226
(206) 647–1912

Motel 6
3701 Byron Ave., Bellingham, WA 98225
(206) 671–4494

Campground

KOA Lynden
8717 Line Rd., Lynden, WA 98264
(206) 354–4772

30. SAUK RIVER, WASHINGTON

Lodging

Motel 6
10006 Evergreen Way, Everett, WA 98204
(206) 347-2060

Nendel's Motor Inn
2800 Pacific Ave., Everett, WA 98201
(206) 258-4141

Smokey Point Motor Inn
17329 Smokey Point Dr., Arlington, WA 98223
(206) 659-8561

Stagecoach Inn
1100 Seaman St., Darrington, WA 98241
(206) 436-1776

Campground

Cascade Kamloop Campground
P.O. Box 353, Darrington, WA 98241
(206) 436-1003

31. SUIATTLE RIVER, WASHINGTON

See accommodations list for the Sauk River.

32. SKAGIT RIVER, WASHINGTON

Lodging

Clark's Skagit River Cabins
Hwy. 20, Marblemount, WA 98267
(206) 873-2250

Cocusa Motel
200 West Rio Vista, Burlington, WA 98233
(206) 757-6044

Concrete Motel
Hwy. 20, Concrete, WA 98237
(206) 853-8870

Nendel's of Mt. Vernon
2009 Riverside Dr., Mt. Vernon, WA 98273
(206) 424-4141

Campgrounds

Goodell Creek and Newhalem Campgrounds
North Cascades National Park, Sedro Wooley, WA 98284
(206) 855-1331

33. SKYKOMISH RIVER, WASHINGTON

Lodging

Brookside Motel
19930 U.S. Hwy. 2, Monroe, WA 98272
(206) 794-8832

Dutch Cup Motel
P.O. Box 336, Sultan, WA 98294
(206) 793-2215

Fairground Inn
18950 U.S. Hwy. 2, Monroe, WA 98272
(206) 794-5401

Campground

Wallace Falls State Park
U.S. Hwy. 2, Gold Bar, WA 98251
(206) 793-0420

34. GREEN RIVER, WASHINGTON

Lodging

Auburn Motel
1202 Auburn Way S., Auburn, WA 98002
(206) 833-7470

Pony Soldier Motor Inn
1521 D St. N.E., Auburn, WA 98002
(206) 939-5950

Campground

Kanaskat-Palmer State Park
Farman Rd., Palmer, WA 98048
(206) 886-0148

35. CISPUS RIVER, WASHINGTON

Lodging

Mountain View Lodge
13163 U.S. Hwy. 12, Packwood, WA 98361
(206) 494–5555

Campground

Packwood RV Park & Campground
P.O. Box 309, Packwood, WA 98361
(206) 494–5145

36. TOUTLE RIVER, WASHINGTON

Lodging

Aladdin Motor Inn
310 Long Ave., Kelso, WA 98626
(206) 425–9660

Motel 6
106 Minor Rd., Kelso, WA 98626
(206) 425–3229

Campground

Volcano View Resort & Campground
4220 Spirit Lake Hwy., Castle Rock, WA 98645
(206) 274–7087

37. OLYMPIC RAIN-FOREST RIVERS, WASHINGTON

Lodging

Forks Motel
P.O. Box 510, Forks, WA 98331
(206) 374–6243

Olympic Inn
616 West Heron St., Aberdeen, WA 98520
(206) 533–4200

Campground

Rain Forest Resort Campground
Rt. 1, Box 40, Quinault, WA 98575
(206) 288–2535

38. ELWHA RIVER, WASHINGTON

Lodging

Uptown Motel
101 E. 2nd St., Port Angeles, WA 98362
(206) 457–9434

Campground

KOA Port Angeles
2065 Hwy. 101E, Port Angeles, WA 98362
(206) 457–5916

39. ROGUE RIVER, OREGON

Lodging

Galice Resort
11744 Galice Rd., Merlin, OR 97532
(503) 476–3818

Morrison's Rogue River Lodge
8500 Galice Rd., Merlin, OR 97532
(800) 826–1963
(503) 476–3825

Motel 6
1800 N.E. 7th St., Grants Pass, OR 97526
(503) 474–1331

Redwood Motel
815 N.E. 6th St., Grants Pass, OR 97526
(503) 476–0878

Riverside Inn
971 S.E. 6th St., Grants Pass, OR 97526
(503) 476–6873

Shilo Inn
1880 N.W. 6th St., Grants Pass, OR 97526
(503) 479–5381

Campgrounds

Indian Mary Park Campground
7100 Galice Rd., Merlin, OR 97532
(503) 474–5285

KOA Gold 'n Rogue
P.O. Box 320, Gold Hill, OR 97525
(503) 855–7710

40. ILLINOIS RIVER, OREGON

See accommodations list for the Rogue River.

41. NORTH UMPQUA RIVER, OREGON

Lodging

Best Western Douglas Inn
511 S.E. Stephens, Roseburg, OR 97470
(503) 673–6625

Windmill Inn
1450 N.W. Mulholland, Roseburg, OR 97470
(800) 452–8018

Campground

Twin Rivers Vacation Park
433 River Forks Park Rd., Roseburg, OR 97470
(503) 673–3811

42. MCKENZIE RIVER, OREGON

Lodging

Shilo Inn
3350 Gateway Rd., Springfield, OR 97477
(503) 747–0332

Sleepy Hollow Motel
54791 McKenzie Hwy., Blue River, OR 97413
(503) 822–3805

Wayfarer Resort
46725 Goodpasture Rd., Vida, OR 97488
(503) 896–3613

Campground

Lazy Days Campground
52511 McKenzie Hwy., Blue River, OR 97413
(503) 822–3889

43. NORTH SANTIAM RIVER, OREGON

Lodging

Motel 6
2250 Mission St. S.E., Salem, OR 97302
(503) 588–7191

Pony Soldier Motor Inn
315 Airport Rd. S.E., Albany, OR 97321
(503) 928–6322

Rodeway Inn
745 Commercial St., Salem, OR 97301
(503) 363–2451

Campground

Detroit Lake State Park
Hwy. 22, Detroit, OR 97342
(503) 854–3346

44. CLACKAMAS RIVER, OREGON

Lodging

Days Inn
9717 S.E. Sunnyside Rd., Clackamas, OR 97015
(503) 654–1699

Monarch Motel
12566 S.E. 93rd Ave., Clackamas, OR 97015
(503) 652–1515

Campground

Milo McIver State Park
Oregon Hwy. 211, Estacada, OR 97023
(503) 630–7150

45. DESCHUTES RIVER, OREGON

Lodging

Inn at The Dalles
3550 S.E. Frontage Rd., The Dalles, OR 97058
(503) 296–1167

Portage Inn
3223 N.E. Frontage Rd., The Dalles, OR 97058
(503) 298–5502

Sonny's Motel
1539 S.W. U.S. Hwy. 97, Madras, OR 97741
(503) 475–7217

Tillicum Motor Inn
2114 W. 6th St., The Dalles, OR 97058
(503) 298–5161

Campgrounds

Beavertail Campground
BLM Prineville District, Deschutes River Rd., Maupin, OR
  97037
(503) 447–4115

Wasco County Fairgrounds
Tygh Valley Rd., Tygh Valley, OR 97063
(503) 483–2288

46. JOHN DAY RIVER, OREGON

See accommodations list for the Deschutes River.

47. GRANDE RONDE RIVER, OREGON-WASHINGTON

Lodging

Motel 6
325 S.E. Nye Ave., Pendleton, OR 97801
(503) 276–3160

Ponderosa Motel
102 S.E. Greenwood St., Enterprise, OR 97828
(503) 426–3186

Pony Soldier Motor Inn
2612 Island Ave., LaGrande, OR 97850
(503) 963–7195

Rivertree Inn
1257 Bridge St., Clarkston, WA 99403
(509) 758–9551

Stardust Lodge
402 Adams Ave., LaGrande, OR 97850
(503) 963–4166

Campground

Minam State Recreation Area
Oregon Hwy. 82, Elgin, OR 97827
(503) 432–4185

48. OWYHEE RIVER, OREGON

Lodging

Basque Station Motel
Main and Blackaby, Jordan Valley, OR 97910
(503) 586–9244

Sahara Motel
P.O. Box 169, Jordan Valley, OR 97910
(503) 586–2500

THE NORTHERN ROCKY MOUNTAIN STATES

49. SALMON RIVER (Middle Fork), IDAHO

Lodging

Best Western Christiana
651 Sun Valley Rd., Ketchum, ID 83340
(208) 726–3351

Heidelberg Inn
P.O. Box 304, Ketchum, ID 83340
(208) 726–5361

Mountain Village Lodge
P.O. Box 150, Stanley, ID 83278
(208) 774–3661

Redwood Motel
P.O. Box 55, Stanley, ID 83278
(208) 774–3340

Campgrounds

KOA Sun Valley
P.O. Box 548, Ketchum, ID 83340
(208) 726–3429

Red Top Meadows RV Park & Campground
P.O. Box 386, Ketchum, ID 83340
(208) 726–5445

50. SALMON RIVER (Upper Main), IDAHO

See accommodations list for the Salmon River (Middle Fork).

51. SALMON RIVER (Main), IDAHO

Lodging

Best Western Wagons West Motel
P.O. Box 574, Salmon, ID 83467
(208) 756–4281

Motel Deluxe
P.O. Box 1044, Salmon, ID 83467
(208) 756–2231

Stagecoach Inn Motel
201 Hwy. 93N, Salmon, ID 83467
(208) 756–4251

Suncrest Motel
705 Challis St., Salmon, ID 83467
(208) 756–2294

Campground

Salmon Meadows Campground
P.O. Box 705, Salmon, ID 83467
(208) 756–2640

52. SALMON RIVER (Lower), IDAHO

Lodging

Monty's Motel
700 W. Main St., Grangeville, ID 83530
(208) 983–2500

Pony Soldier Motor Inn
1716 Main St., Lewiston, ID 83501
(208) 743–9526

Riggins Motel
P.O. Box 1157, Riggins, ID 83549
(208) 628–3456

Sacajawea Motor Inn
1824 Main St., Lewiston, ID 83501
(208) 746–1393

Salmon River Motel
1203 S. U.S. Hwy. 95, Riggins, ID 83549
(208) 628–3231

Campground

Hells Gate State Park
Snake River Ave., Lewiston, ID 83501
(208) 743–2363

53. LOCHSA RIVER, IDAHO

Lodging

Ida-Lee Motel
P.O. Box 16, Kooskia, ID 83539
(208) 926–0166

Snooky's Carriage Inn
U.S. Hwy. 12, Kamiah, ID 83536
(208) 935–2531

Campground

Three Rivers Resort & Campground
HC75, Box 61, Kooskia, ID 83539
(208) 926–4708

54. SELWAY RIVER, IDAHO

See accommodations list for the Lochsa River.

55. MOYIE RIVER, IDAHO

Lodging

Best Western Kootenai River Inn
Kootenai River Plaza, Bonners Ferry, ID 83805
(208) 267–8511

Campground

Blue Lake Campground & RV Park
P.O. Box 655, Bonners Ferry, ID 83805
(208) 267–2029

56. ST. JOE RIVER, IDAHO

Lodging

The Pines Motel
1117 Main, St. Maries, ID 83861
(208) 245–2545

Campground

Benewah Campground
Rt. 1, Box 50, St. Maries, ID 83861
(208) 245-3288

57. SNAKE RIVER (Hells Canyon), IDAHO–OREGON

See accommodations list for the Salmon River (Lower).

58. SNAKE RIVER (Birds of Prey), IDAHO

Lodging

The Pepper Mill Inn
908 3rd St. S., Nampa, ID 83651
(208) 466-3594

Shilo Inn
617 Nampa Blvd., Nampa, ID 83651
(208) 466-8993

Campground

Given's Hot Springs
P.O. Box 103, Melba, ID 83641
(208) 495-2437

59. SNAKE RIVER (Middle), IDAHO

Lodging

Best Western Canyon Springs Inn
1357 Blue Lakes Blvd., Twin Falls, ID 83301
(208) 734-5000

Motel Evergreen
1331 S. Main St., Gooding, ID 83330
(208) 934-9987

Campground

KOA Twin Falls–Jerome
5431 U.S. 93, Jerome, ID 83338
(208) 324-4169

60. PAYETTE RIVER, IDAHO

Lodging

Landmark Inn
2155 N. Garden, Boise, ID 83704
(208) 344–4030

Mountain View Motel
P.O. Box 1053, Cascade, ID 83611
(208) 382–4238

Rodeway Inn
1115 N. Curtis Rd., Boise, ID 83706
(208) 376–2700

Sun-Liner Motel
3433 Chinden Blvd., Garden City, ID 83714
(208) 344–7647

Campgrounds

Americana Overnight Kampground
3600 American Terrace, Boise, ID 83706
(208) 342–9691

Silver Creek Plunge
HC 76, Box 2666, Garden Valley, ID 83622
(208) 344–8688

61. JARBIDGE-BRUNEAU RIVERS, IDAHO

Lodging

Best Western Foothills Motor Inn
1080 Hwy. 20, Mountain Home, ID 83647
(208) 587–8477

Motel Thunderbird
910 Sunset Strip, Hwy. 30W, Mountain Home, ID 83647
(208) 587–7927

Campground

Golden Rule KOA
220 E. 10th St. N., Mountain Home, ID 83647
(208) 587–5111

62. OWYHEE RIVER, IDAHO–OREGON

See accommodations list for the Jarbidge–Bruneau rivers.

63. FLATHEAD RIVER (North Fork), MONTANA

Lodging

Glacier Highland Motel
P.O. Box 397, West Glacier, MT 59936
(406) 888–5427

River Bend Motel
P.O. Box 398, West Glacier, MT 59936
(406) 888–5662

Village Inn
P.O. Box 115, West Glacier, MT 59936
(406) 888–5632

Campgrounds

Glacier Campground
P.O. Box 447, West Glacier, MT 59936
(406) 387–5689

KOA West Glacier
P.O. Box 215, West Glacier, MT 59936
(406) 387–5341

64. FLATHEAD RIVER (Middle Fork), MONTANA

See accommodations list for the Flathead River (North Fork).

65. FLATHEAD RIVER (South Fork), MONTANA

Lodging

Days Inn
1830 Hwy. 93S, Kalispell, MT 59901
(406) 755–3798

Diamond Lil's Motel
1680 U.S. 93S, Kalispell, MT 59901
(406) 752–3467

Super 8 Motel
P.O. Box 318, Polson, MT 59860
(406) 883–6251

Campground

Spruce Park Campground
1985 Hwy. 35, Kalispell, MT 59901
(406) 752–6321

66. FLATHEAD RIVER (Lower), MONTANA

See accommodations list for the Flathead River (South Fork).

67. CLARK FORK RIVER, MONTANA

Lodging

Days Inn
Hwy. 93 and I-90, Missoula, MT 59802
(406) 721–9776

Super 8 Motel
3901 S. Brooks St., Missoula, MT 59801
(406) 251–2255

Travelodge
420 W. Broadway, Missoula, MT 59802
(406) 728–4500

Campground

KOA El Mar–Missoula
3695 Tina Ave., Missoula, MT 59802
(406) 549–0881

68. BLACKFOOT RIVER, MONTANA

See accommodations list for the Clark Fork River.

69. GALLATIN RIVER, MONTANA

Lodging

Best Western Buck's T-4
P.O. Box 279, Big Sky, MT 59716
(406) 995–4111

Golden Eagle Lodge
P.O. Box 8, Big Sky, MT 59716
(406) 995–4800

Campground

KOA West Yellowstone
P.O. Box 327, West Yellowstone, MT 59758
(406) 646–7607

70. MADISON RIVER, MONTANA

Lodging

Rainbow Valley Motel
P.O. Box 26, Ennis, MT 59729
(406) 682–7600

Campground

Bear Trap Hot Spring
P.O. Box 2944, Norris, MT 59745
(406) 685–3303

71. YELLOWSTONE RIVER, MONTANA

Lodging

Hillcrest Motel
P.O. Box 130, Gardiner, MT 59030
(406) 848–7353

Wilson's Yellowstone River Motel
P.O. Box 223, Gardiner, MT 59030
(406) 848–7303

Campground

Rocky Mountain Campground
Jardine Rt., Box 10, Gardiner, MT 59030
(406) 848–7251

72. SNAKE RIVER (Upper), WYOMING

Lodging

Antler Motel
43 W. Pearl St., Jackson, WY 83001
(307) 733–2535

Executive Inn
325 W. Pearl St., Jackson, WY 83001
(307) 733–4340

49'er Motel
330 W. Pearl St., Jackson, WY 83001
(307) 733–7550

Motel 6
1370 W. Broadway, Jackson, WY 83001
(307) 733–9666

Super 8 Motel
1520 S. Hwy. 89, Jackson, WY 83001
(307) 733–6833

Campgrounds

A-1 Campground
125 Virginia Lane S., Jackson, WY 83001
(307) 733–2697

Jackson Hole Campground
P.O. Box 2802, Jackson, WY 83001
(307) 733–2927

73. SHOSHONE RIVER, WYOMING

Lodging

Buffalo Bill Village
1701 Sheridan Ave., Cody, WY 82414
(307) 587–5544

Super 8 Motel
730 Yellowstone Hwy., Cody, WY 82414
(307) 527–6214

Campgrounds

Cody KOA
5561 Greybull Hwy., Cody, WY 82414
(307) 587–2369

Ponderosa Campground
P.O. Box 1477, Cody, WY 82414
(307) 587–9203

THE SOUTHWEST STATES

74. ARKANSAS RIVER, COLORADO

Lodging

Arkansas River Campground
3745 E. Hwy. 50, Salida, CO 81201
(719) 539–2381

Best Western Salida
352 W. Rainbow Blvd., Salida, CO 81201
(719) 539–2514

Budget Lodge
1146 W. Rainbow Blvd., Salida, CO 81201
(719) 539–6695

Economy 9 Motel
7350 W. Highway 50, Salida, CO 81201
(719) 539–6733

Great Western Sumac Lodge
U.S. Hwy. 24, Buena Vista, CO 81211
(719) 395–8111

Old Town Inn
209 N. 19th St., Canon City, CO 81212
(719) 275–8687

Red Wood Lodge
7310 Hwy. 50, Salida, CO 81201
(719) 539–2528

Salida Motel
1312 E. Rainbow Blvd., Salida, CO 81201
(719) 539–2895

Campgrounds

Brown's Campground
11430 County Rd. 197, Nathrop, CO 81236
(719) 395–8301

KOA Kampground
21435 U.S. Hwy. 50, P.O. Box 387, Cotapaxi, CO 81223
(719) 275–9308

Royal View Campground
0227 8-Mile Hill, Canon City, CO 81212
(719) 275–1900

75. CLEAR CREEK, COLORADO

Lodging

Argo Motor Inn
2622 Colorado Blvd., Idaho Springs, CO 80452
(303) 567–4473

Campground

KOA Central City Black Hawk
Rt. 6, Box 111, Golden, CO 80403
(303) 582–9979

76. NORTH PLATTE RIVER, COLORADO-WYOMING

Lodging

Platte's Bed & Breakfast
Star Rt. 49, Encampment, WY 82325
(307) 327–5539

Campgrounds

Northgate Mini Mart & Campground
P.O. Box 136, Cowdrey, CO 80434
(303) 723–4200

Stephens Lake John Resort
P.O. Box 303, Walden, CO 80480
(303) 723–4552

77. CACHE LA POUDRE RIVER, COLORADO

Lodging

Comfort Inn
1638 E. Mulberry, Fort Collins, CO 80524
(303) 484–2444

Days Inn
3625 E. Mulberry, Fort Collins, CO 80524
(303) 221–5490

Motel 6
3900 E. Mulberry, Fort Collins, CO 80524
(303) 482–6466

University Park Holiday Inn
425 W. Prospect, Fort Collins, CO 80524
(303) 482–2626

Campground

KOA Mile High
6670 Hwy. 287N, Box 600, La Porte, CO 80535
(303) 493–9758

78. BLUE RIVER, COLORADO

Lodging

Comfort Inn
560 Silverthorne Ln., Silverthorne, CO 80498
(303) 468–6200

Green Mountain Inn
Blue River Rt., Box 82A, Dillon, CO 80435
(303) 724–9748

Campground

Kremmling RV Park & Campground
P.O. Box 532, Kremmling, CO 80459
(303) 724–9593

79. EAGLE RIVER, COLORADO

Lodging

Best Western Raintree Inn
2211 N. Frontage Rd., Vail, CO 81657
(303) 476–3890

Comfort Inn
0161 W. Beaver Creek Blvd., Avon, CO 81620
(303) 949–5511

Lodge at Cordillera
51 Grand Traverse, Edwards, CO 81632
(303) 926–2200

Lodging and Campground

Best Western Eagle Lodge & RV Park
200 Loren Ln., Eagle, CO 81631
(303) 328–6316

80. ROARING FORK RIVER, COLORADO

Lodging

Best Western Aspenalt Lodge
160 Hwy. 82, Basalt, CO 81621
(303) 927–3191

Tyrolean Lodge
200 W. Main, Aspen, CO 81611
(303) 925–4595

Campground

Aspen Basalt KOA
P.O. Box 880, Basalt, CO 81621
(303) 927–3532

81. COLORADO RIVER (Upper), COLORADO

See accommodations lists for the Blue River, Eagle River, and
Colorado River (Glenwood).

82. COLORADO RIVER (Glenwood), COLORADO

Lodging

Budget Host
51429 U.S. Hwy. 6 & 24, Glenwood Springs, CO 81601
(303) 945–5682

Cedar Lodge
2102 Grand Ave., Glenwood Springs, CO 81601
(303) 945–6579

Frontier Lodge
2834 Glen Ave., Glenwood Springs, CO 81601
(303) 945–8545

Holiday Inn
51359 U.S. Hwy. 6 & 24, Glenwood Springs, CO 81601
(303) 945–8551

Ramada Inn
124 6th St., Glenwood Springs, CO 81601
(303) 945–2500

Campground

New Castle KOA
0581 County Rd. 241, New Castle, CO 81647
(303) 984–2240

83. COLORADO RIVER (Horsethief-Ruby), COLORADO

Lodging

American Family Lodge
721 Horizon Dr., Grand Junction, CO 81506
(303) 243–6050

Best Western Horizon Inn
754 Horizon Dr., Grand Junction, CO 81506
(303) 245–1410

Grand Junction Motor Inn
733 Horizon Dr., Grand Junction, CO 81506
(303) 245–7200

Campgrounds

Fruita Junction RV Park & Campground
607 Hwy. 340, Fruita, CO 81521
(303) 858–3155

KOA Grand Junction
613 E. I-70 Business Loop, Clifton, CO 81520
(303) 434–6644

84. TAYLOR RIVER, COLORADO

Lodging

A-B-C Motel
212 E. Tomichi Ave., Gunnison, CO 81230
(303) 641–2400

Bennett's Western Motel
403 E. Tomichi Ave., Gunnison, CO 81230
(303) 641–1722

Swiss Inn Motel
312 E. Tomichi Ave., Gunnison, CO 81230
(303) 641–9962

Campgrounds

Shady Island RV Park & Campground
2776 Hwy. 135N, Gunnison, CO 81230
(303) 641–0416

Tall Texan Campground
2460 Hwy. 135N, Gunnison, CO 81230
(303) 641–2920

85. SLATE RIVER, COLORADO

Lodging

Cristiana Guesthaus
621 Maroon Ave., Crested Butte, CO 81224
(303) 349–5326

Manor Lodge
P.O. Box 729, Crested Butte, CO 81224
(800) 826–3210 (outside Colorado)
(800) 548–2454 (inside Colorado)

Rozman's Motor Lodge
P.O. Box 909, Crested Butte, CO 81224
(303) 349–6669

86. GUNNISON RIVER, COLORADO

See accommodations list for the Taylor River.

87. GUNNISON RIVER (Lake Fork), COLORADO

See accommodations list for the Gunnison River and Taylor River.

88. GUNNISON RIVER (Gorge), COLORADO

Lodging

Black Canyon Friendship Inn
Hwy. 50E, Montrose, CO 81401
(303) 249–3495

Trapper Motel
1225 E. Main, Montrose, CO 81401
(303) 249–3426

Campground

Hanging Tree RV Park & Campground
17250 Hwy. 550S, Montrose, CO 81401
(303) 249–9966

89. PIEDRA RIVER, COLORADO

Lodging

Best Western Oak Ridge Motor Inn
158 Light Plant Rd., Pagosa Springs, CO 81147
(303) 264–4173

San Juan Motel
191 E. Pagosa St. (Hwy. 160), Pagosa Springs, CO 81147
(303) 264–2262

Super 8 Motel
Hwy. 160 & Piedra Rd., Pagosa Springs, CO 81147
(303) 731–4005

Campground

Pagosa Springs KOA Campground
P.O. Box 268, Pagosa Springs, CO 81147
(303) 264–5874

90. ANIMAS RIVER, COLORADO

Lodging

Best Value Four Winds
20797 Hwy. 160W, Durango, CO 81301
(303) 247–4512

Caboose Motel
3363 Main Ave., Durango, CO 81301
(303) 247–1191

Comfort Inn
2930 N. Main Ave., Durango, CO 81301
(303) 259–5373

Edelweiss Motel
689 C.R. 203, Durango, CO 81301
(303) 247–5685

Thunderbird Motel
2701 Main Ave., Durango, CO 81301
(303) 259–2540

Campgrounds

Durango N. Ponderosa KOA
13391 C.R. 250, Durango, CO 81301
(303) 247–4499

Lightner Creek Campground
1567 C.R. 207, Durango, CO 81301
(303) 247–5406

Molas Lake Park & Campground
P.O. Box 776, Silverton, CO 81433
(303) 387–5410

91. DOLORES RIVER, COLORADO-UTAH

Lodging

Best Western Sands of Cortez
1000 E. Main St., Cortez, CO 81321
(303) 565–3761

Best Western Turquoise Motor Inn
535 E. Main St., Cortez, CO 81321
(303) 565–3778

Ramada Inn
666 S. Broadway, Cortez, CO 81321
(303) 228–2828

Campground

Dolores River RV Park and Camping
18680 Hwy. 145, Dolores, CO 81323
(303) 882–7761

92. SAN MIGUEL RIVER, COLORADO

Lodging

Best Western Tomboy Inn
P.O. Box 325, Telluride, CO 81435
(303) 728-3871

Johnstone Inn
P.O. Box 546, Telluride, CO 81435
(303) 728-3316

Campground

Weber's Campground
20725 Hwy. 550, Ridgeway, CO 81432
(303) 626-5383

93. YAMPA RIVER, COLORADO

Lodging

Antlers Best Western Motel
423 W. Main, Vernal, UT 84078
(801) 789-1202

Best Western Dinosaur Inn
251 E. Main, Vernal, UT 84078
(801) 789-2660

Econo Lodge
311 E. Main, Vernal, UT 84078
(801) 789-2000

Split Mountain Motel
1015 E. Hwy. 40, Vernal, UT 84078
(801) 789-9020

Campground

Campground Dina
930 N. Vernal Ave., Vernal, UT 84078
(801) 789-2148

94. GREEN RIVER (Dinosaur National Monument), COLORADO-UTAH

See accommodations list for the Yampa River.

95. GREEN RIVER (Desolation), UTAH

Lodging

Best Western River Terrace Motel
880 E. Main St., Green River, UT 84525
(801) 564–3401

Bookcliff Lodge
395 E. Main St., Green River, UT 84525
(801) 564–3406

Robbers Roost Motel
135 W. Main St., Green River, UT 84525
(801) 564–3452

West Winds Rodeway Inn
525 E. Main St., Green River, UT 84525
(801) 564–3421

Campground

KOA Green River
P.O. Box 14, Green River, UT 84525
(801) 564–3651

96. COLORADO RIVER (Professor Valley), UTAH

Lodging

Best Western Green Well
105 S. Main St., Moab, UT 84532
(801) 259–6151

Bowen Motel
169 N. Main St., Moab, UT 84532
(801) 259–7132

Moab Travelodge
550 S. Main St., Moab, UT 84532
(801) 259–6171

Ramada Inn
182 S. Main St., Moab, UT 84532
(801) 259–7141

Campgrounds

Canyonlands Campark
555 S. Main St., Moab, UT 84532
(801) 259–6848

Devils Garden Campground
Arches National Park
125 W. 200S, Moab, UT 84532
(801) 259–8161

97. COLORADO RIVER (Westwater), UTAH

See accommodations lists for the Colorado River (Professor Valley) and the Colorado River (Horsethief–Ruby).

98. COLORADO RIVER (Cataract), UTAH

See accomodations list for the Colorado River (Professor Valley).

99. SAN JUAN RIVER, UTAH

Lodging

Canyonlands Motel
P.O. Box 11, Mexican Hat, UT 84531
(801) 683–2230

San Juan Inn
P.O. Box 535, Mexican Hat, UT 84531
(801) 683–2220

Campground

Valle's Trailer Park Campground
P.O. Box 516, Mexican Hat, UT 84531
(801) 683–2226

100. COLORADO RIVER (Grand Canyon), ARIZONA

Lodging

Cliff Dwellers Lodge
Hwy. U.S. 89A, Marble Canyon, AZ 86036
(602) 355–2228

Days Inn
2320 E. Lucky Ln., Flagstaff, AZ 86004
(602) 526-1150

Holiday Inn
1000 W. Hwy. U.S. 66, Flagstaff, AZ 86001
(602) 774-5221

Royal 8 Inn
424 W. Beale St., Kingman, AZ 86401
(602) 753-9222

Weston's Lamplighter
207 N. Lake Powell Blvd., Page, AZ 86040
(602) 645-2451

Campground

Lee's Ferry Campground
Glen Canyon National Recreation Area
Lee's Ferry Rd., Marble Canyon, AZ 86036
(602) 645-2471

101. VERDE RIVER, ARIZONA

Lodging

Best Western Cottonwood Inn
993 S. Main St., Cottonwood, AZ 86326
(602) 634-5575

Campground

KOA Black Canyon
P.O. Box 569, Black Canyon City, AZ 85324
(602) 374-5318

102. SALT RIVER, ARIZONA

Lodging

Best Western Copper Hills
U.S. Hwy. 60, Globe, AZ 85501
(602) 425-7151

Copper Manor Motel
637 E. Ash St., Globe, AZ 85501
(602) 425–7124

103. RIO CHAMA RIVER, NEW MEXICO

Lodging

Chamisa Inn
920 N. Riverside Dr., Espanola, NM 87532
(505) 753–7291

La Quinta Motel
4298 Cerrillos Rd., Santa Fe, NM 87505
(505) 471–1142

Rodeway Inn
2900 Cerrillos Rd., Santa Fe, NM 87501
(505) 473–4281

Campground

Abiquiu Dam Campground
U.S. Army Corps of Engineers
N.M. Hwy. 96, Abiquiu, NM 87510
(505) 685–4371

104. RIO GRANDE RIVER, NEW MEXICO

Lodging

Rodeway Inn
S. Santa Fe Rd., Taos, NM 87571
(505) 758–2200

Sagebrush Inn
P.O. Box 557, Taos, NM 87571
(505) 758–2254

Taos Inn
N. Pueblo Rd., Taos, NM 87571
(505) 758–2233

Campground

Taos Mid-Town Campground
P.O. Box 3273, Taos, NM 87571
(505) 758–8581

105. RIO GRANDE RIVER, TEXAS

Lodging

Badlands Hotel
Rt. 70, Box 400, Lajitas, TX 79852
(915) 424–3471

Big Bend Motor Inn
Hwys. 118 & 170, P.O. Box 336, Terlingua, TX 79852
(915) 371–2218

Chisos Mountain Lodge
Chisos Basin–Big Bend National Park
Big Bend National Park, TX 79834
(915) 477–2291

The Gage Hotel
P.O. Box 46, Marathon, TX 79842
(915) 386–4205

Plaza Inn
Hwy. U.S. 290W, Fort Stockton, TX 79735
(915) 336–5277

Sunday House Inn
P.O. Box 578, Alpine, TX 79830
(915) 837–3363

Campgrounds

Cottonwood Campground
Big Bend National Park
Big Bend National Park, TX 79834
(915) 477–2251

Lajitas Rio Grande Campground
Star Rt. 70, Box 400, Lajita, TX 79852
(915) 424–3471

Lodging and Campground

Terlingua Ranch Lodge
Terlingua Rt., Box 220, Alpine, TX 79830
(915) 371–2416

106. ALSEK-TATSHENSHINI RIVERS, YUKON-BRITISH COLUMBIA-ALASKA

Call or write river outfitter for recommended accommodations and transportation arrangements.

107. CHITINA-COPPER RIVERS, ALASKA

Call or write river outfitter for recommended accommodations and transportation arrangements.

108. LOWE RIVER, ALASKA

Lodging

Totem Inn
P.O. Box 648, Valdez, AK 99686
(907) 835–4443

Village Inn
P.O. Box 365, Valdez, AK 99686
(907) 835–4445

Westmark Inn
P.O. Box 1915, Valdez, AK 99686
(907) 835–4485

Campground

Bearpaw Camper Park
P.O. Box 93, Valdez, AK 99686
(907) 835–4558

109. TONSINA RIVER, ALASKA

Lodging

Caribou Lodge
P.O. Box 329, Glennallen, AK 99588
(907) 822–3302

Campground

KROA–Kamping Resorts of Alaska
Mile 152 Glenn Hwy., Glennallen, AK 99588
(907) 822–3346

110. TAZLINA RIVER, ALASKA

See accommodations list for the Tonsina River.

111. TALKEETNA RIVER, ALASKA

Lodging

Fairview Inn
P.O. Box 379, Talkeetna, AK 99676
(907) 733–2423

The Talkeetna Motel
Talkeetna, AK 99676
(907) 733–2323

Talkeetna Roadhouse
P.O. Box 388, Talkeetna, AK 99676
(907) 733–2341

112. NENANA RIVER, ALASKA

Lodging

Carlo Creek Lodge
Mile 223.9 Parks Hwy., P.O. Box 185, Denali National Park,
    AK 99755
(907) 683–2512

Reindeer Mt. Lodge
Mile 209.5 Parks Hwy., P.O. Box 7, Cantwell, AK 99729
(907) 768–2420

Campgrounds

KOA McKinley
P.O. Box 34, Healy, AK 99743
(907) 683–2379

Lynx Creek Campground
Denali National Park, AK 99755
(907) 683–2547

Lodging and Campground

Denali Grizzly Bear Cabins & Campground
P.O. Box 7, Denali National Park, AK 99755
(907) 683–2696

113. FORTYMILE RIVER, ALASKA

Lodging

Tok Lodge
P.O. Box 135, Tok, AK 99780
(907) 883–2851

Campground

Sourdough Campground
P.O. Box 47, Tok, AK 99780
(907) 883–5543

114. BROOKS RANGE RIVERS (East), ALASKA

Call or write river outfitter for recommended
accommodations and transportation arrangements.

115. BROOKS RANGE RIVERS (Central), ALASKA

Call or write river outfitter for recommended
accommodations and transportation arrangements.

116. BROOKS RANGE RIVERS (West), ALASKA

Call or write river outfitter for recommended
accommodations and transportation arrangements.

117. CHILKO RIVER, BRITISH COLUMBIA

Lodging

Drummond Lodge and Motel
1405 Hwy. 97S, Williams Lake, BC, Canada V2G 2W3
(604) 392–5334

Jamboree Motel
845 Carson Dr., Williams Lake, BC, Canada V2G 3N7
(604) 398–8208

Valley View Motel
1523 Caribou Hwy., Williams Lake, BC, Canada V2G 2W3
(604) 392–4655

118. TASEKO RIVER, BRITISH COLUMBIA

See accommodations list for the Chilko River.

119. CHILCOTIN RIVER, BRITISH COLUMBIA

See accommodations list for the Chilko River.

120. FRASER RIVER, BRITISH COLUMBIA

For Soda Creek to Lillooet section, see accommodations list for the Chilko River.

Lodging (Lytton to Yale section)

Lytton Hotel
P.O. Box 113, Lytton, BC, Canada V0K 1Z0
(604) 455–2211

Lytton Pines Motel
P.O. Box 249, Lytton, BC, Canada V0K 1Z0
(604) 455–2322

Campground

Shaw Springs Resort
P.O. Box 49, Spences Bridge, BC, Canada V0K 2L0
(604) 458–2324

121. THOMPSON RIVER, BRITISH COLUMBIA

See accommodations list for the Fraser River (Lytton to Yale section).

122. NAHATLATCH RIVER, BRITISH COLUMBIA

See accommodations list for the Fraser River (Lytton to Yale section).

123. CLEARWATER RIVER, BRITISH COLUMBIA

Lodging

Dutch Lake Motel
P.O. Box 5116, Clearwater, BC, Canada V0E 1N0
(604) 674–3325

Wells Gray Inn
P.O. Box 280, Clearwater, BC, Canada V0E 1N0
(604) 674–2214

124. ADAMS RIVER, BRITISH COLUMBIA

Lodging

Salmon Arm Manor Hotel
P.O. Box 909, Salmon Arm, BC, Canada V1E 4P1
(604) 832–2129

Campground

KOA Salmon Arm
381 Hwy. 97, Salmon Arm, BC, Canada V1E 4M4
(604) 832–6489

125. CHEHALIS RIVER, BRITISH COLUMBIA

Lodging

Chilliwack River Campground
50801 O'Byrne Rd., Sardis, BC, Canada V2R 2P1
(604) 858–4443

Malibu Motel
46607 Yale Rd. E., Chilliwack, BC, Canada V2P 2R6
(604) 792–9375

Rainbow Motel
45620 Yale Rd. W., Chilliwack, BC, Canada V2P 2N2
(604) 792–6412

Campground

Rainbow's End Camping Resort
606 Hot Springs Rd., Harrison Hot Springs, BC, Canada
   V0M 1K0
(604) 796–9417

126. CHILLIWACK RIVER, BRITISH COLUMBIA

See accommodations list for the Chehalis River.

127. CHEAKAMUS RIVER, BRITISH COLUMBIA

Lodging

Listel Whistler Hotel
P.O. Box 93, Whistler, BC, Canada V0N 1B0
(800) 663–5472
(604) 932–1133

Whistler Fairways Hotel
P.O. Box 1012, Whistler, BC, Canada V0N 1B0
(604) 932–2522

Campground

KOA Whistler Kampground
P.O. Box 749, Whistler, BC, Canada V0N 1B0
(604) 932–5181

128. BIRKENHEAD RIVER, BRITISH COLUMBIA

See accommodations list for the Cheakamus River.

129. SQUAMISH RIVER, BRITISH COLUMBIA

See accomodations list for the Cheakamus River.

130. BABINE RIVER, BRITISH COLUMBIA

Call or write river outfitter for recommended accommodations and transportation arrangements.

131. ILLECILLEWAET RIVER, BRITISH COLUMBIA

Lodging

Alpine Motel
P.O. Box 414, Revelstoke, BC, Canada V0E 2S0
(604) 837–2116

Canyon Motor Inn
P.O. Box 740, Revelstoke, BC, Canada V0E 2S0
(604) 837–5221

Campground

Canyon Hot Springs Campground
P.O. Box 2400, Revelstoke, BC, Canada V0E 2S0
(604) 837–2420

132. KICKING HORSE RIVER, BRITISH COLUMBIA

Lodging

Beaverfoot Lodge
P.O. Box 1560, Golden, BC, Canada V0A 1H0
(604) 346–3216

Rondo Motel
904 Park Dr., Golden, BC, Canada V0A 1H0
(604) 344–5295

Campground

Golden Municipal Campground
P.O Box 350, Golden, BC, Canada V0A 1H0
(604) 344–5412

133. RED DEER RIVER, ALBERTA

Lodging

Highlander Motel
1818 16th Ave. N.W., Calgary, AB, Canada T2M 0L8
(403) 289–1961

Parkwood Motor Inn
P.O. Box 11, Sundre, AB, Canada T0M 1X0
(403) 638–4424

Red Deer Lodge
4311 49th Ave., Red Deer, AB, Canada T4N 5Y7
(403) 346–8841

Sundre Motor Inn
P.O. Box 810, Sundre, AB, Canada T0M 1X0
(403) 638–4440

Campgrounds

Red Deer River Campground
Sundre, AB, Canada T0M 1X0
(403) 427–3582

Tall Timbers Campground
P.O. Box 24, Sundre, AB, Canada T0M 1X0
(403) 638–3555

134. MALIGNE RIVER, ALBERTA

Lodging

Diamond Motel
925 Connaught Dr., Jasper, AB, Canada T0E 1E0
(403) 852–3143

Marmot Lodge
94 Connaught Dr., Jasper, AB, Canada T0E 1E0
(403) 852–4471

135. ATHABASCA RIVER (Upper), ALBERTA

See accommodations list for the Maligne River.

136. ATHABASCA RIVER, ALBERTA

Call or write river outfitter for recommended
accommodations and transportation arrangements.

137. BOW RIVER, ALBERTA

Lodging

Hotel Kananaskis
Trans-Canada Hwy., Kananaskis Village, AB, Canada T0L
  2H0
(403) 591–7711

Kananaskis Inn
Trans-Canada Hwy., Kananaskis Village, AB, Canada T0L
  2H0
(403) 591–7500

Rimrock Inn
P.O. Box 1110, Banff, AB, Canada T0L 0C0
(403) 762–3356

Campgrounds

Bow Valley Campground
Bow Valley Provincial Park
P.O. Box 280, Exhaw, AB, Canada T0L 2C0
(403) 673–3663

Willow Rock Campground
Bow Valley Provincial Park
P.O. Box 280, Exhaw, AB, Canada T0L 2C0
(403) 673–3663

138. KANANASKIS RIVER, ALBERTA

See accommodations list for the Bow River.

139. HIGHWOOD RIVER, ALBERTA

Lodging

Best Western Hospitality Inn
135 Southland Dr. S.E., Calgary, AB, Canada T2J 5X5
(403) 278–5050

140. GREAT SLAVE RIVER, ALBERTA-NORTHWEST TERRITORIES

Call or write river outfitter for recommended
accommodations and transportation arrangements.

Bailer: An open-ended container or bucket used to remove water from the raft.

Chute: A narrow channel through which the flow of water is swifter and deeper than the normal flow.

Ducky: An inflatable kayak.

Eddy: A current of reverse water flow sometimes creating a small whirlpool.

Gradient: Drop in elevation during the downstream flow of a river. Rate of gradient is usually expressed in number of feet decreased per mile.

Hole: A depression in the river caused by reverse water flow. Also may be called a hydraulic.

Hydraulic: A very large hole with reverse water flow.

Hypothermia: A lowering of body core temperature, caused by losing heat faster than it is produced by the body. Hypothermia is a threat when water temperatures are below sixty degrees Fahrenheit, or air temperatures are below fifty degrees Fahrenheit.

Pool: An area of flatwater without rapids.

Pool drop: A whitewater rapid, usually of short duration, that begins and ends with fairly calm water rather than continuous water flow.

Portage: To carry a raft around unraftable or unsafe rapids or falls.

Put-in: The starting point of a rafting trip where rafts are put into the river.

Rapids: A series of waves and turbulences.

Riffle: A very small rapid or wave caused by a shallow sand bar or rocks extending across a stream bed.

Scouting: To visually survey a rapid from the riverbank to select the best route.

Sportyak: A small oar-guided rowing craft fairly unique to the American Southwest. Most commonly seen on Utah's Green and San Juan rivers.

Standing waves: A series of stationary waves caused by water converging at the end of a tongue or a submerged object.

Photo courtesy of **ECHO: The Wilderness Company**/Mary Ann Harrel

Take-out: The point where the rafting trip ends and the rafts are removed from the river.

Tongue: A narrow depression between waves.

Whitewater: Moving water whose surface becomes turbulent or frothy by passing either over rocks, through a narrow river channel, or down a steeper gradient.

INDEX

Rio Grande	165	104	New Mexico
Rio Grande	166	105	Texas–Mexico
Roaring Fork	132	80	Colorado
Rogue	72	39	Oregon
Sacramento (Upper)	54	21	California
Salmon	49	17	California
Salmon (Lower)	96	52	Idaho
Salmon (Main)	95	51	Idaho
Salmon (Middle Fork)	91	49	Idaho
Salmon (Upper Main)	94	50	Idaho
Salt	161	102	Arizona
San Juan	154	99	Utah
San Miguel	144	92	Colorado
Sauk	65	30	Washington
Scott	48	16	California
Selway	99	54	Idaho
Shoshone	119	73	Wyoming
Skagit	67	32	Washington
Skykomish	68	33	Washington
Slate	137	85	Colorado
Snake (Birds of Prey)	102	58	Idaho
Snake (Hells Canyon)	101	57	Idaho–Oregon
Snake (Middle)	103	59	Idaho
Snake (Upper)	116	72	Wyoming
Squamish	198	129	British Columbia
St. Joe	100	56	Idaho
Stanislaus	37	8	California
Stehekin	61	25	Washington
Suiattle	65	31	Washington
Talkeetna	179	111	Alaska
Taseko	189	118	British Columbia
Taylor	136	84	Colorado
Tazlina	179	110	Alaska
Thompson	193	121	British Columbia
Tieton	62	26	Washington
Tonsina	178	109	Alaska
Toutle	70	36	Washington
Trinity	51	19	California
Truckee	35	5	California
Tuolumne	39	9	California
Verde	161	101	Arizona
Wenatchee	59	23	Washington
White Salmon	63	28	Washington
Wooley	50	18	California
Yampa	145	93	Colorado
Yellowstone	114	71	Montana
Yuba (North Fork)	34	4	California

CALIFORNIA

River		Class	Season	Days
1.	American (South Fork)	II–III	Apr.–Oct.	1–2
2.	American (Middle Fork)	II–IV +	Apr.–Oct.	1–3
3.	American (North Fork)			
	Chamberlain Falls	IV +	Apr.–June	1–2
	Giant Gap	V	Apr.–June	1–2
4.	Yuba (North Fork)			
	Upper	V	Apr.–June	1
	Lower	III–IV	Apr.–June	1–2
5.	Truckee	III–IV	Apr.–Oct.	1–2
6.	Carson (East Fork)			
	Upper	III	Apr.–June	1–2
	Wilderness Run	II	Apr.–June	1–2
7.	Mokelumne	II +	Mar–Sept.	$^1/_2$
8.	Stanislaus			
	North Fork	III–IV +	Apr.–June	1
	Middle Fork	IV–V +	Apr.–June	1–2
	Lower	I–II, III–IV +	June–Oct.	1
9.	Tuolumne			
	Main	III–IV +	Apr.–Oct.	1–3
	Upper	IV–V +	Apr.–Aug.	1
10.	Merced	III–IV +	Apr.–July	1–2
11.	Kings	III–IV	Apr.–Aug.	1–2
12.	Kern			
	Forks	IV–V +	Apr.–July	2–3
	Upper	III–IV +	May–July	1–2
	Lower	III–IV	May–Oct.	1–2
13.	Kaweah	III–V +	Apr.–June	1–2
14.	Klamath (Upper)	IV–V	May–Sept.	1–2
15.	Klamath (Lower)	II–III	May–Sept.	1–3
16.	Scott	IV–V	Apr.–June	1–2
17.	Salmon	IV–V	Apr.–July	1–2
18.	Wooley	V	Apr.–June	1–3
19.	Trinity			
	Upper	II–III +	Apr.–Oct.	1–5
	Burnt Range Gorge	IV–V	June–Sept.	1–2
20.	Eel (Middle)	I–III	Apr.–June	1–3
21.	Sacramento (Upper)	III–IV	Apr.–June	1–3
22.	Cache Creek	II–III	May–Sept.	1–2

River		Class	Season	Days
23.	Wenatchee	II–III +	Apr.–July	1
24.	Methow	III–IV	Apr.–July	1–2
25.	Stehekin	I–II	May–Aug.	1
26.	Tieton	II–III +	Sept.	1
27.	Klickitat	III–IV	Apr.–June	1–2
28.	White Salmon	III–IV +	May–Aug.	1
29.	Nooksack (North Fork)	II–III	July–Sept.	1
30.	Sauk	II–IV	May–July	1
31.	Suiattle	I–III	May–Aug.	1
32.	Skagit			
	Upper	II–III	July–Sept.	1
	Lower	I–II	Dec.–Feb.	1/2
33.	Skykomish	III–V	Mar.–July	1
34.	Green	III–IV	Feb.–Apr.	1
35.	Cispus	II–III	Apr.–June	1
36.	Toutle	III–IV	Feb.–Apr.	1
37.	Olympic Rain Forest	I–II	Apr.–Sept.	1
38.	Elwha	I–II	May–Sept.	1/2
39.	Rogue			
	Wild and Scenic	III–IV	May–Oct.	3–5
	Recreation	I–II	May–Oct.	1/2, 1
40.	Illinois	III–V	Mar.–May	3–4
41.	North Umpqua	II–III +	Apr.–July	1/2, 1–3
42.	McKenzie	II–IV	May–Oct.	1
43.	North Santiam	II–III	Apr.–June, Sept.–Oct.	1
44.	Clackamas	I–II, III–IV	Mar.–June	1
45.	Deschutes	II–III	Apr.–Oct.	1–5
46.	John Day	I–II +	Apr.–June	2–5
47.	Grande Ronde	I–II +	Apr.–July	3–5
48.	Owyhee	II–IV +	Apr.–June	3–7

THE NORTHERN ROCKY MOUNTAIN STATES

River	Class	Season	Days
49. Salmon (Middle Fork)	III–IV +	May–Oct.	5–6
50. Salmon (Upper Main)	II–III +	May–Oct.	1/2, 1
51. Salmon (Main)	III–IV	May–Oct.	4–5
52. Salmon (Lower)	I–III	June–Oct.	3–5
53. Lochsa	III–IV +	May–Aug.	1–3
54. Selway	III–IV +	June–July	3–5
55. Moyie	II–III	May–June	1
56. St. Joe	II–IV	May–July	1
57. Snake (Hells Canyon)	III–IV	May–Oct.	3–6
58. Snake (Birds of Prey)	I–II	Apr.–June	1
59. Snake (Middle)			
Hagerman	I–II, III	Apr.–Sept.	1
Murtaugh	III–V	Mar.–June	1
60. Payette			
North Fork	III–IV	May–Sept.	1
South Fork	II–IV	May–Sept.	1/2, 1–3
Main	I–III	May–Sept.	1/2, 1
61. Jarbidge–Bruneau			
Jarbidge	III–VI	May–June	6–7
Bruneau	III–IV +	May–June	3–4
62. Owyhee			
South Fork	III–IV +	Apr.–June	6–9
East Fork	III–VI	Apr.–June	6–9
63. Flathead (North Fork)	I–II	June–Aug.	3–4
64. Flathead (Middle Fork)	II–IV +	May–Sept.	1/2, 1–4
65. Flathead (South Fork)	II–IV	June–Aug.	4–6
66. Flathead (Lower)	II–III +	June–Aug.	1/2
67. Clark Fork	II–III	July–Sept.	1
68. Blackfoot	II–III	May–July	1–3
69. Gallatin	II–IV	June–Aug.	1/2, 1
70. Madison	II–IV	June–Aug.	1
71. Yellowstone	II–III	May–Oct.	1/2, 1
72. Snake (Upper)			
Grand Teton National			
Park	I–II	May–Sept.	1/4, 1/2, 1
Canyons	I–III	May–Sept.	1/2, 1
73. Shoshone	II–III	May–Sept.	1/4, 1/2, 1

THE SOUTHWEST STATES

River	Class	Season	Days
74. Arkansas			
The Numbers	III–IV +	May–Sept.	1
Browns Canyon	II–III +	May–Sept.	$1/2$, 1, 2
Salida–Cotapaxi–			
Parkdale	II–III	May–Sept.	$1/2$, 1
Royal Gorge	III–IV +	May–Sept.	1
75. Clear Creek	IV–V +	May–July	1
76. North Platte	III–IV	May–July	1–3
77. Cache la Poudre	III–IV	May–July	1
78. Blue	II–III	May–July	$1/2$, 1
79. Eagle	II–IV +	May–July	$1/2$, 1
80. Roaring Fork	II–IV	May–July	$1/2$, 1
81. Colorado (Upper)	II–III +	May–Sept.	$1/2$, 1–3
82. Colorado (Glenwood)			
Glenwood Canyon	I–II +	June–Sept.	$1/2$, 1
Shoshone Run	III–IV +	June–Sept.	$1/4$
83. Colorado (Horsethief–			
Ruby)	I–II	Apr.–Sept.	2–3
84. Taylor	III–IV	May–Sept.	$1/2$, 1
85. Slate	V–V +	May–June	$1/2$
86. Gunnison	I–II	May–Sept.	1–2
87. Gunnison (Lake Fork)	III–IV +	May–June	$1/2$, 1
88. Gunnison (Gorge)	II–III +	May–Sept.	1–3
89. Piedra	III–V	May–July	1–2

ALASKA

River	Class	Season	Days
106. Alsek–Tatshenshini	II–IV	June–Sept.	9–12
107. Chitina–Copper	I–III	June–Sept.	6–12
108. Lowe	II–III	May–Sept.	1/4
109. Tonsina	III–IV	May–Sept.	1
110. Tazlina	I–II +	June–Sept.	4–5
111. Talkeetna	III–IV +	June–Sept.	4–5
112. Nenana	III–IV	May–Sept.	1/4, 1/2
113. Fortymile	II–III	June–Sept.	7
114. Brooks Range (East)	I–II	June–Sept.	5–12
115. Brooks Range (Central)	I–II	June–Sept.	7–14
116. Brooks Range (West)	I–II	June–Sept.	10–15

River	Class	Season	Days
117. Chilko	I–V	June–Sept.	2–3
118. Taseko	II–IV	June–Sept.	4
119. Chilcotin	III–V	June–Sept.	4–12
120. Fraser			
Soda Creek	III–V	July–Sept.	6–7
Lytton	III–V +	July–Sept.	1–3
121. Thompson	III–IV	May–Sept.	$^1/_2$, 1–2
122. Nahatlatch	III–IV +	May–Aug.	1
123. Clearwater	III–IV +	June–Sept.	1–2
124. Adams	II–III +	May–Sept.	$^1/_4$
125. Chehalis	II–III	Apr.–June	$^1/_2$
126. Chilliwack	II–IV +	Apr.–Aug.	1
127. Cheakamus	III–IV	June–July	$^1/_4$
128. Birkenhead	II–III	June–July	$^1/_2$
129. Squamish	III–IV	June–Sept.	1
130. Babine	II–IV	Aug.–Sept.	4–5
131. Illecillewaet	III–IV	June–Aug.	$^1/_4$
132. Kicking Horse			
Upper	II–III	May–Sept.	$^1/_2$, 1
Lower	III–IV +	Aug.	$^1/_2$, 1
133. Red Deer	II–III	May–Sept.	1–2
134. Maligne	II–III	June–July	$^1/_2$
135. Athabasca (Upper)	II–III	June–Sept.	$^1/_2$
136. Athabasca	II–IV +	July–Aug.	8
137. Bow			
Banff National Park	I +	June–Aug.	$^1/_4$
East of Park Boundary	I–II	May–Sept.	$^1/_4$
138. Kananaskis	I–III	May–Sept.	$^1/_4$
139. Highwood	III–IV	May–July	1
140. Great Slave	I–V	June–Aug.	$^1/_2$, 1–6